DAY HIKING

Glacier National Park
and Western Montana

Previous page: *Waterton Lake from Goat Haunt Overlook (Hike 53)*

Sunset from Star Peak, in the West Cabinets (Hike 5)

Winter's first ice, Bramlet Lake, Cabinet Mountains Wilderness (Hike 16)

Striking evening panorama at Big Hole Lookout, southern Cabinets (Hike 22)

Late evening at McGuire Mountain Lookout (Hike 26)

Autumn's colors reflected in the Swan River, Swan River Nature Trail (Hike 36)

On the Highline Trail above the Going-to-the-Sun Road (Hike 43)

A hiker and child enjoy St. Mary Falls on the Three Falls Loop (Hike 47).

A cow moose and calf bed down among spring's first leaves, Swiftcurrent Valley (Hike 50).

Early autumn color lights up the Reservation Divide near Three Lakes Peak (Hike 79).

Sunrise alpenglow reflects in Crescent Lake in the Mission Mountains Wilderness (Hike 71).

Late afternoon light picks out spring's lingering snow above Stanton Lake in the Flathead Range (Hike 59).

Late evening sunlight breaks through a passing storm above Missoula, as viewed from Mount Sentinel (Hike 81).

The author hikes among autumn larch lining the Burdette Creek Trail (Hike 100).

A lone larch lights up the forest above Crystal Lake in the northern Bitterroots (Hike 90).

A sunrise rainbow reflects in Lower Blossom Lake in the northern Bitterroots (Hike 88).

Summer wildflowers carpet Rock Candy Mountain in the Northwest Peak Scenic Area (Hike 2).

A hiker ascends a granite slab en route to Aichele Lake from Knaack Lake in the Selway-Bitterroot Wilderness (Hike 109).

The sun dips behind Sky Pilot from Bear Creek Overlook in the Selway-Bitterroot Wilderness (Hike 107).

A hushed Hemlock Lake reflects autumn color in the Mission Mountains Wilderness (Hike 73).

A hiker crosses a log over Blodgett Creek on the Blodgett Canyon Trail, Selway-Bitterroot Wilderness (Hike 111).

Casting for a dinner of pan-size trout in Tamarack Lake, Selway-Bitterroot Wilderness (Hike 118)

DAY HIKING

Glacier National Park
and Western Montana

cabinets · mission and swan ranges
missoula · bitterroots

Aaron Theisen

MOUNTAINEERS
BOOKS

MOUNTAINEERS BOOKS is the publishing division of
The Mountaineers, an organization founded in 1906 and dedicated to the
exploration, preservation, and enjoyment of outdoor and wilderness areas.

1001 SW Klickitat Way, Suite 201, Seattle, WA 98134
800.553.4453, www.mountaineersbooks.org

Printed in the United States of America
Distributed in the United Kingdom by Cordee
First edition, 2018

Copyeditor: Rebecca Friedman
Book & cover design: Mountaineers Books
Layout: McKenzie Long
Cartographer: Pease Press

Cover photograph: *Avalanche Lake (Hike 42) off the Going-to-the-Sun Road in Glacier National Park*
Frontispiece: *The return hike from Little Rock Creek Lake, with the Como Peaks in the background (Hike 117)*
Photo on page 6: *Crossing a log footbridge at high water en route to Glacier Lake in the Mission Mountains Wilderness (Hike 71)*
All photographs copyright © by the author unless otherwise noted.

Library of Congress Cataloging-in-Publication Data
Names: Theisen, Aaron, author.
Title: Day Hiking Glacier National Park and Western Montana : Cabinets, Mission and Swan Ranges,
Missoula Bitterroots / Aaron Theisen.
Description: First edition. | Seattle, WA: Mountaineers Books, 2018. | Includes bibliographical
references and index.
Identifiers: LCCN 2017057622| ISBN 9781680510485 (pbk) | ISBN 9781680510492 (ebook)
Subjects: LCSH: Day hiking—Montana—Glacier National Park—Guidebooks. | Day hiking—
Montana, Western—Guidebooks. | Glacier National Park (Mont.)—Guidebooks. | Montana,
Western—Guidebooks.
Classification: LCC GV199.42.M92 T47 2018 | DDC 796.5109786/52—dc23
LC record available at https://lccn.loc.gov/2017057622

Printed on FSC® -certified materials
ISBN (paperback): 978-1-68051-048-5
ISBN (ebook): 978-1-68051-049-2

MIX
Paper from
responsible sources
FSC® C005010

Table of Contents

Flathead Range

Swan Range

Mission Mountains

Reservation Divide

Missoula Area

Bitterroot Range

Sapphire Mountains

Hikes at a Glance

HIKE	DISTANCE	RATING	DIFFICULTY	KID-FRIENDLY	DOG-FRIENDLY
YAAK VALLEY					
1. Northwest Peak	4.4 miles	*****	3	•	•
2. Rock Candy Mountain	7.8 miles	*****	5		•
3. Fish Lakes Canyon	11.8 miles	****	3	•	•
4. Pink Mountain	6.4 miles	***	3		•
CABINET MOUNTAINS					
West Cabinets					
5. Star Peak	8.4 miles	*****	5		•
6. Little Spar Lake	6.8 miles	****	3	•	•
7. Ross Creek Cedars	0.9 mile	*****	2	•	•
8. Berray Mountain	10.2 miles	****	5		•
Cabinet Mountains Wilderness					
9. Rock Lake	7.8 miles	*****	4	•	•
10. Engle Lake	6.4 miles	****	4	•	•
11. Cedar Lakes	10 miles	*****	3	•	•
12. Sky Lakes	11.2 miles	****	5		•
13. Granite Lake	12.4 miles	****	5		•
14. Leigh Lake	2.8 miles	****	3	•	•
15. Ozette Lake	7.2 miles	*****	5		•
16. Bramlet Lake	4 miles	***	3	•	•
17. Geiger Lakes	5.8 miles	*****	3	•	•
18. Bear and Baree Lakes Loop ~~1 hr~~ ~~15 Mies~~	8.6 miles	****	4		•
Southern Cabinets					
19. Four Lakes Loop	8.5 miles	*****	4		•
20. Priscilla Peak	9 miles	****	5		•
21. Terrace Lake	3.4 miles	***	3	•	•
22. Big Hole Lookout	5.4 miles	****	3	•	•
23. Baldy Mountain and Baldy Lake	5 miles	****	3	•	•
UPPER KOOTENAI RIVER					
24. Flagstaff Mountain	4 miles	****	3		•
25. Boulder Lakes	4.8 miles	****	3	•	•

EXCEPTIONAL WILDFLOWERS	EXCEPTIONAL WATERFALLS	EXCEPTIONAL OLD GROWTH	HISTORICAL RELEVANCE	EXCEPTIONAL BERRY PICKING	EXCEPTIONAL FISHING	BICYCLES PERMITTED
		•	•			•
•			•			•
	•	•			•	
•		•	•			•
			•	•		
•					•	
		•				
		•	•			•
			•		•	
				•	•	
					•	
•					•	
	•	•			•	
	•				•	
	•			•	•	
				•	•	
	•			•	•	
•			•		•	•
•		•	•			•
		•			•	•
			•			•
			•			•
•			•			•
				•	•	•

HIKE	DISTANCE	RATING	DIFFICULTY	KID-FRIENDLY	DOG-FRIENDLY
26. McGuire Mountain	4.6 miles	***	2	•	•
WHITEFISH RANGE					
Ten Lakes Scenic Area					
27. Ten Lakes Loop	10 miles	*****	4	•	•
28. Stahl Peak	6.2 miles	*****	4	•	•
North Fork Wildlands					
29. Tuchuck Mountain	11.6 miles	****	5		•
30. Mount Thompson-Seton	10 miles	****	5		•
31. Whale Lake and Huntsberger Lake	10.4 miles or 8.2 miles	**** or ****	4 or 4	•	•
32. Link Lake and Nasukoin Mountain	10.2 miles	*****	5		•
FLATHEAD VALLEY					
Whitefish Area					
33. Danny On Trail	8.4 miles	***	4	•	•
34. Whitefish Trail to Smith Lake	5.5 miles	***	3	•	•
Kalispell Area					
35. Lone Pine State Park	2.6 miles	***	2	•	•
36. Swan River Nature Trail	4 miles	***	2	•	•
GLACIER NATIONAL PARK					
North Fork					
37. Bowman Lake	13.6 miles	*****	4	•	
38. Quartz Lakes Loop	12.7 miles	****	4		
39. Logging Lake	10 miles	****	3	•	
Going-to-the-Sun Road					
40. Apgar Lookout	7 miles	***	4	•	
41. Sperry Chalet	12 miles	****	5		
42. Trail of the Cedars and Avalanche Lake	1 mile or 5.4 miles	**** or *****	1 or 3	•	
43. Highline Trail to Granite Park Chalet	14.8 miles	*****	4	•	
44. Hidden Lake Overlook and Hidden Lake	4.8 miles	*****	3	•	
45. Siyeh Pass	9.5 miles	*****	4		
46. Gunsight Lake	12 miles	****	4		

EXCEPTIONAL WILDFLOWERS	EXCEPTIONAL WATERFALLS	EXCEPTIONAL OLD GROWTH	HISTORICAL RELEVANCE	EXCEPTIONAL BERRY PICKING	EXCEPTIONAL FISHING	BICYCLES PERMITTED
			•			•
•				•	•	•
			•	•		•
			•	•		•
•			•	•		•
				•	•	•
			•	•		•
•				•		
						•
•						•
•						•
					•	
				•	•	
					•	
			•			
			•			
	•	•				
•			•			
•						
•			•			
	•				•	

HIKE	DISTANCE	RATING	DIFFICULTY	KID-FRIENDLY	DOG-FRIENDLY
47. Three Falls Loop	5.1 miles	★★★	3	•	
48. Otokomi Lake	10.4 miles	★★★★	4		
Many Glacier					
49. Iceberg Lake and Ptarmigan Tunnel	9.4 miles or 10.4 miles	★★★★★ or ★★★★★	4 or 5		
50. Swiftcurrent Valley	7.2 miles	★★★★	3	•	
51. Grinnell Glacier	10 miles	★★★★★	4	•	
52. Cracker Lake	12.6 miles	★★★★★	4		
Goat Haunt					
53. Kootenai Lakes and Goat Haunt Overlook	5.6 miles or 2 miles	★★★ or ★★★★	3 or 3	•	
54. Rainbow Falls	1.8 miles	★★★	2	•	
Two Medicine Area					
55. Triple Divide Pass	14 miles	★★★★★	5		
56. Dawson-Pitamakan Loop	18.2 miles	★★★★★	5		
57. Appistoki Falls and Scenic Point	7.4 miles	★★★★	4	•	
FLATHEAD RANGE					
58. Great Northern Mountain	7.2 miles	★★★★★	5		•
59. Stanton Lake	3.6 miles	★★★	3	•	•
60. Marion Lake	4.2 miles	★★★★	3	•	•
SWAN RANGE					
61. Columbia Mountain	11 miles	★★★★	5		•
62. Birch Lake	6 miles	★★★★★	3	•	•
63. Jewel Basin Loop	9.9 miles	★★★★★	4	•	•
64. Hall Lake	8 miles	★★★★	4		•
65. Bond and Trinkus Lakes	11.4 miles	★★★★	4		•
66. Inspiration Point	10.8 miles	★★★★	5		•
67. Holland Falls and Upper Holland Lake Loop	3 miles or 12.1 miles	★★★★ or ★★★★★	2 or 5	•	•
68. Morrell Falls	5.4 miles	★★★★	3	•	•
69. Pyramid Lake	10.6 miles	★★★★	4	•	•
MISSION MOUNTAINS					
East-Side Mission Mountains					
70. Cold Lakes	5 miles	★★★★	3	•	•

EXCEPTIONAL WILDFLOWERS	EXCEPTIONAL WATERFALLS	EXCEPTIONAL OLD GROWTH	HISTORICAL RELEVANCE	EXCEPTIONAL BERRY PICKING	EXCEPTIONAL FISHING	BICYCLES PERMITTED
•	•					
•	•				•	
•	•		•			
•	•			•		
•						
•			•			
•					•	
	•					
•				•		
				•	•	
	•		•			
				•		
				•	•	
•						•
•						
•				•	•	
				•	•	•
				•	•	•
•			•			•
•					•	•
	•					•
					•	
					•	

HIKE	DISTANCE	RATING	DIFFICULTY	KID-FRIENDLY	DOG-FRIENDLY
71. Glacier Lake and Heart and Crescent Lakes	3.2 miles or 7.9 miles	***** or *****	3 or 4	•	•
72. Turquoise Lake	11.6 miles	*****	5		•
73. Hemlock Lake	6.8 miles	****	4	•	•
74. Crystal Lake	4.6 miles	****	3	•	•
75. Lake Elsina to Lake Dinah	4.4 miles	****	3	•	•
Mission Mountains Tribal Wilderness					
76. Terrace Lake	8.6 miles	*****	4		•
77. Mission Falls	4.6 miles	****	3	•	•
78. Lost Sheep Lake	7.8 miles	****	5		•
RESERVATION DIVIDE					
79. Three Lakes Peak	12.4 miles	****	5		•
80. Ch-paa-qn	7 miles	*****	4	•	•
MISSOULA AREA					
81. Crazy Canyon to Mount Sentinel	6.6 miles	***	3	•	•
82. Mount Jumbo	4.1 miles	***	3	•	•
83. South O'Brien Creek Loop	7.1 miles	***	3	•	•
84. Sawmill Gulch and Curry Cabin Loop	5 miles	***	3	•	
85. Stuart Peak	18.4 miles	*****	5		•
86. Boulder Point and Boulder Lake	12.4 miles	****	4		•
87. Sheep Mountain	7.4 miles	****	4	•	•
BITTERROOT RANGE					
Northern Bitterroot Range					
88. Blossom Lakes	7.1 miles	****	4	•	•
89. St. Regis Lakes	5.4 miles	****	3	•	•
90. Crystal Lake	3.2 miles	***	3		•
91. Hazel and Hub Lakes	6.4 miles	*****	3	•	•
92. Diamond and Cliff Lakes	2 miles	****	2	•	•
93. Lost Lake	7.6 miles	***	3	•	•
94. Oregon Lakes	1.2 miles	***	2	•	•
95. Stateline Trail to Bonanza Lakes	5.4 miles	*****	3	•	•
96. Stateline Trail to Illinois Peak	8 miles	*****	3		•

EXCEPTIONAL WILDFLOWERS	EXCEPTIONAL WATERFALLS	EXCEPTIONAL OLD GROWTH	HISTORICAL RELEVANCE	EXCEPTIONAL BERRY PICKING	EXCEPTIONAL FISHING	BICYCLES PERMITTED
				•	•	
				•	•	
					•	
		•		•		
					•	•
•					•	
	•					
				•		
•			•			•
			•			•
•						•
•						
•						•
•			•			•
			•			
•					•	
•						•
					•	•
•					•	•
			•	•	•	•
	•	•				
•					•	•
•	•					•
					•	•
•					•	•
•			•			•

HIKE	DISTANCE	RATING	DIFFICULTY	KID-FRIENDLY	DOG-FRIENDLY
97. Heart Lake	5.4 miles	*****	3	•	•
98. Straight Creek	10.4 miles	****	3	•	•
99. Kid and Mud Lakes	9 miles	****	3	•	•
100. Burdette Creek	9.8 miles	***	3		•
Bitterroot Mountains					
101. Lolo Peak	11.4 miles	*****	5		•
102. Sweeney Creek Lakes	12.6 miles	****	5		•
103. Bass Lake	15.4 miles	*****	5		•
104. Kootenai Creek	14.6 miles	*****	5	•	•
105. Saint Mary Peak	7 miles	*****	3	•	•
106. Glen Lake	5.4 miles	****	3	•	•
107. Bear Creek Overlook	4 miles	*****	3	•	•
108. Bear Creek to Bryan Lake	16.5 miles	*****	5		•
109. Sheafman Creek Lakes	13.8 miles	*****	5		•
110. Mill Creek Falls	6.2 miles	****	3	•	•
111. Blodgett Canyon	9.8 miles	*****	3	•	•
112. Blodgett Canyon Overlook and Canyon Lake	2.8 miles or 9 miles	***** or ****	2 or 5	•	•
113. Camas Lake	5.6 miles	****	3	•	•
114. Bailey Lake	2.4 miles	****	2	•	•
115. Fish Lake	8.6 miles	*****	4		•
116. Lake Como Loop	7.7 miles	****	3	•	•
117. Little Rock Creek Lake	8.4 miles	*****	4		•
118. Chaffin Creek Lakes	12.2 miles	*****	4		•
119. Trapper Peak	8 miles	*****	5		•
120. Boulder Creek Falls	8 miles	****	3	•	•
121. Boulder Point Lookout	4.6 miles	*****	5		•
122. Nelson Lake	5.6 miles	****	4		•
123. Castle Rock	5 miles	***	3		•
SAPPHIRE MOUNTAINS					
124. Welcome Creek	5.2 miles	***	4		•
125. Stony Lake and Dome-Shaped Mountain	7 miles or 13.2 miles	*** or ****	4 or 5		•

EXCEPTIONAL WILDFLOWERS	EXCEPTIONAL WATERFALLS	EXCEPTIONAL OLD GROWTH	HISTORICAL RELEVANCE	EXCEPTIONAL BERRY PICKING	EXCEPTIONAL FISHING	BICYCLES PERMITTED
•					•	•
•	•					•
					•	•
		•				•
			•			
		•			•	
					•	
	•					
			•			
					•	
		•			•	
		•			•	
•	•					
	•					•
					•	
				•	•	•
				•	•	
						•
	•				•	
				•	•	
	•					
			•			
				•		
			•	•		•
		•	•	•	•	
•					•	•

Introduction

Considered the backbone of the world by the Blackfeet Indians of the northern Rocky Mountains, the region now protected as Glacier National Park is one of the pillars of the national parks system, the archetype of big, wild America. A smattering of trappers and miners traipsed through the area beginning in the early 19th century, and in 1891, completion of the Great Northern Railway brought a wave of settlers bewitched by the scenic splendor and fertile valleys of northwest Montana. Recognizing the intrinsic value of the area, influential leaders pressed for its protection. Chief among them was George Bird Grinnell, "the Father of Glacier National Park," childhood next-door-neighbor to John James Audubon, respected naturalist in his own right, and founding member of Boone and Crockett Club with Teddy Roosevelt. The efforts of Grinnell and others culminated when President William Taft signed the bill establishing Glacier as the tenth national park in the United States in 1910.

At more than a million acres, Glacier is far from the largest national park—it ranks a mere fifteenth among the sites managed by the National Park Service—but its dramatic landscapes of glacier-scoured granite peaks, lively rivers, alpine lakes, and wildflower-decorated meadows earn it the distinction of America's favorite park. Although several glaciers still cling to life on the park's highest cirques, Glacier is named not for these but for the great glacial activity of twenty thousand years ago that carved the park's peaks and scooped out its 762 lakes. The park provides refuge to a panoply of some of the continent's most charismatic critters. Grizzly bears, mountain goats, moose, wolves, and even wolverines wander among its cirques and hanging valleys.

More than two million visitors come to Glacier National Park every year, with the average visit lasting a scant three hours. Less than 2 percent of visitors log time in the backcountry, which means hikers can easily enjoy a crowd-free experience with a little effort. Glacier's high season runs roughly from Memorial Day to Labor Day, but the park offers unique recreation opportunities in every season. In early spring, the wildlife have become active but the crowds have not; brilliant wildflowers stun in early summer, followed by huckleberries; visitors in autumn marvel at the golden carpet of larch that drapes the forested foothills; and snow-shoers and Nordic skiers have unfettered and uncrowded access to the park in winter.

But, more than other grand dames of the national parks system, Glacier is a hiker's park, with its highlights accessible only with hiking boots.

WHAT'S IN THIS BOOK?

This guidebook focuses on the best day hikes within Glacier National Park and western Montana, but these hikes are only a fraction of what Montana has to offer hikers. Weekend-worthy wilderness hikes throughout the region—the 100,000-acre Cabinet Mountains Wilderness, where alpine

Opposite: *Enjoying the last light over Middle Oregon Lake in the northern Bitterroots (Hike 94)*

lakes hide among sheer shelves of rock; the shallow, grass-fringed pools of the Whitefish Range, just shy of the Canadian border in northwest Montana; the jeweled basins of the Swan Range; the granite bastions of the Selway-Bitterroot Wilderness—await explorers in western Montana's Glacier Country.

PERMITS, REGULATIONS, AND FEES

Hikers have a responsibility to know, understand, and abide by regulations governing the areas they explore. As our public lands have become increasingly popular and as state and federal funding have continued to decrease, regulations and permits have become components in managing and maintaining our natural heritage. The US Forest Service, National Park Service, Montana State Parks, and other land managers have implemented a sometimes complex set of land-use rules and regulations.

Glacier National Park charges an entrance fee. Hikers who frequent national parks and forests should consider buying the America the Beautiful Annual Pass (interagency pass; http://store.usgs.gov/pass) for $80. This pass grants the driver and three other adults in a vehicle access to all federal recreation sites that charge a day-use fee (children under sixteen are admitted free). These sites include national parks, national forests, national wildlife refuges, and Bureau of Land Management areas throughout the country.

State lands: Residents of Montana receive free access to Montana State Parks. Nonresidents will need to purchase either a day-use pass or an annual pass, available at all state parks.

Mission Mountains Tribal Wilderness: Nontribal visitors to the Mission Mountains Tribal Wilderness will need to purchase either a multiday or annual recreation permit. Visitors planning to camp, either in the backcountry or at one of the primitive front-country campgrounds on tribal lands, will need to purchase an additional overnight permit. First-time purchasers will need to buy a permit in person at one of the vendors listed on the Confederated Salish and Kootenai Tribes website (http://nrd.csktribes.org/fwrc/recreation). Subsequent permits can be purchased through the Montana Fish, Wildlife, and Parks website (http://fwp.mt.gov).

WEATHER

The weather in mountainous regions is famously unpredictable, but Montana holds special disdain for the mores of meteorology. Browning, on the eastern edge of Glacier National Park, holds the national record for a twenty-four-hour temperature drop: on January 23, 1916, the temperature plunged from forty-four degrees Fahrenheit to fifty-six degrees below zero. Meteorologically, Montana west of the Continental Divide is considered part of the Pacific Northwest, with a maritime-influenced climate in which Pacific Ocean currents create a more temperate climate. East of the Continental Divide, a continental climate produces colder, drier winters and warmer summers. In the mountains, where the two climates mix, is where generalities break down. And that's where hikers go. Generally, though, snow blankets the high country from late October through late May but it can fall any time of year. Summers are generally mild with extended periods of no or low rainfall. July through early October is usually a delightful time to hike the region.

Plan your hike according to your weather preference. No matter where in the region you hike, always pack raingear and extra layers of clothing. Being caught in a sudden rain- or windstorm with inadequate clothing can lead to hypothermia (loss of body temperature), which is deadly if not treated immediately.

Other weather-induced hazards to be aware of result from past episodes of rain and snow. River and creek crossings can be extremely dangerous after periods of heavy rain or snowmelt. Always use caution and sound judgment when fording any body of water. Be aware, too, that the National Park Service installs many of its larger bridges in the spring and removes them in the fall to ward against snowload and runoff damage; if you are hiking outside high season, it is best to check the park's trail conditions report to see whether your water crossings will be aided by a bridge.

Snowfields remaining from the previous winter's snowpack can be hazardous, especially for hikers who head into steep high-country slopes early in the hiking season. Depending on the severity of the past winter and the weather conditions of the spring and early summer, some trails may not melt out until well into summer. In addition to treacherous footing and route-finding difficulties, lingering snowfields can be prone to avalanches or slides. Use caution when crossing them and review techniques for self-arrest before traversing them.

Strong winds can happen anywhere in the region, particularly at higher elevations and in combination with heavy rainfall. Avoid hiking during high winds and windy periods, which carry with them the hazards of falling trees and branches.

Short-term forecasts are the key to planning the safest and most enjoyable trip. A high-pressure system could offer a week of premier weather in May, while a low-pressure system could present a week of wetness in June. I have hiked in or on snow every month of the year in western Montana.

Before setting out, check the National Weather Service forecast for the region and plan accordingly. And, forecast aside, be prepared, especially in the milder months when hikers can be caught in unpredicted temperature shifts and storms.

ROAD AND TRAIL CONDITIONS

Trails generally change little from year to year. But change can occur, sometimes very quickly. A heavy storm can cause a river to jump its channel, washing out sections of a trail or access road in moments. Windstorms can blow down trees across trails by the hundreds, obstructing paths. Avalanches, landslides, and forest fires can damage or obliterate trails. Lack of agency funding for trail repair and maintenance also leads to trail neglect and degradation.

Change, however, is not always bad. Trails are also created, improved, or rerouted over the course of time. Groups such as the Montana Wilderness Foundation, Selway-Bitterroot Frank Church Foundation, Bob Marshall Wilderness Association, and friends groups for state parks and federal wildlife refuges have been sources of countless hours of volunteer labor, helping local, state, and federal crews build and maintain trails in the areas covered by this book. These groups and others are listed under "Conservation and Trail Organizations" in the Resources section at the end of the book. You can connect with them—and perhaps add some muscle power or other expertise to the cause.

Management decisions can have greater impact even than floods and fires on our trails, including—but by no means limited to—ever-shrinking trail funding, inappropriate trail use, and conflicting land management policies and practices.

Decades ago the biggest threats to trails were the overharvesting of timber and the wanton building of roads to access it. As timber harvesting has substantially decreased on much of our national forest land, one of the biggest threats to our trails now is access: many roads once used for hauling timber—and by hikers to reach trailheads—are no longer being maintained. Many of these roads are slumping or grown over. They are becoming downright dangerous to drive or have washed out completely, severing access to trails. While the decommissioning of roads that go "nowhere" is economically and environmentally prudent, so is maintaining and keeping open the main roads that see a lot of use for trail access. Once a road has been closed for several years, the trails radiating from it often receive no maintenance and become obstructed or impossible to follow.

Wildfires present a perennial challenge to western Montana's trails. And although wildfires fulfill an important biological role in forest health, decades of fire suppression in the 20th century, exacerbated by the hotter, drier conditions wrought by climate change, mean that contemporary wildfires burn hotter, faster, and farther than in the past. The summers of 2015 and 2017 saw some of the worst fire seasons in recent memory, with conflagrations in every region in western Montana ranging from spot burns to complete devastation of old-growth forests.

Although it is beyond the scope of this book to keep every hike description up to date with recent fire activity, hikers entering recently burned areas should be aware of increased deadfall on the trail and the presence of hazardous standing snags overhead.

And, during fire season, hikers should contact the appropriate land manager (see Contacts) before setting out to ensure their trail of choice is not closed owing to fire activity.

Many of our trails are also threatened by increased motorized use. The speed and noise of motors don't mix well with horseback riders, hikers, and quiet muscle-powered modes of backcountry travel. Motorcycles and all-terrain vehicles have a heavy impact on trails. Even when users obey rules and regulations—and most do—wheels tear up tread far more than boots, and this is especially true in the fragile soils and lush meadows of the high country. Motor noise is incompatible with Leave No Trace backcountry principles. Although the majority of motorcyclists with whom we share trails are decent people, motorcycles simply preclude a wilderness experience. And while I support the rights of motorized recreation users to have access to public lands, many of the trails currently open to motorcycles should never have been opened to them. Although Montana has fared better than many of its neighbors in protecting traditional, nonmotorized recreational use on its public lands, several trails in this book, such as Hike 95 to Bonanza Lakes in the Northern Bitterroots, are open to motorized use. Motorized user groups would like to see more added to that list. The value of these routes, and the importance of maintaining a hiker presence on them, overrides the potential for having to put up with the bray of motorbikes.

WILDERNESS ETHICS

Ensuring the long-term survival of our trails and the wildlands they cross requires a group effort. To avoid fouling our own nest, hikers have nourished a "wilderness ethic" to leave the land as good as or better than we found it.

Hikers watch a sunset from Blodgett Canyon Overlook in the Bitterroot Mountains (Hike 112).

Instead of merely complying with no-litter rules, bring a bag and take some time to pick up after others. Avoid creating unauthorized trails. Rest on rock and camp on bare ground when possible to avoid trampling or killing vegetation in fragile dryland or alpine areas. Don't pollute streams or lakes with soaps or chemicals. As the adage says, take only pictures, leave only footprints.

Wilderness ethics, most of which apply when visiting all public open-space lands, rise from attitude and awareness rather than rules and regulations. The following are the accepted principles of Leave No Trace:

Plan ahead. Know the regulations of the area you plan to visit. Call ahead for current conditions. Check the weather forecast. Bring proper gear and prepare for emergencies.

Consider the abilities of your group, and assure that everyone understands wilderness ethics. Protect food from bears and other critters to avoid turning wild animals into a nuisance—or dangerous beggars.

Travel and camp on durable surfaces. Stay on the trail. Avoid tramping parallel trails to talk with a companion or widening trails to avoid mud. Don't cut switchbacks. Choose rocky off-trail routes when possible and avoid meadows. Picnic and camp on hard, dry surfaces such as rock, sand, gravel, or conifer-needle duff rather than on vegetation or meadows. Take special care to avoid tramping or camping within 100 feet of backcountry streams or lake shorelines.

Dispose of waste properly. Pack out everything you pack in. Human food and

A hiker and her trail dogs make an early season crossing of Bear Creek in the Selway-Bitterroot Wilderness (Hike 108).

trash is unhealthy for animals and leads to harmful habituation by animals to human presence and food. Bury human waste at least 200 feet from water sources, trails, or campsites. Use toilet paper sparingly and pack it out. A plastic bag confines odors effectively, and double bagging prevents any accidental contamination.

Leave what you find. Wildflowers, fossils, and other natural objects of beauty or interest should be left for others to discover and enjoy.

Minimize campfire impacts. Where fires are permitted, use existing fire rings if possible. Never cut live trees or branches for firewood. Most fires are unnecessary, but if you must build one, be sure it's dead out when you leave. A small, thoughtfully built fire can be completely extinguished and the ashes removed or buried to leave no trace.

Respect wildlife. Never feed wild animals or leave food available to them. This is for your own good and the protection of those who follow. Observe from a distance, for your safety as well as to prevent the animal from unnecessary exertion or danger. Keep pets under control so they don't disturb wildlife.

Be considerate of other visitors. Read on to find out how.

TRAIL ETIQUETTE

While wilderness ethics hone our respect for the land, trail etiquette steers us into balance with others we might see along the way. Many of the trails in this book are open to an array of trail users. Some trails are only for hikers, but others allow equestrians, mountain bikers, and even motorcycles. Common sense and courtesy will smooth out the possible bumps in any encounter. Beyond that, keep the guidelines below in mind to help make things better for everyone.

Right-of-way: When meeting other hikers, the uphill group has the right-of-way.

There are two general reasons for this. First, on steep ascents, hikers heading up may be watching the trail and might not notice the approach of descending hikers until they are face-to-face. More importantly, it's easier for descending hikers to break their stride and step off the trail than it is for those who have gotten into a good climbing rhythm. But by all means, if you're the uphill trekker and you wish to grant passage to oncoming hikers, go right ahead with this act of trail kindness.

Moving off-trail: When meeting other user groups (like bicyclists and horseback riders), the hiker should yield. This is because hikers are more mobile and flexible than other users, making it easier for them to step off the trail.

Encountering horses: When meeting horseback riders, the hiker should step off the downhill side of the trail unless the terrain makes this difficult or dangerous. All hikers in a group should move to the same side of the trail. Remain visible and talk in a normal voice to the riders. This calms the horses. If hiking with a dog, keep your buddy very close and under control.

Hiking with dogs: One of the most contentious issues in hiking circles is whether dogs should be allowed on trails. Although pets are prohibited from trails in Glacier National Park, many of the areas in this book allow dogs. Hikers who take dogs on the trails should have their dog on a leash or under strict voice command at all times. Some areas require dogs to be on leash, such as designated pet areas within the Rattlesnake National Recreation Area. Too many dog owners flagrantly disregard this regulation, setting themselves up for tickets, hostile words from fellow hikers, and the possibility of losing the right to bring Fido on that trail in the future. Some people are uncomfortable with loose dogs that rush toward them—and they may have had a bad experience to justify that. Respect their right to a dog-free space. On the other hand, a well-behaved, leashed dog can help warm up these hikers to canine companions.

Never roll rocks off trails or cliffs: You risk injuring someone or something below.

WATER

As a general rule, assume that all water is contaminated, and treat all backcountry water sources to avoid *Giardia*, waterborne parasites, and other aquatic nasties. Treating water can be as simple as boiling it, using an ultraviolet light purifier, chemically purifying it with iodine tablets, or pumping it through a water filter and purifier. Note: Pump units labeled as filters generally remove everything but viruses, which are too small to be filtered out. Pumps labeled as purifiers use a chemical—usually iodine—to render viruses inactive after filtering all the other bugs out.

FISHING

Some hikers consider a fishing rod essential gear in their daypacks. However, fishing is a highly regulated sport, with seasons, gear restrictions, and catch limits that can vary by fish species as well as by stream or lake. Anglers age twelve and older must have a Montana fishing license and a conservation license. Regulations and requirements are spelled out in the *Montana Fishing Guide* pamphlet available at the Montana Fish, Wildlife, and Parks website (http://fwp.mt.gov/fishing/) and at most retail locations. Glacier National Park operates under its own fishing regulations: anglers there need no permit, but they must abide by the regulations and requirements spelled out on the park's website (www.nps.gov/glac/planyourvisit/fishing.htm).

HIKING AMONG HUNTERS

Many public lands are open to hunting. The season dates vary, but generally big-game hunting begins in early August and ends in December. While hiking in areas frequented by hunters, it's best to make yourself visible by donning an orange cap and vest. If hiking with a dog, put an orange vest on your buddy too. The majority of hunters are responsible, decent folks (and conservationists who provide significant support for public lands), and you should have little concern when encountering them in the backcountry. Still, if being around outdoors-people schlepping rifles is unnerving to you, stick to hiking where hunting is prohibited—within the scope of this book, that means Glacier National Park and state and local parks.

WILDLIFE

While for the most part wildlife wants little to do with humans, it pays to be prepared for encounters with certain creatures. In Glacier and western Montana, those creatures include rattlesnakes, ticks, grizzly bears, and cougars.

Rattlesnakes

In low-elevation, dry canyon areas, such as the lower Rattlesnake Creek Valley in Missoula, hikers may encounter the western rattlesnake. As intent on avoiding you as you are of them, rattlesnakes generally keep to themselves. But if you get too close, they'll set off an alarm by rattling their tails. Walk away, allowing the rattler to retreat; never try to catch, provoke, or pursue one. Rattlesnake bites in western Montana are rare; deaths by rattlesnake bite even more so. If you are bit, remain calm. Wash the bite, immobilize the limb, apply a wet wrap, and seek medical attention immediately.

Ticks

Parasites that live off the blood of their hosts, ticks are arachnids whose role as a disease vector is what should concern you. Generally active in the springtime throughout western Montana, particularly at low elevations, ticks inhabit shrubs and tall grasses. When hikers brush up against these plants, ticks have the opportunity to hitch a ride. During tick season, wear long sleeves and tuck pant legs into socks.

Do a full-body check after hiking; ticks prefer dark, damp areas, so pay particular attention to armpits and the scalp. And if a tick has fastened itself to you, get out your tweezers. Gently squeeze its head (try not to break it off, or it may become lodged and infected) until it lets go. Wash and disinfect the bite area. Most ticks in the Northwest do not carry Lyme disease or other diseases. Still, it's best to monitor the bite. If a rash develops, seek medical help immediately.

The Bear Essentials

Although grizzlies have not been definitively sighted in the Bitterroots since the 1950s, save an errant radio-collared sow who wandered through from the Missions in 2008, the other areas covered by this book are in grizzly country. And western Montana harbors one of the densest black bear populations in the state.

Most hikers consider themselves lucky to catch a glimpse of a bear's bottom as it reacts normally to human contact—by running away. But occasionally a bruin may want to get a look at you. In very rare cases, a bear may act aggressively. And while many visitors to western Montana consider a glimpse of a grizzly to be a once-in-a-lifetime experience, it's up to you to make sure it's not for all the wrong reasons. To avoid an un-*bear*-able

A grizzly bear makes a border crossing of its own, just outside Waterton Lakes.

encounter, heed the following advice compiled from bear experts:

- **Respect a bear's need for space.** If you see a bear in the distance, make a wide detour around it. If that's not possible, leave the area.
- **Make lots of noise**—more than you think you need. Wind, crashing creeks, and the muffling effect of thick vegetation can diminish a bear's chances of hearing you before you're too close. And, no, bear bells do not help: they are much too quiet to alert a bear to your presence over ambient noise, and they often lull their wearers into a false sense of security. Your best bets: clapping, singing, or striking the tip of a trekking pole on trailside rocks.
- **Avoid direct eye contact** if you encounter a bear at close range, and, most important, do not run.
- **Talk in a low, calm manner** to the bear to help identify yourself as a human.
- **Wave your arms slowly** above your head to make yourself look taller.
- **Slowly move upwind** of the bear if you can do so without crowding the bear.

The bear's strongest sense is its sense of smell, and if it can sniff you and identify you as human, it may retreat.

- **Know how to interpret bear actions.** A nervous bear will often rumble in its chest, clack its teeth, and "pop" its jaw. It may paw the ground and swing its head violently side to side. If the bear does this, watch it closely (without staring directly at it). Continue to speak low and calmly.
- If you cannot safely move away from the bear, and the animal does not flee, **try to scare it away** by clapping your hands or yelling.
- **A bear may bluff-charge**—run at you but stop well before reaching you—to try to intimidate you. Resist the urge to run, as that would turn the bluff into a real charge and you will *not* be able to outrun the bear.
- **In the case of a bear attack,** a human without the benefit of bear spray should react differently depending on whether the bear is being predatory or defensive. **In a predatory confrontation** (more typical of the rare black bear that's

stalking you), fight back aggressively. **In a defensive confrontation** (more typical of grizzly encounters, especially sows with cubs or food caches), drop to the ground and play dead if contact is about to be made. Lie on your stomach, clasp your hands behind your neck, and use your elbows and toes to avoid being rolled over. If the bear succeeds in rolling you over, keep rolling until you're on your stomach. Remain still and try not to struggle or scream. A defensive bear will no longer attack once it feels it has stopped the threat. Do not move until you're sure the bear has left the area.

Where Cougars Roam

University of Montana fans might disagree, but western Montana is cougar country. Cougars, also called mountain lions, are among the most secretive of the apex predators lurking in the wilds of western Montana. Very few hikers ever see cougars in the wild. But Montana supports a healthy population of *Felix concolor*; they are linked to virtually any habitat where deer are found in good numbers, which encompasses the entire coverage area of this book. While cougar encounters are extremely rare in the region, they do occur. To make sure the encounter is a positive one (at least for you), it is important to understand a bit about these wildcats.

Cougars are curious critters (after all, they're cats). They will follow hikers simply to see what kind of beasts we are, but they almost never attack adult humans. If you do encounter one, remember that cougars rely on prey that cannot, or will not, fight back. So, as soon as you see the cat, heed the following recommendations of Montana Fish, Wildlife, and Parks.

While recreating in cougar habitat:

- Hike in small groups and make enough noise to avoid surprising a cougar.
- Keep small children close to the group, preferably in plain sight just ahead of you.
- Do not let pets run unleashed.
- Minimize your activity during dawn and dusk hours.

If you encounter a cougar:

- **Stop, don't run.** Running triggers a cougar's instinct to chase. Make sure to pick up and hold small children.
- **Don't approach the animal,** especially if it's near a kill or with cubs.
- **Try to appear larger than the cougar.** Never take your eyes off the animal or turn your back. Don't crouch or try to hide.
- **Maintain eye contact** to establish your dominance.
- **Be vocal,** talking calmly and regularly.
- If the animal displays aggressive behavior, **shout, wave your arms, and throw rocks.** The idea is to convince the cougar that you are a potential danger—not prey.
- If the cougar attacks, **use bear spray** or, if you have one, a firearm.

DAY HIKING GEAR

Although gear is beyond the scope of this book (which is about where to hike, not how to hike), it's worth noting a few points. No hiker should venture up a trail without being properly equipped. Starting with the feet, a comfortable pair of boots—and well-fitting socks—can make all the difference between a wonderful hike and a blistering affair. Keep your feet happy and you'll be happy.

For clothing, wear whatever is most comfortable except for cotton. Cotton is a wonderful fabric, but not the best for hiking. When it gets wet, it stays wet and lacks insulation value. In

A hiker keeps her boots dry while swimming in Lower St. Regis Lake (Hike 89).

fact, wet cotton sucks away body heat, leaving you susceptible to hypothermia. Far better: layers of synthetics or wool.

While every hiker's gear list will vary, some items should be in every daypack. Hikers who venture deep into the woods should be prepared to spend the night out, with emergency food and shelter. Mountain storms or whiteouts can whip up quickly, catching fair-weather hikers by surprise. And there's always the chance of an illness or injury that could delay or prevent you from returning to the trailhead. Be prepared with the Ten Essentials.

The Ten Essentials

The point of the Ten Essentials, originated by The Mountaineers, has always been to answer two basic questions: Can you prevent emergencies and respond positively should one occur (items 1–5)? And can you safely spend a night—or more—outside (items 6–10)? Use this list as a guide and tailor it to the needs of your outing.

1. **Navigation:** Always bring a map and compass as a backup for your GPS device. Also consider packing an altimeter and a personal locator beacon or other device to contact emergency first responders.

2. **Headlamp:** A headlamp (don't forget extra bulb and batteries) is more functional than a flashlight, because it leaves your hands free.

3. **Sun protection:** For protection from the sun, wear a wide-brimmed hat, good sunglasses, lip protectant, and sun-protective clothes, and use a strong sunblock with both UVA and UVB protection.

4. **First aid:** A good basic wilderness first-aid kit should include bandages; skin closures; gauze pads and dressings; roller bandage or wrap; tape; antiseptic; blister prevention and treatment supplies; nitrile gloves; tweezers; needle; nonprescription painkillers; anti-inflammatory, anti-diarrheal, and antihistamine tablets; topical antibiotic; and any important personal prescriptions, including an EpiPen if you are allergic to bee or hornet venom.

5. **Knife:** A knife comes in handy for both first-aid and emergency kindling. Also consider a multitool, strong tape, some cordage, and gear repair supplies.

6. **Fire:** Carry a butane lighter or two (and some waterproof matches) in addition to firestarter, which helps with wet wood.

7. **Shelter:** In addition to a rain shell, carry a single-use bivy sack, plastic tube tent, or jumbo plastic trash bag.

8. **Extra food:** For shorter trips a one-day supply is reasonable.

9. **Extra water:** Carry sufficient water and have the skills and tools required to obtain and purify additional water.

10. **Extra clothes:** Extra clothes are essential, even if you think you know exactly what the weather will be. Pack extra layers of quality clothes in your daypack; temperatures can drop suddenly, winds can kick up, or an unexpected storm can suddenly move in over a ridgetop.

Before You Go

Always give somebody reliable information—best to write it down—about where you're going, what you're doing, and when you plan to be home. Also include which land manager, agency, or emergency operator to contact should you not return in a reasonable time.

TRAILHEAD CONCERNS

Sadly, the topic of trailhead and trail crime must be addressed. As urban areas encroach upon our green spaces, societal ills follow along. By and large our hiking trails are safe places—far safer than most city streets—and violent crimes are extremely rare. Common sense and vigilance, however, are the rule. This is true for all hikers, but especially for solo hikers. Be aware of your surroundings at all times. Leave your itinerary with someone back home. If something doesn't feel right, it probably isn't. Take action by leaving the place or situation immediately.

If you arrive at a trailhead and someone looks suspicious, don't discount your intuition. Take notes on the person and his or her vehicle. Record the license plate and report the behavior to the authorities. Do not confront the person. Leave and go to another trail. Remember, though, most hikers are friendly, decent people. Some may be a little introverted, but that's no cause for worry.

By far your biggest concern should be with trailhead theft. While most car break-ins are crimes of opportunity by drug addicts looking for loot to support their fix, organized gangs intent on stealing IDs have also been known to target parked cars at trailheads. There's no sure way of preventing this from happening to you other than being dropped off at the trailhead or taking the bus (rarely an option), but you can make your car less of a target by not leaving anything of value in it. Take your wallet, cell phone, and listening devices with you—or better yet, don't bring them along in the first place. Don't leave anything in your car that may appear valuable. A duffle bag on the backseat may contain dirty T-shirts, but a thief may think there's a laptop in it. Save yourself the hassle of returning to a busted window by not giving criminals a reason to clout your car. And contact your government officials and demand that law enforcement be a priority in our national forests. We taxpayers have a right to recreate safely on our public lands.

Using This Book

The Day Hiking guidebooks were developed to be easy to use and to provide enough detail to help you explore a region. They include all the information you need to find and enjoy the hikes but leave enough room for you to make your own discoveries. I have hiked every mile of trail described in *Day Hiking: Glacier National Park and Western Montana*, so you can follow the directions and advice with confidence.

WHAT THE RATINGS MEAN

Each hike starts with two subjective assessments: a rank of 1 to 5 stars for an overall rating, and a numerical score of 1 to 5 for a route's difficulty. The overall appeal rating is based on my impressions of each route's scenic beauty, natural wonder, and other unique qualities, such as solitude potential and wildlife-viewing opportunities.

***** Unmatched hiking adventure, great scenic beauty, and wonderful trail experience

**** Excellent experience, sure to please all

*** A great hike, with one or more fabulous features to enjoy

** May lack the "killer view," but offers lots of little moments to enjoy

* Worth doing as a refreshing walk, especially if you're in the neighborhood

Making a safe stream crossing on the way to Heart Lake in the northern Bitterroots (Hike 97)

MAP LEGEND

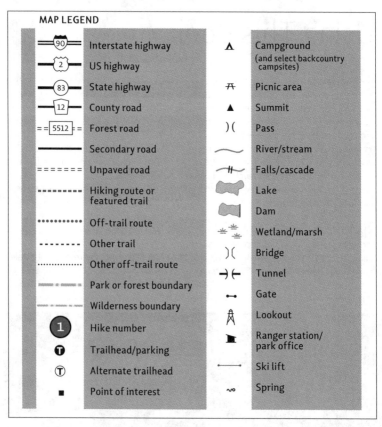

Interstate highway	Campground (and select backcountry campsites)
US highway	Picnic area
State highway	Summit
County road	Pass
Forest road	River/stream
Secondary road	Falls/cascade
Unpaved road	Lake
Hiking route or featured trail	Dam
Off-trail route	Wetland/marsh
Other trail	Bridge
Other off-trail route	Tunnel
Park or forest boundary	Gate
Wilderness boundary	Lookout
Hike number	Ranger station/park office
Trailhead/parking	Ski lift
Alternate trailhead	Spring
Point of interest	

The **difficulty** score is based on trail length, overall elevation gain, steepness, and trail conditions. Generally, trails that are rated more difficult (4 or 5) are longer and steeper than average. But it's not a simple equation. A short, steep trail over talus slopes may be rated 5 while a long, smooth trail with little elevation gain may be rated 2.

5   Extremely difficult: Excessive elevation gain and/or more than 5 miles one-way

4   Difficult: Some steep sections, possibly rough or poorly maintained trail

3   Moderate: A good workout, but no real problems

2   Moderately easy: Relatively flat or short route with good trail

1   Easy: A relaxing stroll in the woods

To help explain a hike's difficulty score, you'll also find **roundtrip** mileage (unless otherwise noted as loop or one-way mileage), total **elevation gain**, and the hike's **high point.** While I consulted maps and measured the hikes using GPS, a trip's distance

Drinking in the view of the Many Glacier area of Glacier National Park from Ptarmigan Tunnel (Hike 49)

can vary depending on how you customize the route. The elevation gain measures the *cumulative* gain and loss you'll encounter on a trip, accounting for all significant changes in elevation along the way. As for the trip's high point, it's worth noting that not all high points are at the end of the trail—a route may run over a high ridge before dropping to a lake basin, for instance.

The recommended **season** information will help you choose a hike. Many trails can be enjoyed from the time they lose their winter snowpack up until they're buried in fresh snow the following fall. But snowpack varies from year to year, so a trail that's open in May one year may be snow-covered until July the next. The hiking season for each trail is an estimate. Contact land managers for current conditions before you go.

Hikes in this guidebook typically reference the standard 7.5-minute USGS topographical **maps**. However, I also list maps available from local groups, agencies, or national forests. And each hike is depicted on a map based on my visits to the area. While it's a great map to give you a sense of the scope and terrain, you should always carry a reliable, up-to-date topographic map.

Under **contact** I include the area's governing agency, which has information about localized maps as well as current access and trail conditions. You will find the phone numbers and websites for these agencies in Resources at the back of this guidebook. **Notes** for each trip comprise permits required, road conditions, possible hazards, and seasonal closures. **GPS** coordinates are provided to help get you to the

A NOTE ABOUT SAFETY

Safety is an important concern in all outdoor activities. No guidebook can alert you to every hazard or anticipate the limitations of every reader. Therefore, the descriptions of roads, trails, routes, and natural features in this book are not representations that a particular place or excursion will be safe for your party. When you follow any of the routes described in this book, you assume responsibility for your own safety. Under normal conditions, such excursions require the usual attention to traffic, road and trail conditions, weather, terrain, the capabilities of your party, and other factors. Keeping informed on current conditions and exercising common sense are the keys to a safe, enjoyable outing.

—*Mountaineers Books*

trailhead—and back to your car should you wander off-trail. They are given in decimal degrees, with the north value followed by the west value (the negative number) and are calculated basd on the WGS84 datum.

Finally, **icons** at the start of each hike give a quick overview of what each trail has to offer:

 Kid-friendly

 Dog-friendly

 Exceptional wildflowers in season

 Exceptional waterfalls

 Exceptional old growth

 Historical relevance

 Exceptional berry picking in season

 Exceptional fishing opportunities

Getting there includes thorough driving directions that will get you to the trailhead from the nearest large town or geographic feature. **On the trail** route descriptions tell you what might be found on the hike, including geographic features, scenic potential, flora and fauna, and more. Options for **extending your trip** round out many hikes.

ENJOY THE TRAILS

Most importantly, be safe and enjoy the thrill of discovery and exercise on the trails. They exist for our enjoyment and for the enjoyment of future generations of hikers.

Consider stepping up to be an advocate for trails. Your involvement can be as simple as picking up trash, signing up for a volunteer work party, joining a trail advocacy group, educating fellow citizens, or writing a letter to Congress or your state representatives. Introduce children to our trails. We need to continue a legacy of good trail stewardship. These seemingly small acts can make a big difference. At the end of this book is a list of organizations working on behalf of trails and wildlands in western Montana. Several of them organize great group hikes into the areas covered by this book and beyond. Check them out.

Happy hiking!

Opposite: Sunset over the Northwest Peak Scenic Area, as viewed from Northwest Peak (Hike 1)

yaak valley

The far northwest corner of Montana was once known for the trees that came out of it on the back of log trucks. Slowly it is becoming known for the trees that remain—perhaps the most diverse mid-elevation forest in the state. Most of the Purcells lay thickly ensconced under glaciers during the last ice age, so with few exceptions they lack the chiseled features of their neighbors. Instead, explorers will find quiet forests, lakes tucked in tiny canyons, graceful aspens, and willow-dense meadows; no wonder this is grizzly and moose country.

① Northwest Peak

RATING/ DIFFICULTY	ROUNDTRIP	ELEV GAIN/ HIGH POINT	SEASON
*****/3	4.4 miles	1610 feet/ 7706 feet	July–early Oct

Map: USGS Northwest Peak, MT; **Contact:** Kootenai National Forest, Three Rivers Ranger District; **Note:** Open to horses and bicycles. Open to motorcycles; **GPS:** 48.9630°, -115.9282°

Except for the last quarter mile of talus, this 4.4-mile roundtrip trek is one of the easiest alpine summit hikes in northwest Montana. From the white clapboard walls of the old fire lookout, hikers are likely to have the view all to themselves, and there's never a line for the outhouse—one of Montana's highest-elevation privies—either.

GETTING THERE
From Yaak, drive west on the Yaak River Road (Montana Highway 508) 2 miles, just past milepost 27, to Pete Creek Road (Forest Road 338). Follow this sometimes paved, sometimes gravel road, turning left onto West Fork Road at 13 miles and right onto Winkum Creek Road shortly after, to stay on FR 338. The trailhead (elev. 6130 feet) is 19 miles from Yaak River Road. A pullout on the right shoulder accommodates two vehicles. (For a preview of the Northwest Peak Scenic

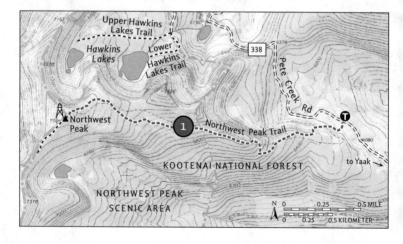

Area, stop at the viewpoint spur road 1 mile before the trailhead to peer over the frequently fog-shrouded Yaak Valley.)

ON THE TRAIL
Tucked into the thick mid-elevation forests of far northwest Montana, the tiny timber community of Yaak is not on the way to anything. And the nearby Northwest Peak Scenic Area is out of the way even for Yaak residents. That alone recommends it for a hike, but the scenery helps—a lonely country of thick forests, glacier-ground peaks, and tiny lakes—this is a quiet neighbor to the Selkirks and Cabinets. At 7706 feet, Northwest Peak is the centerpiece of the 19,000-acre Northwest Peak Scenic Area, and its summit is easily accessible via a long drive and short hike. Although Northwest Peak Trail 169 is one of the few in this book open to motorcycles, hikers needn't worry about the bray of motors interrupting their solitude; the long drive to the trailhead and the unrideable final half mile keep use of any kind light.

The first mile of the hike ascends rather directly through open forest. Waist-high huckleberry shrubs should keep most hikers busy come August. Just be sure to make your presence known: this is key habitat for the Cabinet-Yaak grizzly recovery area.

Under thinning tree cover, cross several small meadows stacked high with granite. At 1.9 miles (elev. 7350 feet), the easy tread ends on the south shoulder of Northwest Peak. Peer down to the pair of Hawkins Lakes to the northeast. Peer up into the gracefully twisted canopies of alpine larch. The high-elevation deciduous conifer—relatively uncommon in northwest Montana—loses its needles in a glorious golden display every fall, making this a great autumn hiking destination.

The stars and bars fly just shy of the Canadian border at Northwest Peak Lookout.

From here, the trail switchbacks up the steep final stretch, gaining 400 feet in 0.3 mile on compacted granite, to reach the summit at 2.2 miles (elev. 7706 feet). Check out the white clapboard lookout anchored solidly in place against the region's heavy snowpack and high winds. Canada lies a mile or so to the north, Idaho the same distance to the west. And directly below lies one of the last and largest unprotected tracts of wild forest in northwest Montana.

EXTENDING YOUR TRIP
Hikers keen on a 2-mile ridgeline rock hop can travel cross-country south from the summit of Northwest Peak to Davis Peak. It's part of the official Pacific Northwest Trail route (see "Crown to Coast: The Pacific Northwest Trail" sidebar). Otherwise, just up Pete Creek Road from the Northwest Peak trailhead, a pair of quarter-mile-long trails accesses Hawkins Lakes; anglers can land successful casts from the granite hunks surrounding the shore. Be sure to plan for every possible type of weather; even in the meteorologically fickle state of Montana, the northwest corner has notoriously capricious conditions.

2 Rock Candy Mountain

RATING/ DIFFICULTY	ROUNDTRIP	ELEV GAIN/ HIGH POINT	SEASON
*****/5	7.8 miles	3150 feet/ 7204 feet	Late June–Oct

Maps: USGS Northwest Peak, MT; USGS Mount Baldy, MT; **Contact:** Kootenai National Forest, Three Rivers Ranger District; **Note:** Open to horses and bicycles; **GPS:** 48.8701°, -115.9357°

Named by early Kootenai National Forest ranger Sam Billings for the rock formations on its summit, Rock Candy Mountain provides some of the sweetest views in northwest Montana. It also puts on one of the best floral shows, its colorful flowers complementing the distinctive granite hunks of its summit.

GETTING THERE
From Yaak, drive 7.4 miles south on the Yaak River Road (Montana Highway 508) to Spread Creek Road (Forest Road 435). Turn right (north) and proceed 6.2 miles, bearing left at 5 miles to remain on FR 435, to the signed trailhead on the right (elev. 4190 feet). The disused roadbed that comprises the initial trail segment accommodates several vehicles.

ON THE TRAIL
Part of the Northwest Peak Scenic Area, but less popular (even by Yaak standards) than Northwest Peak, Rock Candy Mountain is, in many ways, a more captivating hike, with 360-degree vistas for half its length, although there's nothing sweet about its steep climb. Rock Candy Mountain Trail 461 immediately leaves an obscure old

Glacier lilies gild the long ridge of Rock Candy Mountain.

roadbed in favor of a steep pitch through western redcedar and lodgepole pine with talus aprons and towering aspen occasionally breaking up the proceedings. Elk sign is plentiful here, hinting at what is likely the trail's primary use.

After nearly a mile, the trail intersects an old roadbed, briefly relenting from its ascent in a thicket of slide alder and cedar. Soon the trail resumes its upward course, climbing up the apex of the ridge through a phalanx of lodgepole and its beargrass attendants, occasionally closing in with a tiny unnamed stream. The hiking here is typical of northwest Montana mid-elevation forest, if unremarkable, but the plentiful huckleberry

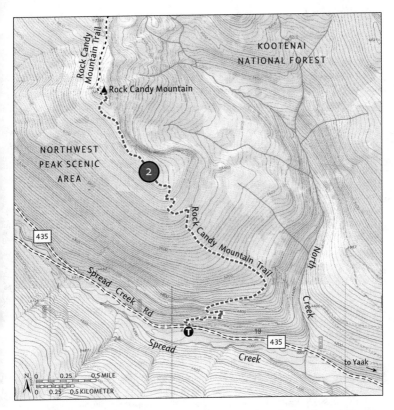

picking helps pass the time (in late summer at least).

At 2.3 miles (elev. 6100 feet), exit the trees for a vast, steep slope of flowers: lupine and lousewort, cat's ears and yarrow. Flowers flank and threaten to overtake the faint trail, but cairns guide the way. A glance to the left (west) shows Buckhorn Lookout, a historic tower, now Forest Service rental, that caps the long run of Buckhorn Ridge. The route levels out through a corridor of stunted sub-alpine fir and small larch before leaving tree line behind just shy of the sub-summit at 3.2

miles (elev. 6800 feet). Follow cairns as the route traverses across the south face of the peak; the main route bends around the flank of the mountain back into forest, but to reach the summit, look for cairns heading upslope at about 3.7 miles (elev. 6980 feet). Follow this faint boot path up through talus and flowers to a level notch; from there it follows rocky scree—listen for the whistle-squeak of pikas here—to the small, windswept summit at 3.9 miles (elev. 7204 feet).

Potshard pieces of quartz and the scattered remnants of an old fire lookout

CROWN TO COAST: THE PACIFIC NORTHWEST TRAIL

In the 1970s, in the midst of a backpacking boom, long-distance hiker Ron Strickland had an epiphany. Strickland, whose trail name was "Pathfinder," realized that an east-to-west long-distance hiking route would sample more of a region's varied topography—mountains, valleys, and everything in between—than the ridge-running routes popularized by the granddaddies of long-distance trails, the Pacific Crest Trail and Appalachian Trail.

A native of the Northeast, Strickland was nonetheless drawn to the Pacific Northwest. In 1970, Strickland hitched a ride to the east end of what is now the Pasayten Wilderness in north-central Washington and hiked westward across the tundra-like terrain over the North Cascades and to the Olympics, the vision of a cross-Washington corridor forming in his mind.

By 1972 Strickland expanded his route to include northern Idaho and western Montana. That year, Strickland conceived the Pacific Northwest Trail (PNT): stretching from Glacier National Park to Cape Alava on the Pacific coast in Olympic National Park, the PNT would tack westward 1200 miles through subalpine spires, sagebrush, cedar groves, and finally to the sea. Unlike the other preeminent long-distance trails, which hew closely to the contours of a particular mountain range, the PNT would climb over four mountain ranges (the Rockies, Selkirks, North Cascades, and Olympics) rather than following one. Over its course the PNT would pass through the varied topography of seven national forests, three national parks, and a patchwork of state and private land.

In 1977, Strickland founded the Pacific Northwest Trail Association (PNTA) and began walking the halls of Congress for federal recognition of the route. The plans stumbled when, in 1980, a congressional study decreed "it is overwhelmingly evident . . . the trail . . . is neither feasible nor desirable."

No stranger to long slogs, Strickland was undeterred. Committed to the idea that the PNT would be volunteer-driven like its long-distance brethren, he began rounding up like-minded adventurers. Since then, Strickland and others have fostered the PNTA to coordinate trail maintenance and act as a community for hikers.

Finally, in 2009, as part of its Omnibus Lands Bill, Congress formally designated the Pacific Northwest Trail a National Scenic Trail, one of eleven such congressionally designated long-distance trails in the United States.

On the ground, the formal designation means little, save for a few small scattered signs with the official PNT logo. The PNT patches together singletrack trails, city streets, cow paths, highway shoulders, logging roads, Native American trade routes, flood-control dikes, and even a ferry. The formal route remains in flux, particularly where the trail enters north Idaho from Montana.

decorate the summit, which is free of vegetation save a few snow-cowed subalpine fir and a carpet of heather. Rock Candy Mountain is the southernmost high point on a long lobe of intersecting ridges that connects it to Davis and Northwest Peaks to the north, the glacial origin of the peaks and the broad U-shaped valleys below immediately evident; note the impressive curved head-wall on the north face of the peak, which would not look out of place in Glacier.

EXTENDING YOUR TRIP

From the southwest face of the peak, the trail continues its long ridge run to Canuck Peak and a network of seldom-used trails that crisscross the Northwest Peak Scenic Area. Savvy shuttlers could arrange a point-to-point trip that connects Northwest Peak to Davis Mountain to Rock Candy Mountain for an 11-mile high-country hike.

3 Fish Lakes Canyon

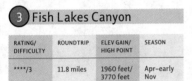

RATING/ DIFFICULTY	ROUNDTRIP	ELEV GAIN/ HIGH POINT	SEASON
****/3	11.8 miles	1960 feet/ 3770 feet	Apr–early Nov

Maps: USGS Yaak, MT; USGS Lost Horse Mountain, MT; USGS Mount Henry, MT; **Contact:** Kootenai National Forest, Three Rivers Ranger District; **Note:** Open to horses and bicycles; **GPS:** 48.8606°, -115.6436°

A quartet of ponds strung out like bobbers on a fishing line in a narrow, talus-packed canyon, the namesake lakes of this long, level ramble are almost incidental to its charm. The true attraction is the expansive and intact low-elevation forest—perhaps the most diverse forest in this book. The sight of 60-foot Turner Falls and the prospect of bagging your limit of fish or a bushel of berries doesn't hurt either.

GETTING THERE

From Yaak, drive south on paved Pipe Creek Road (Forest Road 68) 3.9 miles to Vinal Creek Road (FR 746). Drive north on FR 746 for 5.9 miles, just past the bridge over Vinal Creek, to the trailhead parking area on the right (elev. 3090 feet).

ON THE TRAIL

Plunging immediately into thick forest, Vinal Creek Trail 9 gains and loses little elevation, allowing hikers to focus on their surroundings. Lanky old-growth larch and western redcedar tower over perhaps every wild berry variety found in Montana; huckleberry, thimbleberry, raspberry, and gooseberry invite trailside tasting. It's increasingly rare to find low-elevation landscape like this intact.

Enter an open burn area and the first of seven crossings of Vinal Creek, all on small, sturdy footbridges. At times, thimbleberry

Backpackers cross talus in Fish Lakes Canyon.

The plunge pool of Turner Falls makes a fine swimming hole.

and gooseberry threaten to swallow the tread. The spectacular canyon walls begin to open up; larch and aspen perch on steep talus slopes.

Enter a small grove of impressive western redcedar, and at 3 miles (elev. 3520 feet), take the short spur to Turner Falls. The 60-foot horsetail cascades splash into a deep pool before funneling down a handful of smaller cascades. In late summer, low water levels expose an inviting rock lip that encircles the plunge pool, the perfect place for dangling sore feet.

Just past Turner Falls, next to a shallow, slow-moving stream channel—moose country to be sure—bear left at a junction (the way right climbs to Mount Henry; see Extending Your Trip). Now on the Pacific Northwest Trail (PNT) route (see "Crown to Coast" sidebar above), pass a few incongruous junipers, cross another small bridge, and, at 3.4 miles (elev. 3580 feet), bear right at the outlet of the lowest of the quartet of Fish Lakes. (The way left, the continuation of the PNT, rounds Bunker Hill and provides access to Hoskins Lakes.) Shallow and marshy, ringed by larch, this lake has mosquito- and mouse-friendly campsites. Walk across the talus at water's edge, cross the bridge at the head of the lake, and pass through thick brush and towering larch to the second lake at 3.9 miles (elev. 3620 feet). The long, sinuous canyon pinches the lake to some six feet across in the middle; great picnic and campsites can be found at this sandy waist of the lake and near its outlet.

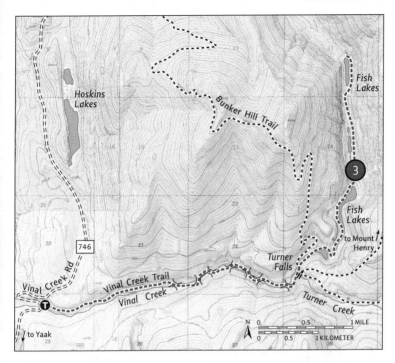

Skirt the left side of the lake on ankle-testing talus. Past the second lake, the trail gets significantly brushier; you may find yourself swimming in thimbleberry rather than water. As the canyon narrows, climb well above the hidden third lake. The trail then tops out in head-high brush before descending slightly to the fourth lake at 5.4 miles (elev. 3740 feet). The trail skirts its talus pile shore to end at a small campsite at the head of the lake. Stand on one of the rocky outcroppings to survey the scenery— or perhaps cast a line—before returning the way you came. Some old maps show the trail continuing farther up the canyon to Okaga Lake, but that tread is long gone.

EXTENDING YOUR TRIP

From the junction just north of Turner Falls, climb more than three thousand feet on brutally steep, sometimes obscure tread northeast to Mount Henry. The vista from the intact lookout on its summit is worth every drop of sweat. From here the trail continues on a much more calf-friendly course to Boulder Lakes (see Hike 25).

4 Pink Mountain

RATING/ DIFFICULTY	ROUNDTRIP	ELEV GAIN/ HIGH POINT	SEASON
***/3	6.4 miles	2250 feet/ 6597 feet	June–Oct

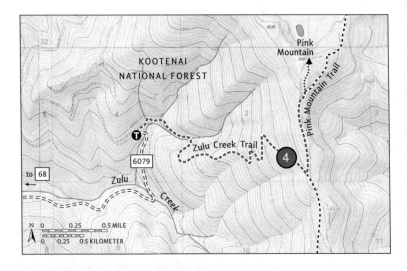

Map: USGS Pink Mountain, MT; **Contact:** Kootenai National Forest, Three Rivers Ranger District; **Note:** Open to horses and bicycles; **GPS:** 48.7364°, -115.6093°

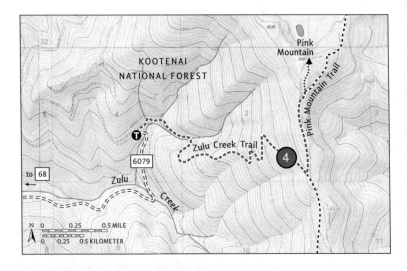 *Named not for its hue but for an early Forest Service ranger, Pink Mountain boasts plenty of summertime color on its high-elevation meadows. The former site of a fire lookout, Pink Mountain's gently rounded profile is typical of the Purcells; its expansive summit offers panoramic views of neighboring mountain ranges. While Pink may be petite, its trees are not; some of the area's few remaining old-growth white pines grow on Pink's forested skirts.*

GETTING THERE

From Yaak, drive south on Pipe Creek Road (Forest Road 68) for 8.4 miles. Turn left (east) on FR 6079 and proceed 2.5 miles to the signed trailhead on the right (elev. 4500

feet). Wide spots on the road's shoulder accommodate several vehicles.

ON THE TRAIL

Climbing through thick forest on Zulu Creek Trail 202, immediately cross an obscure roadbed; the Yaak area has a long and dubious history of roads-to-nowhere, so it's always a pleasure to find one reclaimed by nature. Like the Fish Lakes Canyon hike (see Hike 3), the mid-elevation forest flanking Pink Mountain features perhaps every tree species in Montana, including some lofty larch and a handful of the now-rare white pine. It's no wonder the 1980s Timber Wars that provoked so much conflict, and, ultimately, collaboration, between timber outfits and conservationists across the Northwest originated in the Yaak. After crossing a couple mossy rivulets, the trail bends toward the ridge and begins climbing more steeply through a hall of larch

A hiker descends the trailless top of Pink Mountain.

and lodgepole. The lightly maintained trail tends to accumulate blowdowns, none large. Beargrass, pipsissewa, and kinnikinnick carpet the numerous erratic boulders, ice-age emigrants deposited by valley glaciers as they ground their way south out of Canada.

Having gained the ridge, turn left onto Pink Mountain Trail 7 at 2.3 miles (elev. 6250 feet). Initially in a tight corridor of subalpine trees, the trail eventually breaks out to an open, forested ridgeline of lodgepole and purple lupine. Large mounds, clearly manmade and now grass-covered, suggest the presence of old mining test pits.

As the trail continues north, Pink Mountain's summit reveals itself. At about 2.9 miles (elev. 6410 feet), as the trail begins to angle northeast, leave the tread behind in favor of the first broad meadow to the left

of the trail. There's little in the way of even a boot-built path to guide the way, but cross-country travel couldn't be easier than on this grassy expanse. Tack to the northeast, skirting whitebark pine, to reach the summit at 3.2 miles (elev. 6597 feet).

Named for early Forest Service ranger J. K. "Pink" Dwinille, the rounded helm of Pink Mountain—a remarkably flat parkland of snow-cowed crowns of whitebark pine—provides a panoramic view of the Purcells, Mount Henry and its lookout tower most prominent to the northeast and Roderick's rocky summit fin obvious to the west. In contrast to the mellow summit of Pink Mountain and its American Purcells neighbors, the Canadian Purcell peaks to the north. Having stayed above the tops of the major valley glaciers that proceeded south from Canada, they are significantly craggier, as are the peaks of the Whitefish Range and Glacier National Park to the east and A Peak and its Cabinets' kin to the west. All are visible on a sunny day. Also visible, unfortunately, is the crisscrossing patchwork of clear-cuts that culminated in Yaak's Timber Wars. Fortunately, a few pristine pockets of land survived the saw—Pink Mountain is one.

EXTENDING YOUR TRIP

From below the summit, the main trail continues some two miles through increasingly thick north-facing forest of fir and fool's huckleberry to Lost Horse Mountain.

Opposite: *Sunrise alpenglow reflects in the unusually smooth surface of Upper Cedar Lake (Hike 11).*

cabinet mountains

The "modern" lookout atop Star Peak overlooks Montana's first fire lookout cabin.

West Cabinets

The Cabinet Mountains straddle the Idaho-Montana border for some hundred miles, from Hope, Idaho, to Paradise, Montana. Separated from the main part of the range, the core of which is protected by the Cabinet Mountains Wilderness, by a two-lane state highway—and from formal wilderness designation by an act of congress—the 88,000-acre Scotchman Peaks Wilderness Study Area straddles the Idaho-Montana border and is perhaps the largest intact tract of unprotected wildlands in the Cabinet Mountain range. Although it lacks the abundance of glittering alpine lakes of the nearby wilderness, the Scotchman Peaks are no less wild. Bounded by the Clark Fork and Bull rivers, the Scotchmans boast jagged summits, avalanche-scraped cirques, subalpine meadows and rugged, brushy drainages.

5 Star Peak

RATING/ DIFFICULTY	ROUNDTRIP	ELEV GAIN/ HIGH POINT	SEASON
*****/5	8.4 miles	3920 feet/ 6167 feet	June–Oct

Map: USGS Heron, MT; **Contact:** Kootenai National Forest, Cabinet Ranger District; **Note:** Open to horses and bicycles; **GPS:** 48.0692°, -115.9240°

Star Peak boasts an active fire lookout at its 6167-foot summit with 360-degree views of the Bull River Valley, Lake Pend Oreille, and the two highest peaks in the Cabinet Mountains Wilderness: A Peak and Snowshoe Peak. Just below the lookout sits a century-old rock shelter and one of the best outhouse views in the region.

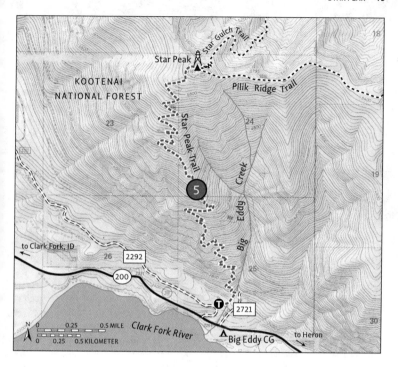

GETTING THERE

From the junction of Montana Highways 56 and 200 southeast of Heron, head northwest on MT 200 for 9.4 miles to Forest Road 2292. The trailhead (elev. 2250 feet), up that road 0.1 mile, has limited parking; most hikers park on the wide pullout on the south side of MT 200 and walk the short distance up the dirt road.

ON THE TRAIL

Five trails gain the summit of Star Peak (né Squaw Peak; the old appellation still appears in some maps and guidebooks), from the packhorse-friendly Pilik Ridge Trail from MT 56 to the Big Eddy Trail from MT 200. The

recently restored historic trail to Star Peak is slightly easier than its predecessor, the Big Eddy Trail, which used an impossibly steep mining road on its lower half. Not that your legs or lungs will notice the difference—it still gains about 4000 feet of elevation over a little more than four relentless miles. But it's more visually appealing. And the destination still looks as good as ever.

Beginning at the "new" historic trailhead, climb alongside Big Eddy Creek, young sun-dappled cedars paralleling both sides of the trail. Cross the creek—the old "new" trailhead lies just on the other side—and continue on the historic route past a couple of viewpoints with views of the Clark Fork

Sketching en plain air above Horseshoe Lake

delta. A vista at 1.2 miles (elev. 3550 feet) provides a nice breather from the climbing—1300 feet in 1.2 miles! Continue on narrow, off-camber tread under tall Douglas-firs as the trail tacks on another thousand feet of elevation in another mile. Then, at 2.2 miles (elev. 4590 feet), bear left and switchback through a thicket of huckleberries, the picking of which offers a welcome respite from the preceding climb.

Continue on. The lodgepole forest thins, but the summit doesn't appear until you're almost on top of it. Round the north side of the summit—pause here for a fir-framed view of flat-topped Billiard Table Mountain—and, at 4.1 miles (elev. 6070 feet), reach an old cabin on the shoulder of Star Peak. Constructed by Granville "Granny" Gordon, the first forest ranger of the Cabinet Ranger District (now Kootenai National Forest), and his wife Pauline, the squat dry-stone cabin was the first fire lookout in Montana. It's the work of an experienced stonemason; the doors and windows are all perfectly square—no small feat considering its perch on a peak that routinely receives 10 feet or more of snow each winter. An old privy hides in the trees fifty feet away. A steep stone path climbs another 0.1 mile to the modern lookout. From here, peer down into the Bull River and Clark Fork River Valleys almost a vertical mile below. Berray Mountain and its companion lookout tower sit directly across the Bull River; beyond Berray stand the highest peaks of the Cabinets. To the northeast lie smooth rock shelves. This is mountain goat country; scan the scopes for their shaggy white coats.

EXTENDING YOUR TRIP

It's possible, with two vehicles, to make an open loop using the Pilik Ridge Trail. Popular with stock users, the 11-mile Pilik Ridge Trail comes by its elevation change much more slowly as its descends to a trailhead on the Bull River Valley. Experienced off-trail

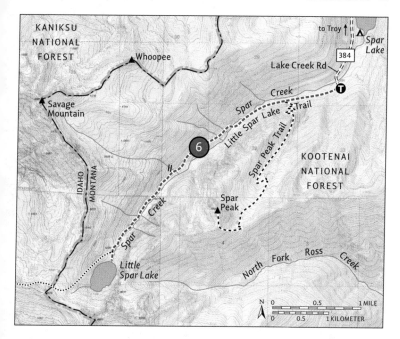

navigators can also follow the rugged ridge-line over to Billiard Table Mountain.

6 Little Spar Lake

RATING/ DIFFICULTY	ROUNDTRIP	ELEV GAIN/ HIGH POINT	SEASON
****/3	6.8 miles	2200 feet/ 5260 feet	Late June–Oct

Maps: USGS Scotchman Peak, ID; USGS Sawtooth Mountain, MT; **Contact:** Kootenai National Forest, Three Rivers Ranger District; **Note:** Open to horses and bicycles; **GPS:** 48.2429°, -115.9582°

The only trail-accessible tarn in the Scotchman Peaks Wilderness Study Area, Little Spar Lake attracts anglers and picnickers alike. Never steep for long, this kid-friendly trail passes acres of avalanche slopes awash in color.

GETTING THERE
Two miles east of Troy, turn south off US Highway 2 onto Lake Creek Road (Forest Road 384). Drive 17 miles to Spar Lake Campground. From the campground, continue 2 miles to the large trailhead (elev. 3440).

ON THE TRAIL
Beginning a little beyond Spar Lake, the cedar-shaded shores of which feature a quiet campground, Little Spar Lake Trail 143 begins on old roadbed among cedars before turning to true tread amid pleasant hemlock

forest. Pass a junction with the Spar Peak Trail at 0.6 mile (elev. 3630 feet), then, at 1.3 miles (elev. 3900 feet) descend to Spar Creek for a crossing that can be dicey early in the season.

The trail then traverses a brushy avalanche slope high above Spar Creek. Shaded by steep Star Peak on the far side, this drainage may harbor snow until July. Blooms abound, from the musty smell of fool's huckleberry to the minty fragrance of hyssop. Bears abound, too: Montana Fish, Wildlife, and Parks have relocated several grizzly sows from Glacier National Park to this drainage over the years. While these bruins have room to roam well away from the trail corridor, it's best to practice bear-aware hiking.

At 2.1 miles (elev. 4400 feet) pass a steep stream pouring into Spar Creek. Just upstream of the trail lies a hidden waterfall that's worth the minute or two of bushwhacking.

Back on the trail, continue through thickening flowers, and at 3.4 miles (elev. 5260 feet),

Little Spar Lake awaits at the base of a steep talus slope. Good and well-used tent sites by the lake's outlet fill up quickly on summer weekends—relative to its western Montana neighbors, at least. Van-sized granite boulders on the shore are perfect for lounging.

EXTENDING YOUR TRIP

Most hikers will be content to relax at this picturesque lake, but seasoned cross-country travelers can bushwhack about a mile northwest of the lake to shallow Horseshoe Lake in the high heart of the Scotchmans.

7 Ross Creek Cedars

RATING/ DIFFICULTY	ROUNDTRIP	ELEV GAIN/ HIGH POINT	SEASON
*****/2	0.9 mile	80 feet/ 2890 feet	May–Nov

Map: USGS Sawtooth Mountain, MT; **Contact:** Kootenai National Forest, Three Rivers

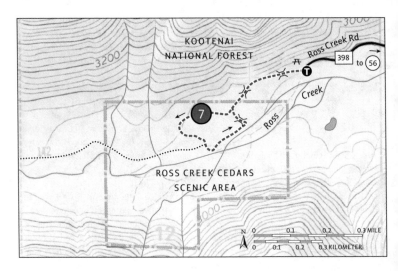

Ranger District; **Note:** Dogs must be on leash; **GPS:** 48.2083°, -115.9157°

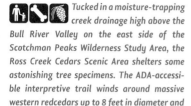 *Tucked in a moisture-trapping creek drainage high above the Bull River Valley on the east side of the Scotchman Peaks Wilderness Study Area, the Ross Creek Cedars Scenic Area shelters some astonishing tree specimens. The ADA-accessible interpretive trail winds around massive western redcedars up to 8 feet in diameter and 175 feet tall—some of Montana's largest, oldest trees. Although an easy walk, it will exhaust your vocabulary of superlatives.*

GETTING THERE

From Troy, drive east 2 miles on US Highway 2. Turn right (south) on Montana Highway 56, and continue 18.5 miles to Ross Creek Road (Forest Road 398). Turn right and drive 1 mile, then turn left to continue on FR 398 another 3.4 miles to the road's end and trailhead (elev. 2860 feet). Privy available.

ON THE TRAIL

Beginning among hemlocks and ferns, the wide, wheelchair-friendly path crosses two bridges over a small braid of Ross Creek before entering the cathedral-like cedar grove. Bear right as two paths diverge. Devil's club and Douglas maple garland the bases of deeply fluted cedars that look like elephant's feet. Many of the cedars have heart rot typical of this species, the hollowed-out hulks providing homes for numerous birds and mammals. Notice the titanic twins growing from the same nurse log; it's hard to imagine with trees that have outlasted nations, but they once had to struggle for survival. Now, a moisture- and cold-trapping canyon protects them from wind and wildfire.

At 0.4 mile, bear left at a signed junction (the narrower trail to the right goes to the South and North Forks of Ross Creek; see Extending Your Trip). Now paralleling the broad, rocky bed of Ross Creek, bear left to cross a wide footbridge and then

Resting amid the shade and sun of the Ross Creek Cedars

immediately bear right to close the cherry-stem loop and return to the trailhead.

EXTENDING YOUR TRIP

The interpretive loop surveys only a fraction of the giants residing near Ross Creek. From the far end of the main loop, head up the creek drainage on a noticeably narrower and rougher trail. Massive cedars and a few hardy hemlocks shade the drainage. In 2.2 miles the trail reaches Ross Creek. Cross carefully, aiming for the mouth of South Fork Ross Creek straight ahead; you want the trail that picks up on the right (west) side of that stream. A bit of steep climbing ensues on the crude path, but then the trail levels out before fading entirely just past the South Fork Ross Creek Cascades.

Most of the few hikers who make it this far stop near the cascades, where the creek splashes some thirty feet down stairsteps of smooth granite; still fewer pursue the summit of Sawtooth Peak beyond, a grueling off-trail scramble best suited for an overnight trip. Either way, unlike the popular interpretive loop, you're likely to have this special place all to yourself.

8 Berray Mountain

RATING/ DIFFICULTY	ROUNDTRIP	ELEV GAIN/ HIGH POINT	SEASON
****/5	10.2 miles	4020 feet/ 6177 feet	June–Oct

Maps: USGS Smeads Bench, MT; USGS Ibex Peak, MT; **Contact:** Kootenai National Forest, Cabinet Ranger District; **Note:** Open to horses and bicycles; **GPS:** 48.1162°, -115.7965°

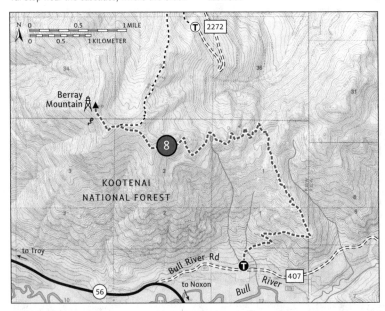

Hike to a shuttered lookout with next-door-neighbor views of the interior of the Cabinet Mountains Wilderness on the 10-mile roundtrip trek to Berray Mountain. Located outside the boundaries of the wilderness and the Scotchmans, Berray boasts great views of both.

GETTING THERE

From Noxon, drive 5 miles west on Montana Highway 200. Turn right (north) onto MT 56 and drive 8 miles to Bull River Road (Forest Road 407). (From Troy, drive east 2 miles on US Highway 2. Turn right, south, on MT 56, and drive 28.5 miles to FR 407.) Drive east on FR 407 for 1 mile to the Berray Mountain trailhead parking area on the left side of the road (elev. 2370 feet).

ON THE TRAIL

As is typical with many Cabinets' summits, Berray boasts impressive vertical relief, all of it exploited by a trail that starts from the valley floor. While there is a shorter route to Berray's summit, it's a long drive to the trailhead on a rough road. The route described here is much easier to access and offers plenty of visual rewards. And, unlike neighbor Star Peak, it mercifully gains its 4000 feet of elevation in 5 miles rather than 4.

The first mile of the trail dips into and out of tiny creek drainages, steadily gaining elevation under stately Douglas-firs. Occasional openings reveal the broad delta of the Bull River Valley below, and, beyond, Government Mountain. At 1.1 miles (elev. 3230 feet), the trail turns straight up the spine of the ridge, gaining almost 500 feet in 0.4 mile.

At 1.5 miles (elev. 3680 feet), reach an open rock perch. A 2015 wildfire cleared out much of the serviceberry and other shrubs, opening up views into the Lost Girl Creek

drainage to the southeast. Continue back into the trees as the trail winds steadily upward through cool cedar forest and dry Douglas-fir; balsamroots and maples add spring and fall color, respectively. A small pond at 3.5 miles offers a good opportunity to spot moose and white-tailed deer.

Traverse steep talus slopes and under towering lodgepole, and at 4.8 miles, continue straight at a junction (the trail entering from the right comes from the upper Berray Mountain trailhead) and, shortly after, pass a signed junction—the steep, 0.4-mile spur accesses a small spring that provided water for the fire lookout.

The trail levels on beargrass-clad ridge and, in a broad opening surrounded by subalpine firs, reaches the summit and its shuttered lookout at 5.1 miles (elev. 6177 feet).

Climb to the catwalk of the thirty-foot tower for impressive views of Dad, Saint Paul, and Chicago Peaks in the heart of the Cabinet Mountains Wilderness. Across the Bull River Valley, spot Star Peak Lookout and

The now-shuttered lookout tower on Berray Mountain

Resting above Rock Lake en route to Libby Lakes

the distinctive glacier-shaved plane of Billiard Table Mountain. Close at hand, keep a keen eye out for bighorn sheep: Berray Mountain is home to a herd of about a hundred, which augment smaller populations throughout the state.

EXTENDING YOUR TRIP

A faint footpath continues for a half mile past the lookout along Berray's summit ridge, eventually reaching a clearing with even better views of the Snake Creek drainage and seldom-visited Dad Peak in the Cabinet Mountains Wilderness beyond.

Cabinet Mountains Wilderness

When French-Canadian fur trappers first surveyed the mountain range straddling the Idaho-Montana border, they dubbed it the

Cabinet Mountains, for the shelves of rock that loomed over the rivers below. In the intervening two hundred years, the hiking technology used to cross the Cabinets may have changed, but little else has.

The Cabinet Mountains are commonly regarded as one of the wildest mountain ranges in the Lower 48. Grizzly bears, mountain goats, and even wolverines take refuge among its glacier-carved cirques and hanging valleys. The Cabinet Mountains Wilderness protects almost 100,000 acres of alpine lakes and knife-edge peaks in the heart of the range. Think of it as an off-the-beaten-path alternative to Glacier National Park.

9 Rock Lake

RATING/ DIFFICULTY	ROUNDTRIP	ELEV GAIN/ HIGH POINT	SEASON
*****/4	7.8 miles	2340 feet/ 4980 feet	June–Oct

Maps: USFS Cabinet Mountains Wilderness; USGS Elephant Peak, MT; **Contact:** Kootenai National Forest, Cabinet Ranger District; **Notes:** Wilderness rules apply. Open to horses; **GPS:** 48.0399°, -115.6794°

A disused access road to a defunct mine offers easy access to this popular Cabinets' destination, its many islets and coves occupying one of the most spectacular hanging valleys in the Cabinets, all under the sheer-faced spectacle of Ojibway Peak. The mining history here evokes a rich story but also portends a troubling mining future; a mine proposed for just outside the wilderness boundary has the potential to permanently drain the lake.

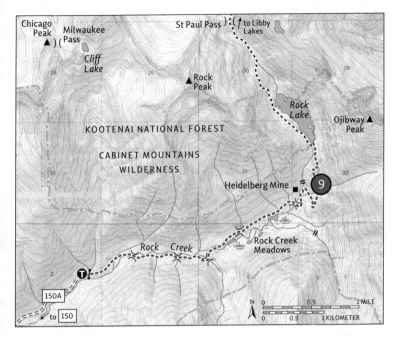

GETTING THERE

From Montana Highway 200 about 1.8 miles east of the Noxon turnoff, and just past the railroad crossing (milepost 17.1), turn north onto Rock Creek Road (Forest Road 150). Drive 0.2 mile and bear right under the powerlines to stay on FR 150. Continue 5.8 miles to the junction with FR 150A, bearing right onto it and continuing 1.6 increasingly rough miles to the trailhead (elev. 3270 feet).

ON THE TRAIL

From the trailhead, pass the gate and walk the wide roadbed originally used to access the Heidelberg Mine; cedar and hemlock line the route but do little to calm the raucous sounds of Rock Creek. Crossing a trio of sturdy bridges at 0.6, 1.4, and 1.6 miles,

the road-trail gains elevation in short, steep bursts typical of old mining roads. Shortly past the third bridge, pass a dilapidated, mouse-inhabited cabin; there's little reason to go in.

Cross the creek again on a small footbridge and pass a group camp at the foot of Rock Creek Meadows at 1.9 miles (elev. 3830). The site of a beaver farm a century ago, the meadow's expansive willows and grasses are a good place to spot moose—and a popular grizzly gathering spot. The meadows also offer the first views of the Cabinets' crenellated bedrock buttresses, most prominently Ojibway's summit horn.

Pass a second group camp and old cabin at 2.5 miles—a wise place to camp if you have gotten a late start on a backpacking trip. Cross another new footbridge and reach Rock Creek Falls and the Heidelberg Mine at 2.9 miles (elev. 4140 feet). Here, at the end of the old mining road, where Rock Creek tumbles out of the lake and sluices through a small canyon, rusting mining relics and concrete mineworks still mark early efforts to yield precious metals from the base of the Cabinets' bedrock. A proposed mine, its plans in the works off and on for well over a decade, would do the same, tunneling into the Cabinets' crest from just outside the wilderness and potentially draining several of its pristine lakes.

Just before the road's end, a dozen or so switchbacks climb quickly away from the mine, with increasingly good views of broad Rock Creek Meadows below; scan the marsh for moose and grizzly—a much better vantage point from which to see them than close up. On the far side of the meadow, an unnamed waterfall cascades down a narrow hanging valley below Flat Top Mountain.

Having leveled out, the trail reaches the outlet of Rock Lake at 3.9 miles (elev. 4970 feet). Steep granite and talus plunge straight down to the lake's east shore; numerous islets and coves harbor excellent, albeit hard-to-access, fishing. A limited number of tent sites crowd one large popular spot on the south side of the lake; late arrivals on a weekend may be out of luck. Rock Peak's many gendarmes and needles rise to the west, while Ojibway, identifiable by its almost blemish-free upthrust bedrock west face, looms to the southeast. Sunset comes early to this tightly cradled subalpine lake.

EXTENDING YOUR TRIP
Rock Lake provides the best access to the Libby Lakes, the highest pools in the Cabinets. From the campsite at the lake's outlet,

cross the log jam and follow a well-trod boot path about 75 feet above the lake as it traverses talus aprons and extensive brush to the inlet creek in a hanging valley above Rock Creek, the superb subalpine scene here reminiscent of much higher elevations elsewhere in the Rockies.

Reaching the mine pits atop St. Paul Pass 1.7 miles from Rock Lake, bear right, directly up the ridge, for a steep climb over often-slick beargrass and around stunted subalpine fir to the high rocky outlet of the uppermost Libby Lake. From St. Paul Pass to here it's a climb of 800 feet in 0.3 mile, but this trio of pools—easily the most stunning in the Cabinets, and ranking high on the list of anywhere in western Montana—is worth every bit of sweat.

10 Engle Lake

RATING/ DIFFICULTY	ROUNDTRIP	ELEV GAIN/ HIGH POINT	SEASON
****/4	6.4 miles	2900 feet/ 6580 feet	June–Oct

Maps: USFS Cabinet Mountains Wilderness; USGS Elephant Peak, MT; USGS Howard Lake, MT; **Contact:** Kootenai National Forest, Cabinet Ranger District; **Notes:** Wilderness rules apply. Open to horses; **GPS:** 48.0061°, -115.6672°

A high-elevation trailhead, a high subalpine lake, ridgetop walking through one of the best beargrass displays in the Cabinets, and the possibility to bag a peak sans scrambling recommend this as a 6-mile sampler of what the Cabinets have to offer. But make no mistake: even with a high-elevation trailhead, Engle Lake doesn't skimp on steepness—that other classic Cabinets characteristic.

GETTING THERE

From Montana Highway 200 about 1.8 miles east of the Noxon turnoff, and just past the railroad crossing (milepost 17.1), turn north onto Rock Creek Road (Forest Road 150). Drive 0.2 mile and bear right under the powerlines to stay on FR 150. Continue 4.5 miles and, just before the bridge, turn right onto Orr Creek Road (FR 2285). Drive this good gravel road 7.4 miles to the road's end and trailhead (elev. 4940 feet).

ON THE TRAIL

From the trailhead, Engle Lake Trail 932 briefly follows the continuation of an old roadbed before commencing with single-track switchbacks. In contrast to other Cabinets' trails, though, the hike to Engle Lake starts above the brush zone, so the views may be sparse the first mile, but it doesn't have the closed-in forest feel some find claustrophobic. At 1.3 miles (elev. 6340 feet), gain the ridge, which forms the wilderness boundary. Quickly leave lodgepole forest behind for an old burn, its shadeless west face exposed to the withering sun and summer storms. Walking the ridge, eye

Taking a brisk summer dip in Engle Lake

Engle Lake and its five nameless neighbors below—can you spot them all?—and Noxon Reservoir to the west. Mimicking the swaying snags are the white-capped colonnades of beargrass, one of the best such floral displays in the Cabinets. These tall flowers—not grass at all but a member of the lily

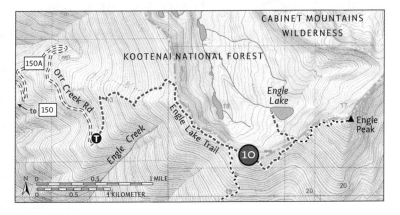

GRIZZLY BEARS: BACK FROM THE BRINK

Grizzly bears once roamed the West from northern Mexico to British Columbia. Researchers have estimated there were 50,000–100,000 grizzlies in the Lower 48 at the time Lewis and Clark explored the West. In the last century, those numbers have plummeted to around 1000 bears.

Protected in 1975 under the Endangered Species Act, grizzlies have slowly recovered some of their territory in the Northwest. The Northern Continental Divide Ecosystem, which stretches from the southern tip of the Rattlesnake Wilderness north of Missoula through Glacier National Park, maintains about a thousand grizzlies; the Cabinet-Yaak Ecosystem in the far northwest corner of the state struggles to maintain about fifty.

Wildlife biologists attribute the growing numbers of bears to several factors, including road closures that have been in place since the 1980s and that have greatly limited potential poachers, campers learning to store food properly, and changing public perception—bears are simply not as reviled as they used to be.

Now to address the elephant—or grizzly—in the room: despite recent gains in grizzly populations, most hikers are unlikely to ever see one, let alone have a nasty encounter. Over the course of thousands of miles hiking in grizzly country, I have seen one bruin—and that was from the comfort of my car while it crossed a highway. Close encounters with grizzlies are rare; deaths, even less so. Only a handful of grizzly-related deaths have been recorded in the history of Glacier National Park; by comparison, deaths owing to falls number in the single digits each year. Keep in mind that's out of the more than 2 million visitors the park sees each year.

That said, a little vigilance (see The Bear Essentials in the Introduction) will go a long way toward ensuring that, if you're lucky enough to spot a grizzly, the encounter is a positive one for all involved.

Before venturing out in bear country this summer and fall, visit the Grizzly Bear Outreach Project website (http://bearinfo.org/) for tips on differentiating between grizzly and black bears and contact information for reporting a grizzly sighting.

family—bloom every three to five years, so fields of genetically related plants tend to mature en masse.

Returning to the trees, the trail reaches a junction at 2.1 miles (elev. 6340 feet); bear left (the trail coming in from the right is a steeper, longer approach and infrequently used). The route descends for a time, its course seeming to stray, maddeningly, from what would appear be the most direct route to the lake. After a short distance the trail heads uphill, skirting a broad talus apron and regaining the ridge. At 2.8 miles (elev. 6570 feet), reach a signed junction; bear left and downhill for the lake (the trail right goes to Engle Peak; see Extending Your Trip). From here, descend steep switchbacks across talus blasted into place for the benefit of equestrians. It's 0.4 mile that feels longer than it is, but the trail finally reaches the lake at 3.2 miles (elev. 6110 feet).

Lying at the base of a mellow cirque and surrounded by spruce and fool's huckleberry,

Engle Lake dutifully reflects the angled talus apron of Engle Peak's north aspect, but the true summit is not visible from the lake; a broad, flat moraine behind the lake hints at its otherwise-hidden neighbors. The well-used tent sites at trail's end offer a good embarkation point for swimming; several flat rocks at or just under the lake's surface invite exploration.

EXTENDING YOUR TRIP

Engle Peak makes an essential side trip; it's one of the few nontechnical, trail-accessible summits in the Cabinet Mountains Wilderness. From the trail junction, steadily switchback across bleached blocks of granite for 0.8 mile, the trees increasingly sparse and the views increasingly excellent, to the summit at 7583 feet. From the long, narrow summit ridge, peer north to the narrow needles and gendarmes of Rock Peak, a significantly more challenging summit, and the deep teardrop basin of Rock Lake below it; distinctive Ojibway, its steep pyramidal summit block seeming to offer little purchase for scramblers; and Flat Top Mountain and Carney Peak, which tower over Wanless Lake.

11 Cedar Lakes

RATING/ DIFFICULTY	ROUNDTRIP	ELEV GAIN/ HIGH POINT	SEASON
*****/3	10 miles	3200 feet/ 5920 feet	June–Oct

Maps: USFS Cabinet Mountains Wilderness; USGS Scenery Mountain, MT; **Contact:** Kootenai National Forest, Libby Ranger District; **Notes:** Wilderness rules apply. Open to horses; **GPS:** 48.4091°, -115.6651°

  *The Cabinets have been called a miniature version of Glacier,*

and the hike to Cedar Lakes explains why: tumbling, tumultuous creeks; indigo subalpine lakes; and the amphitheater-like walls of glaciated peaks. The only thing missing is the crowds. And while its namesake cedars steal the creekside show en route to the lake, it's alpine larch that lights up autumn on the high ridges of the Cabinet Divide.

GETTING THERE

From downtown Libby, drive west on US Highway 2 for 7 miles. Just after crossing Cedar Creek, turn left (south) onto Cedar Creek Road. Drive 2.5 miles to the road's end and large trailhead parking lot (elev. 2920 feet).

ON THE TRAIL

Cedar Creek Trail 141 begins on an old roadbed, ascending through second-growth cedar in the most significant climbing of the hike. At 0.7 mile (elev. 3420 feet), pass the junction where Scenery Mountain Trail takes off to the right. Now maintaining stream gradient, the trail settles in for a nice creekside cruise through pristine western redcedar and spruce forest, clamoring Cedar Creek never far from view to the left. In contrast, the slope of Scenery Mountain to the right consists of the few blackened snags still standing from the 1994 Scenery Mountain Fire; the trail, a convenient firebreak, serves as the demarcation between old growth and regeneration. Unsurprisingly, this trail accumulates blowdowns, both snags and old-growth trees now unprotected from mountain winds; checking the ranger district's trail maintenance schedule might be a good idea before setting off.

At 2.8 miles, enter the wilderness, the trail now increasingly coarser underfoot. Nearing the lower lake, gain ground upslope into the burn area and its bountiful post-fire blooms;

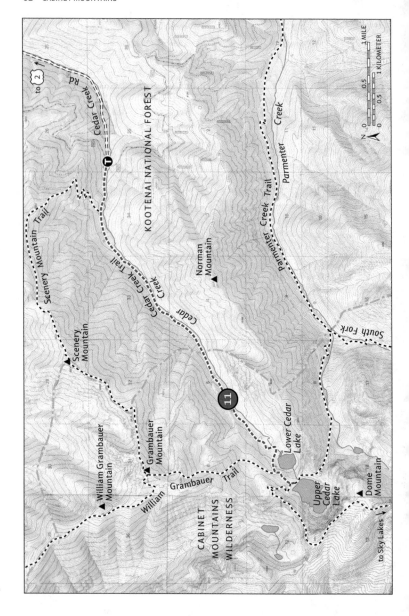

this section of the trail can be witheringly hot on a cloudless day. At 4.6 miles, reach Lower Cedar Lake, tucked tightly against a steep rock wall to the south. By any other measure a pretty pool of water, Lower Cedar Lake is easily upstaged by its larger neighbor less than a half mile distant. Continue through shaded and frequently muddy bottomland forest, passing a junction with the William Grambauer Trail at 4.9 miles, to reach Upper Cedar Lake at 5 miles (elev. 5920 feet).

The third-largest lake in the Cabinet Mountains Wilderness, Upper Cedar Lake reflects, when the water is becalmed, the broad bedrock amphitheater forming the north face of Dome Mountain, the summit of which lies unseen from the lake. A perfect reflection is rare, though, as wind tends to whip across the lake's surface in eddies and twisters, stirring the indigo waters around its myriad coves and jetties. An angular bedrock ramp offers easy wade-in access from the several heavily used campsites at the foot of the lake.

EXTENDING YOUR TRIP

Hikers with two vehicles can combine the trip to Cedar Lakes with Sky Lakes (Hike 12) to form an open loop through perhaps the finest high-country hiking in the Cabinets.

12 Sky Lakes

RATING/ DIFFICULTY	ROUNDTRIP	ELEV GAIN/ HIGH POINT	SEASON
****/5	11.2 miles	3450 feet/ 6210 feet	Late June–Oct

Maps: USFS Cabinet Mountains Wilderness; USGS Treasure Mountain, MT; **Contact:** Kootenai National Forest, Libby Ranger District; **Notes:** Wilderness rules apply. Open to horses; **GPS:** 48.3555°, -115.6357°

A steep trail, frequently coarse underfoot, repays hikers with aptly named Sky Lakes, which occupy a lofty hanging valley hidden in the shadow of Sugarloaf Mountain—some of the highest trail-accessible lakes in the Cabinet Mountains Wilderness.

GETTING THERE

From downtown Libby, drive southeast on US Highway 2 for 1.8 miles, then turn right (west) onto Shaughnessy Hill Road. Drive 0.8 mile to a three-way intersection and bear left, continuing 0.5 mile to Granite Creek Road (Forest Road 618). Turn right and proceed 0.8 mile, then bear right onto Flower Creek Road (FR 128). Continue 5 miles to the trailhead (elev. 3740 feet).

ON THE TRAIL

Immediately retreating upstream under heavily shaded bottomland forest, Flower Creek Trail 137 toys with a casual gradient before proceeding steeply, only the occasional switchback smoothing out the grade. Pass through patches of heavy brush fields typical of the Cabinet Mountains' lower reaches, marking the wilderness boundary at 1.8 miles (elev. 4050 feet), and at 2.6 miles (elev. 4730 feet) reach a junction with the Hanging Valley Trail (see Extending Your Trip). Continue straight, bearing left at another junction at 4.3 miles (elev. 5490 feet), the trail eventually leaving dense tree cover in favor of miniature meadows of yellow groundsel and delicate alpine forget-me-not. Grizzlies can be found foraging here in the summer months.

The trail detours around the distinctive flour-sack shape of Sugarloaf Mountain before crossing two tributaries of Flower Creek in succession at 4.6 miles (elev. 5510

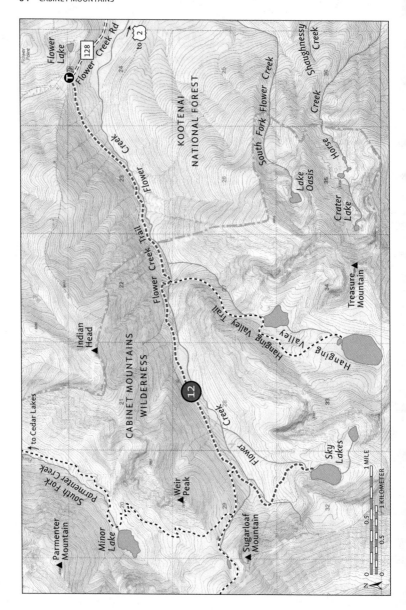

feet). Departing the steep cirque on Sugar-loaf's east face, the final mile climbs sharply on a deeply eroded trail where spring runoff sluices down to the bedrock. Clambering over mud-slick tread and thick spruce blow-downs, reach the raucous outlet stream of Lower Sky Lake at 5.5 miles (elev. 6170 feet). The outlet stream, some thirty feet across, will surely soak shoes early in the summer, but the best lake access is on the far side of the outlet. Cross it, and reach the shores of the lake a few hundred yards later.

Lower Sky Lake inhabits a wide, talus- and timber-clad cirque just shy of the Cabinet Divide. On the south side of the outlet stream, a well-used campsite, popular with equestrians, offers fine fishing and swimming access from its rocky edge; just mind the manure. A boot path taking off around the south side of the lake hints at the hanging valley containing even prettier Upper Sky Lake a half mile away.

EXTENDING YOUR TRIP

Lower Sky Lake makes for a good base camp for a 27-mile open-loop shuttle with Cedar Lakes. From the junction 1.3 miles before Lower Sky Lake, ascend the forested flank over Sugarloaf Mountain, past a remarkable, unnamed tarn set in a steep talus field in its east shoulder. Gaining the Cabinet Divide, head north, passing Minor and Parmenter Lakes well below and lingering under expansive stands of alpine larch—perhaps the largest such population outside the Bitterroot Crest. Round Dome Mountain, its north side capping a gorgeous U-shaped valley—careful, late-lingering snowfields can stymie early-summer hikers—before descending to Upper Cedar Lake.

As good as Upper Cedar Lake is from its shore, the view of its massive bedrock

Backpackers cross Flower Creek on their way out from Lower Sky Lake.

amphitheater from Dome Mountain's shoulder is positively breathtaking. Hikers can also make a lollipop loop with the Hanging Valley Trail, but be aware: this unmaintained angler's path is faint and not for the faint of heart, crossing fast-flowing Flower Creek—a treacherous proposition early in the summer—and climbing more than 2000 feet in less than two miles through head-harrowing brush.

13 Granite Lake

RATING/ DIFFICULTY	ROUNDTRIP	ELEV GAIN/ HIGH POINT	SEASON
****/5	12.4 miles	2570 feet/ 4640 feet	June–Oct

Maps: USFS Cabinet Mountains Wilderness; USGS Little Hoodoo Mountain, MT; USGS Treasure Mountain, MT; USGS Snowshoe Peak, MT; **Contact:** Kootenai National Forest, Libby Ranger District; **Notes:** Wilderness rules apply. Open to horses; **GPS:** 48.2947°, -115.6260°

A combination of creek crossings, blowdowns, and brush makes this hike seem longer than it is, but the destination, a vast, glacier-fed lake at the base of pyramidal A Peak, will reward any sweat—blood and tears optional—that hikers expend.

GETTING THERE

From downtown Libby, drive southeast on US Highway 2 for 1.8 miles, then turn right (west) onto Shaughnessy Hill Road. Drive 0.8 mile to a three-way intersection and bear left, continuing 0.5 mile to Granite Creek Road (Forest Road 618). Turn right and continue 8 miles to the road's end and parking area (elev. 3080 feet).

ON THE TRAIL

The 2015 Klatawa Fire, one of several that charred the Cabinets and elsewhere in one of the worst fire seasons in recent memory, ravaged the Granite Creek drainage, burning down to the bedrock in places. Only season-ending rain and snow finally extinguished the fire. A hike once known for being well in the Cabinets' low-elevation "brush zone" now occasionally resembles the bare-rock Bitterroots. Not to worry: there's still plenty of brush.

Beginning in shade-dappled cedar forest, Granite Creek Trail 136 quickly enters patchy remains of burnt boles and blackened rock. Big-leaved, sun-soaking plants such as thimbleberry have taken advantage of the increased sunlight, as have post-fire colonizing flowers such as fireweed. Well above the rushing creek waters, the trail dips into and out of several brushy dry-creek draws before meeting up with the mainstem creek at 1.9 miles (elev. 3500 feet). This fifty-foot-wide crossing could be sketchy in the spring, but a log jam provides several dry-boot crossing options.

Just beyond the creek, pass the wilderness boundary and reach Granite Falls at 2.6 miles (elev. 3570 feet). Its large plunge pool is now a churning depository for deadfall. There's a fine tent site here—the last before the lake. For a time the trail keeps close to the creek on a particularly pretty stretch of riffles and pools before reaching the first of several creek crossings, some of which can be navigated with careful crossing of downed timber, others of which must be waded. Beyond this first crossing, good routefinding skills are a must, as the Klatawa blaze essentially eradicated the path in

Taking a dip (and finding refuge from mosquitoes) in Granite Lake

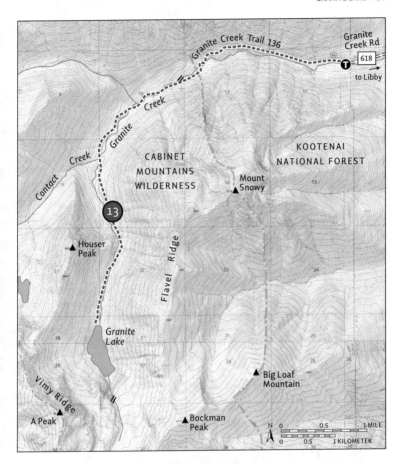

places; charred timber will continue to fall and obstruct trail for years to come. Look for the distinctive downturned exclamation point of old blazes and the "hall of trees" effect typical of trail corridors; when in doubt, stay on the north side of the creek.

At 4 miles (elev. 3880), cross the creek again, just south of its confluence with Contact Creek. Beyond here, the fire had little

effect, likely because the Hauser Peak ridge separating the Granite and Contact Creek drainages acted as a natural firebreak. In untouched timber for the first time, admire the old Douglas-firs that escaped this and centuries of other blazes. The trail grows increasingly brushy as it eventually breaks out onto a north-facing slope that nonetheless gets sun-battered in the summer. At 5.4

miles, cross the creek for a final time—this last crossing necessitates careful foot placement in its knee-high depths—before traversing yet more cow parsnip and horsemint past Granite Lake's marshy and moose-friendly outlet ponds to the main lake at 6.2 miles.

Granite Lake's long, shoe-shaped profile reflects pyramidal A Peak at its head, its bracingly cold waters directly fed from Blackwell Glacier on Snow Peak via a dramatic, several-hundred-foot-high waterfall. The waters, though cold, are nice and deep, perfect for swimming—or taking shelter from Granite Lake's notorious early-season skeeters.

EXTENDING YOUR TRIP

Hikers with a desperate desire to thrash through more thick brush can ascend the steep slope above the north side of the lake to reach Vimy Ridge. While the view is excellent, a similar view can be had by ascending to Snowshoe Peak from Leigh Lake (Hike 14), which will provoke significantly less cursing at shrubs or significant others.

14 Leigh Lake

RATING/ DIFFICULTY	ROUNDTRIP	ELEV GAIN/ HIGH POINT	SEASON
****/3	2.8 miles	1710 feet/ 5210 feet	Mid-June– early Oct

Maps: USFS Cabinet Mountains Wilderness; USGS Snowshoe Peak, MT; **Contact:** Kootenai National Forest, Libby Ranger District; **Notes:** Wilderness rules apply. Camping prohibited within 300 feet of the shoreline; **GPS:** 48.2244°, -115.6412°

Short—albeit steep—access to the second-largest lake in the Cabinet Mountains Wilderness means Leigh Lake is a popular spot: some three thousand people visit its sprawling shores every year. But the destination—a granite-ringed subalpine lake set under the highest peak in the Cabinets—makes up for the lack of elbow room. And a resident mountain goat herd means Leigh Lake is truly a "kid"-friendly hike!

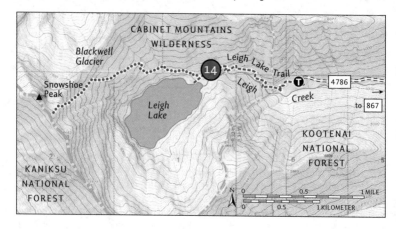

GETTING THERE

From Libby, drive 8 miles south on US Highway 2. Just past milepost 40, turn right on Bear Creek Road (Forest Road 278). Drive 3 miles, then turn right on Cherry Creek Road (FR 867). Drive 4.3 miles and turn right on Leigh Creek Road (FR 4786), negotiating 1.7 rough, rocky, and slow miles to the road's end and trailhead (elev. 4090 feet).

ON THE TRAIL

Immediately set to work climbing. Maple, yew, and some truly huge hemlock shade the steep Leigh Lake Trail 132, the brushy slopes of Leigh Creek occasionally visible below. At 0.3 mile (elev. 4150 feet) enter the wilderness. Cross a dry creek bed and pass through head-high vegetation, careful to make lots of noise—these are prime conditions for grizzly encounters.

Leigh Creek's cascades soon come into view, and at 0.9 mile (elev. 4920 feet) the trail reaches the base of the spectacular multitier waterfall. Bear right and gear down: having gained 900 feet in 0.9 mile, the trail now gains a steep 200 feet in 0.1 mile. Stay left as the trail braids, occasionally requiring the use of handholds and mountain goatlike dexterity. Speaking of these shaggy beasts, a herd regularly hangs out here, lured by handouts and the salt of sweat-soaked pack straps. Keep your distance, for your safety and theirs.

The trail soon levels out for a quarter mile of walking through thick vegetation to the lake's granite shore. The second-largest lake in the Cabinet Mountains Wilderness—only Wanless, on the west side of the range, is bigger—Leigh Lake wears a stunning green hue thanks to glacial flour dissolved in its waters. Tall, mossy firs tower over smooth rock benches just above the lake's surface, worn down by glaciers and generations of hikers' backsides. The rocks are perfect for swimming or reclining. Broad-shouldered Snowshoe Peak, the highest in the Cabinets, towers above the lake, its steep east face streaked black by old waterfalls. Although Leigh Lake sits relatively low in elevation among lakes in the Cabinet Mountains Wilderness, it's above the brush zone; climb the open, flower-covered slopes on the north side of the lake for unobstructed views of this Cabinets' classic.

EXTENDING YOUR TRIP

Leigh Lake is a popular base for off-trail scrambling to Snowshoe's 8738-foot summit. (Camping is prohibited within 300 feet

Leigh Lake's smooth-rock shores make for excellent swimming.

of the shoreline.) The best route is to climb the steep, bare benches above the north side of the lake to the ridgeline, then follow it west to Snowshoe's granite shoulder and the summit block beyond. Snow lingers late into summer; in June and early July, bring crampons and an ice axe.

15 Ozette Lake

RATING/ DIFFICULTY	ROUNDTRIP	ELEV GAIN/ HIGH POINT	SEASON
*****/5	7.2 miles	2590 feet/ 5530 feet	Mid-June– Oct

Maps: USFS Cabinet Mountains Wilderness; USGS Howard Lake, MT; **Contact:** Kootenai National Forest, Libby Ranger District; **Notes:** Wilderness rules apply. Dogs permitted; **GPS:** 48.0518°, -115.5294°

Reflecting the sedimentary sides of Flat Top and Lost Horse Mountains in its peninsula-split pool, Ozette Lake offers one of the most dramatic lake settings in the region. Perhaps to guard against overuse, the trail officially ends some three-quarters of a mile below the lake, but hikers keen on tackling a tangle of slide alder and brush will discover what is perhaps the Cabinets' best-kept secret.

GETTING THERE

From Libby, drive 24 miles southeast on US Highway 2. Shortly after milepost 56, turn right on West Fisher Creek Road (Forest Road 231). Drive 5.8 miles, then turn left on FR 2332. In 0.5 mile, turn right onto FR 6746. Continue on this increasingly narrow and rocky road for 2.5 miles to a large pullout. Low-clearance vehicles should park here; otherwise, continue to the right, on the heavily timbered

jeep road, for 0.7 mile to the nominal trailhead next to an old mining cabin (elev. 3750 feet).

ON THE TRAIL

From the nondescript parking area, continue on the rough roadbed as it parallels the cedar-flanked West Fisher Creek. The road shortly makes a crossing of this cobble-bottomed watercourse, which during early-summer snowmelt could be knee-deep.

Once you are on the other side of the creek, continue on the roadbed, bearing left at two forks, before turning left onto true trail (Mill-Ozette Trail 302) at 1.3 miles (elev. 4020 feet). A large "OZ" carved into a tree is the only clue to this otherwise easily missed junction.

A descent of a tenth of a mile returns the trail to the West Fisher Creek at its confluence with Mill Creek; the joining of the two narrow tree-lined gorges is one of the prettier creekside scenes in the Cabinets. Cross West Fisher Creek again, this time mercifully on a footbridge.

Amid well-spaced western redcedar and yew, the trail ascends the finger ridge formed by the confluence of the two gorges, reeling off a series of switchbacks before settling into a contour high above Mill Creek. The tread here is surprisingly well-tended considering its rude access road and abrupt end—more on that in a minute.

The trail enters the Cabinet Mountains Wilderness and, shortly after, ends in its official capacity at 3.1 miles (elev. 5080 feet). A rough footpath continues from here, picking its way through pocket meadows and small aspen glades. Crossing a steep avalanche chute—which, early in the summer, might be filled with snow or a lingering stream—the trail allows its first look at the lower slopes of Flat Top Mountain above Ozette Lake.

Crossing a footbridge over snowmelt-filled West Fisher Creek

Shouldering your way through slide alder and aspen, continue on the faint track, Ozette Lake's outlet creek always to your left, before reaching the evergreen-shaded moraine at the foot of the lake at 3.6 miles (elev. 5510 feet).

Encircled by a large lateral moraine—the leavings of an ice-age glacier—and the sheer flanks of Flat Top and Lost Horse Mountains, Ozette Lake presents a dramatic sight. Snowmelt cascades carve steep routes down the striated faces of the cirque. By midsummer, a grassy peninsula bisects the shallow pool. A broad slide path of beargrass and talus above the lake's north shore permits an aerial view of this oft-overlooked mountain scene.

EXTENDING YOUR TRIP

Lost Horse Mountain makes a worthwhile objective for hikers overnighting at Ozette. The broad, slide-scrubbed south face permits an easy approach from the head of the lake; from its 7508-foot summit, scramblers can continue south to Flat Top Mountain or content themselves with views of the steep summit ramp of Ojibway to the north.

16 Bramlet Lake

RATING/ DIFFICULTY	ROUNDTRIP	ELEV GAIN/ HIGH POINT	SEASON
***/3	4 miles	1450 feet/ 5580 feet	Late June– early Oct

Maps: USFS Cabinet Mountains Wilderness; USGS Howard Lake, MT; **Contact:** Kootenai National Forest, Libby Ranger District; **Notes:** Wilderness rules apply. Open to horses; **GPS:** 48.0422°, -115.5328°

Lying just barely within the Cabinet Mountains Wilderness—the boundary wraps around the lake's outlet— Bramlet Lake is a minor player when compared to many of its Cabinets' kin, which

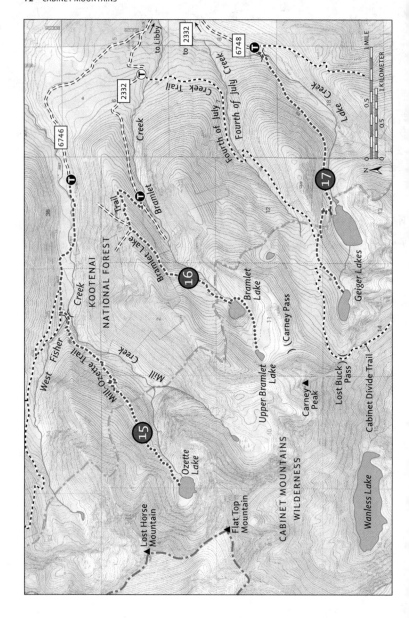

seemed blasted out of granite. But this is a
great early-summer hike that, despite its easy
access, has stayed off the radar of hikers.

GETTING THERE

From Libby, drive 24 miles southeast on US
Highway 2. Shortly after milepost 56, turn
right on West Fisher Creek Road (Forest
Road 231). Drive 5.8 miles, then turn left on
FR 2332. In 0.8 mile, bear right to stay on FR
2332 (continuing straight goes toward Lake
Creek campground) and continue another
2.7 miles to the trailhead (elev. 4600 feet).
The final 1.5 miles is steep and rough; those
with low-clearance vehicles may want to
park at the Fourth of July trailhead and walk
the road, which adds 3 miles and 900 feet of
elevation gain. At the end of FR 2332, a small
pullout on the right shoulder accommodates
two cars. Just beyond the parking area is
private property; do not block the gate.

ON THE TRAIL

The presence of private mining inholdings has
complicated access to Bramlet Lake in the
past—certainly not the only instance of conflict
between mines and wilderness in the Cabinets.
The Forest Service has routed the trail around
the private property, but it's subject to change;
for now, green "reassurance markers" should
help guide hikers. From the Bramlet Creek 658
trailhead, follow an old mining road as it climbs
west then quickly switchbacks away from the
lake. Thick timber—Douglas-fir, hemlock, and
a few western white pines—obscures most of
the views.

At 0.6 mile (elev. 5090 feet), continue
straight at a three-way junction. The road-
trail begins going full bore straight up the
slope. At 0.8 mile (elev. 5260 feet), bear left
and follow the descending road. A path that
better resembles a true trail branches off at

*The first snows of November blanket Bramlet
Lake.*

1.1 miles (elev. 5150 feet); bear right onto
this route as it climbs, the steep, sloughed-
granite canyon walls of Bramlet Creek now
visible far below. Gaps in the timber permit
views east to the southernmost reaches of
the Purcells.

Enter boggy bottomland—keep an eye out
for moose in the thick willow cover—and at 2
miles (elev. 5580 feet), just inside the wilderness boundary, reach Bramlet Lake. The small
body of water rests in a high forested bowl,
the triangular nub of Carney Peak the only
prominent point on the horizon. Subalpine
firs grow right down to the shore around most
of the lake, necessitating a short bushwhack
to reach the water. Directly across the lake, a
waterfall crashes over a small bench into the
placid waters below. Spacious campsites just
above the lake's surface invite lingering. On
the wetter east side of the Cabinets, Bramlet
is one of the earliest lakes to melt out, a fact
not lost on the local mosquito population;
bring bug repellent.

EXTENDING YOUR TRIP

Experienced off-trail hikers may wish to continue to Upper Bramlet Lake, but it's a steep,
slippery, and brushy slog in bear country.

 17 Geiger Lakes

RATING/ DIFFICULTY	ROUNDTRIP	ELEV GAIN/ HIGH POINT	SEASON
*****/3	5.8 miles	1810 feet/ 5400 feet	Mid-June– Oct

Maps: USFS Cabinet Mountains Wilderness; USGS Howard Lake, MT; **Contact:** Kootenai National Forest, Libby Ranger District; **Notes:** Wilderness rules apply. Open to horses; **GPS:** 48.0262°, -115.5042°

Sheltered on timbered shelves below the sprawling subalpine lawns of the Cabinet Divide, this pair of pretty lakes offers a high reward for your effort. Add in an easy and essential side trip to Lost Buck Pass and its bedrock overlook of the interior of the Cabinet Mountains Wilderness, and you have a Cabinets' classic. No surprise, then, that it's quite popular; this is one of the few Cabinets' trails where you're likely to rub elbows with other hikers.

GETTING THERE

From Libby, drive 24 miles southeast on US Highway 2. Shortly after milepost 56, turn right on West Fisher Creek Road (Forest Road 231). Drive 5.8 miles, then turn left on FR 2332. In 0.5 mile, turn left on FR 6748, cross the bridge, and continue for 1.6 occasionally rough miles to the road's end and trailhead (elev. 3750 feet).

ON THE TRAIL

Immediately descend to cross a footbridge over Lake Creek. On well-tended tread wide enough for pack strings, the trail climbs steadily but gently through uniform lodgepole forest, giving hikers plenty of time to harvest huckleberries. The trail's popularity with horses occasionally becomes evident when it crosses shrubby swales, the chewed-up, mud-slick bedrock underfoot testing your balance. The early-summer pink of spirea mixed with slide alder provides a nice distraction, though.

At 1.6 miles, pass the wilderness boundary and, immediately after, the short spur to the outlet of Lower Geiger Lake. The four-foot-wide outlet provides entry to a handful of popular tent sites on the marshy outlet, which is cut off from the main body of the lake. It's a good place to see moose in the morning and mosquitoes any time early in the summer. While it's the more popular of the two lakes by virtue of its shorter hike, the upper lake is worth the work to get there.

From the main trail, proceed on well-graded switchbacks that quickly ascend upslope from the lower lake, the views of Lower Geiger Lake's deep, steep, northeast-facing cirque—and the berry picking—improving as you go. At 2.3 miles, just past a small stone memorial, keep left where the Fourth of July Creek Trail comes in from the north, and keep left again at a signed junction at 2.6 miles. Reaching level ground, cross the moss-draped rocks of a tiny creek before reaching the grassy outlet of Upper Geiger Lake at 2.9 miles.

Flanked by Carney Peak's subalpine meadows to the west, a great bedrock headwall to the south, and thick hemlocks elsewhere, Upper Geiger Lake provides excellent swimming from its silt-bottomed shoreline. Its large grassy outlet is particularly attractive and provides excellent camping once it dries out. Keep an eye out for mountain goats, which nimbly negotiate the steep talus slopes to the west and north. This is a popular overnight spot despite the absence of truly level tent sites.

EXTENDING YOUR TRIP

The granite causeway of Lost Buck Pass, just west of Upper Geiger Lake, is an essential hike. From the final junction before the upper lake, continue climbing as the trail leaves the timber behind for extensive beargrass and berry spreads just below the rocky notch of the pass. It's only 1.1 miles to the wood-and-granite defile at the pass, but a few minutes of walking south on the Cabinet Divide Trail reveals increasingly jaw-dropping views of the heart of the Cabinet Mountains Wilderness, most prominently Wanless Lake—the largest lake in the wilderness—to the west, with Goat Peak's rocky facade prominent behind it.

A hiker and her trail pup admire Upper Geiger Lake from Lost Buck Pass.

18 Bear and Baree Lakes Loop

1 hr 15 mn (handwritten)

RATING/ DIFFICULTY	LOOP	ELEV GAIN/ HIGH POINT	SEASON
****/4	8.6 miles	2640 feet/ 6250 feet	July–Oct

Maps: USFS Cabinet Mountains Wilderness; USGS Goat Peak, MT; USGS Silver Butte Pass, MT; **Contact:** Kootenai National Forest, Libby Ranger District; **Notes:** Wilderness rules apply. Open to horses; **GPS:** 47.9512°, -115.4948°

At the southern end of the Cabinet Mountains Wilderness, this open loop typifies the southern Cabinets: small, tree-lined lakes in the crook of a crest where broad, rounded ridges replace the angular faces of peaks farther to the north. The lakes here lack the granite grandeur of others in the Cabinets, but the open-forest and high-meadow hiking—and huckleberry picking—is superb.

GETTING THERE

From Libby head southeast on US Highway 2 for 29.2 miles, then turn right on Silver Butte Road (Forest Road 148). To reach the Bear Lakes trailhead, drive 9.5 miles, then bear right at the signed trailhead spur and drive 0.25 mile to the parking area (elev. 3730 feet). To reach the Baree Lake trailhead, continue another mile on FR 148, then bear right at the signed trailhead spur and drive 0.25 mile to the large parking area (elev. 3820 feet).

ON THE TRAIL

For this hike, known locally as the Bear-Baree Loop, hikers can start at either trailhead—they are only a mile apart—but I begin at Baree: the initial ascent is gentler, and I prefer the prettier backdrop for an uphill grunt than a final descent.

From the Baree Lake trailhead, climb at creek grade through lodgepole and then lofty larch, huckleberries always within easy reach of the trail. The lightly shaded lodgepole forests of the central and southern Cabinets have been revered for huckleberry picking since pre-European settlement, and it's easy to see why. Following the general course of the creek, never steeply, the trail ventures upon an impressive cascade at 1.3 miles and, shortly after, crosses a strong footbridge. Note the slabby granite of the creek bed; exfoliation has caused rock to slide away in sheets to leave perfect stair steps behind.

Now in thicker north-facing forest, enter the wilderness at 1.8 miles, and, shortly after, cross Baree Creek again to reach a steep slope decorated with talus and rock-garden penstemon and lomatium. The dogleg bend of Baree Creek effectively limits any vistas downstream. Thick brush and centuries-old spruce accompany the now-steeper tread to an unmarked but obvious junction at 2.7 miles (elev. 5530 feet)—if you cross a dry creek bed, you've just missed it. Bear left on level tread to Baree Lake's outlet 0.2 mile later.

Baree Lake doesn't have the rugged granite visage of high Cabinets' lakes, but a nice green headwall reflects onto its waters, and long-submerged logs lie just underneath. Large campsites under a spruce-larch canopy and excellent fishing encourage overnight stays.

To continue the loop, head back to the main trail and turn left, climbing somewhat steeply, first through thick timber and then

Looking out over the interior of the Cabinet Mountains Wilderness from the Cabinet Divide Trail

across steep beargrass slopes, to a junction with the Cabinet Divide Trail after 3.4 miles (elev. 5920 feet). Turn right (north) and savor the broad, beargrass-clad ridgeline, where purple lupine bloom in profusion amid whitebark pine. Head north, feasting on increasingly good vistas of the Swamp Creek drainage and Goat Peak's pyramidal profile to the west and the bare ridge separating the Baree and Bear Lakes basins—your destination—to the east. Clambering onto any of the squared-off rock knobs immediately trailside will give even better views.

Passing through a grassy saddle where it appears there might be an old trail junction—there isn't—the route briefly descends off the west side of the divide before meeting a cairn-marked trail junction at 4.8 miles (elev. 6220 feet). Bear right. The trail gradually loses elevation as it crosses talus slopes amid stunted subalpine fir. Below the trail, in the dry basin, is a bit of interesting geology: a broad bedrock terrace, nearly flat and scattered with fractured granite slabs and small meltwater pools.

After a mile of descending, the trail jogs up and crests the ridge in a timbered defile before dropping north into the Bear Lakes basin. At 5.9 miles, at a switchback junction, continue north onto the Divide Cutoff Trail briefly before following an unofficial yet easy-to-follow boot path to the middle Bear Lake.

Back on the Bear Lakes Trail, continue your descent with a bit of featureless forest hiking through more lodgepole forest. Unlike the Baree Creek drainage, the understory here is fool's, rather than true, huckleberry, so when you reach the Bear Lakes trailhead at 8.6 miles, consider saving some time after the 1-mile trek back to the Baree Lake trailhead for berry picking on the latter trail.

EXTENDING YOUR TRIP

Leave a second vehicle at the Geiger Lakes trailhead (Hike 17), rather than the Bear Lakes trailhead, for two open-looping hiking options. By continuing north on the Cabinet Divide rather than descending to Bear Lakes, hikers can enjoy an added mile of high-country hiking over granite ballast

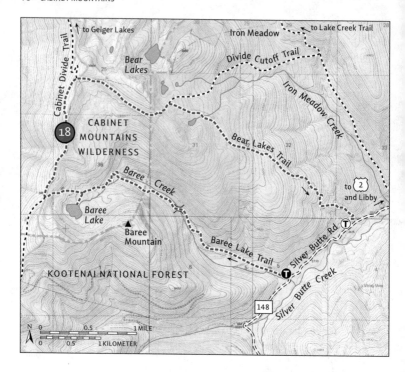

to Lost Buck Pass. From there, it is about a one-mile descent to Upper Geiger Lake. Or, by bearing north at Bear Lakes onto the Iron Meadow Trail, hikers can wander the open elk country of Iron Meadow before reaching their vehicle via the Lake Creek Trail.

Southern Cabinets

At the southernmost extension of the Cabinet Mountains lies a little-known and lightly explored region of rugged ridgelines, expansive wildflower meadows, and steep, glacier-gouged basins pockmarked with tiny lakes. The southern Cabinets do not get the same regard as the lofty peaks of the

Cabinet Mountains Wilderness to the north, but they have their own quiet charm, with lakes such as Cabin, Lawn, and Grass inviting relaxation.

19 Four Lakes Loop

RATING/ DIFFICULTY	LOOP	ELEV GAIN/ HIGH POINT	SEASON
★★★★★/4	8.5 miles	3230 feet/ 7110 feet	Late June–Oct

Map: USGS Mount Headley, MT; **Contact:** Lolo National Forest, Plains/Thompson Falls Ranger District; **Note:** Open to horses and bicycles; **GPS:** 47.7031°, -115.2632°

Hazy summer sunset from Cube Iron Mountain

⬛⬛⬛⬛ Sample four shallow, flower-garlanded ponds and the blocky summit of Cube Iron Mountain on this essential introduction to the Cube Iron–Silcox Roadless Area.

GETTING THERE

From Thompson Falls, drive east on Montana Highway 200 for 5 miles. At milepost 56, just before the bridge over the Thompson River, turn left (north) on Thompson River Road (County Road 556, which turns into Forest Road 56). It's paved the first 4 miles, then good gravel thereafter. At 6.2 miles, bear left onto West Fork Thompson River Road (FR 703), and drive 7.5 miles to the large trailhead parking area (elev. 4760 feet). Privy available.

ON THE TRAIL

From the trailhead parking area, you have two options: to the left is Four Lakes Creek Trail 460, which climbs, first on old roadbed, then on bona fide trail, 3 miles to an avalanche-gouged basin at the foot of Cube Iron Mountain. Straight ahead is Four Lakes

Trail 459. Take it. Although its best lake is at the beginning, after just 2.3 miles—usually a dessert-before-dinner no-no—this route saves Cube Iron Mountain for last, a worthy trade-off.

Immediately cross a bridge over the West Fork Thompson River. The route casually picks its way through an open forest carpeted with huckleberry bushes—and in mid-August, bushels of ripe berries. After crossing a small stream, gear down for a stiff climb through Douglas-fir with occasional glimpses of the rocky spires seen from the trailhead. Note, too, the occasional monolithic western larch.

At 2 miles, enter a meadow of waist-high wildflowers—white plumes of licorice-scented giant hyssop, creamy clusters of lovage, and blue disks of aster—and the intersection with Thompson-Headley Trail 450. To the right, the route ascends through moist meadows to Mount Headley, approximately 5 miles away. For this hike, bear left, and at 2.3 miles (elev. 6030 feet), reach Cabin Lake.

Of the small tarns that make up this part of the southern Cabinets, locally known as

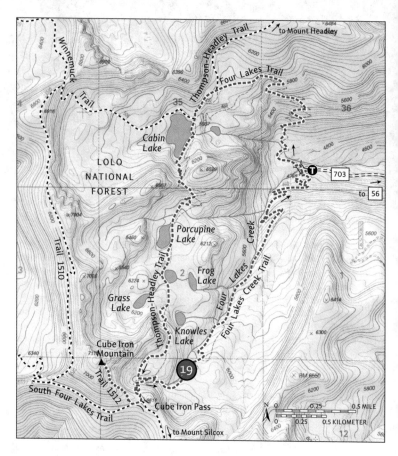

the Cabinet Lakes country, Cabin Lake is the largest and most popular—although "popular" is a relative term here; even on a cloudless August Saturday you are not likely to find more than a handful of equestrians and anglers at the lake. Consider bringing a rod; the trout are active.

From the lake's outlet stream, ascend through increasingly dense forest interspersed with shady rock gardens of penstemon,

paintbrush, stonecrop, and buckwheat. After cresting the ridge at 2.5 miles (elev. 6310 feet), a sunbaked dry meadow grants a stunning view of the heart of the Four Lakes basin. Descend dusty tread into the wooded basin. Amble through asters and arnica, first past Porcupine Lake, where you are just as likely to see a moose, then past an unnamed pond, then to the splendor of Grass Lake. All three lakes are shallow and fish-free but invite lingering.

From Grass Lake, hike gradually upward as the sheer rock walls close in on your right. An opening in the tree canopy provides an aerial view of Knowles Lake, the last of the namesake lakes of this loop. Continue angling uphill through increasingly airy forest to the junction with South Four Lakes Creek Trail in a basin below Cube Iron Pass at 4.1 miles (elev. 6400 feet). Many years, this basin holds snow well into August.

To reach Cube Iron Mountain, bear right at a trail junction in the basin (you'll return to the trailhead on the left trail). Climb to Cube Iron Pass. At a junction with Trail 1512 at 4.4 miles (elev. 6630 feet) turn right, and after a few yards, take another right onto an unmarked lookout's path to the summit of Cube Iron Mountain. The summit route is breathtakingly steep, gaining 500 feet in 0.6 mile, but the views are worth the work.

All that remains at the former lookout site are foundation blocks, a flattened outhouse, and with a little sleuthing, several piles of detritus: door hinges and empty cans from lonely lookouts' dinners. Cube Iron Mountain is so named because of the cube-shaped hunks of pyrite (fool's gold), found here and elsewhere in the Cabinets, in which rusty red iron oxides have replaced most or all of the pyrite (iron sulfide). The prevalence of iron oxides gives the rocks a brick-red hue, although early-morning and late-evening sunlight brings out the gold.

The heart of the southern Cabinets spreads out to the north and west. To the east there are several thousand more acres of pristine ridgelines and plunging meadows, capped by the white cupola of Priscilla Peak's lookout (Hike 20). Thompson Falls lies almost 5000 feet below, to the southwest. Due south looms Mount Silcox, named after Ferdinand Silcox, chief of the US Forest Service during the era of the Civilian Conservation Corps and the Works Progress Administration. Fortunately, little has changed here since Silcox's days. Around 100,000 acres of ridges and mid-elevation forest, including the 39,000-acre Cube Iron–Silcox Roadless Area encompassing the Cabinet Lakes, remain pristine and perfect for modern-day explorers.

To close the loop, return to the basin below Cube Iron Pass. Here, at 5.6 miles, bear right onto Four Lakes Creek Trail 460, which descends 3 uneventful miles to the trailhead on an old roadbed, the mineral-soil substrate sure to tax your feet. Moose frequently inhabit this creek.

EXTENDING YOUR TRIP
Hikers interested in an 11-mile loop with more ridge walking but fewer lakes can take the unmarked junction right before the lake, which climbs up through dense forest before heaving up a sun-parched pass to gain the ridgeline above Cabin Lake.

20 Priscilla Peak

RATING/ DIFFICULTY	ROUNDTRIP	ELEV GAIN/ HIGH POINT	SEASON
****/5	9 miles	4470 feet/ 7005 feet	Mid-June– Oct

Maps: USGS Priscilla Peak, MT; USGS Calico Creek, MT; **Contact:** Lolo National Forest, Plains/Thompson Falls Ranger District; **Note:** Open to horses and bicycles; **GPS:** 47.6641°, -115.1131°

 *A steep, seldom-used trail ascends broad benches of ponderosa pine grassland en route to an abandoned lookout cabin atop Priscilla*

Sun and fog mingle above the rocky prow of Priscilla Peak.

Peak. Here, survey the timbered interior of the southern Cabinets, a landscape that looks much as it did when mapmaker David Thompson passed through two centuries ago.

GETTING THERE

From Thompson Falls, drive east on Montana Highway 200 for 5 miles. At milepost 56, just before the bridge over the Thompson River, turn left (north) on Thompson River Road (County Road 556, which turns into Forest Road 56). It's paved the first 4 miles, then good gravel thereafter. Proceed 9.6 miles, continuing right at the junction with West Fork Thompson River Road (FR 703) at 6.2 miles, to the no-frills trailhead parking area on the left (elev. 2710 feet).

ON THE TRAIL

From the bottomlands of the Thompson River, Sundance Ridge Trail 433 settles into a series of steeply pitched switchbacks. The broad benches of ponderosa pine grassland comprise the terraced remains of the Lake Missoula Floods: between fifteen thousand and thirty thousand years ago, dozens of breaches of glacier-dammed Lake Missoula—a body of water nearly the size of Lake Michigan that spread over western Montana—released a torrent of water west as far as central Washington. The terraces leaven some of the climbing, which, in typical Cabinets' calf-cramping fashion, gains a steady thousand feet or so per mile.

After a mile of climbing, the route curves northwest into a steep, brushy, and occasionally boggy draw, the charred boles of lodgepole and ponderosa here the handiwork of a 2014 fire. The rough tread retreats into deeper forest before connecting with a steep skid road on the ridge crest at 2.3 miles (elev. 5020 feet). Here the trail crosses and re-crosses the skid road several times before angling just off the west side of the ridge; if windfall hides the route, just keep to the left side of the ridgeline.

Nearly a mile later, the skid road ends amid small pocket meadows, the delicate forest flowers—lupine, balsamroot, buckwheat—contrasting with the deep furrows of old-growth Douglas-fir. Now liberated from thick timber, the path permits views of Big Hole Peak and Koo Koo Sint Ridge to the south and the Coeur d'Alene Mountains to the west.

Crossing broad talus washes and scattered subalpine trees, the trail contours around the east side of Priscilla Peak's summit before attaining the ridgetop at 4.5 miles

(elev. 6960 feet). Bear left at an unmarked junction for the last two hundred feet to the summit (elev. 7005 feet).

Priscilla Peak's sculpted bedrock pinnacles punctuate the forested hogback of Sundance Ridge. The summit's white clapboard cabin, complete with charming cupola, was once available to rent from the Forest Service but has been abandoned owing to lack of use. Pack rats have since taken up residence and, in light of the risk of hantavirus, the Forest Service has cordoned off the interior of the structure. It's best to enjoy the cabin and its cupola from the outside. Fortunately, the views compensate, with the timbered latticework of Sundance Ridge and Cube Iron–Silcox Roadless

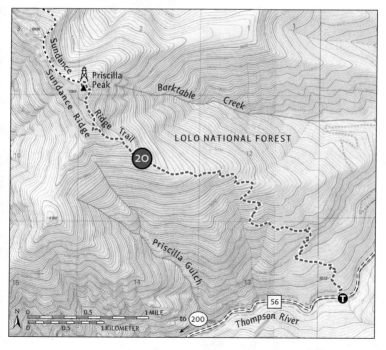

Areas—wilderness candidates both—a contrast to the clear-cuts elsewhere in the southern Cabinets.

The many creeks and streams of the southern Cabinets drain into the Thompson River, named for explorer David Thompson, widely acknowledged as the first European to map the region. The mapmaker's moniker is affixed to numerous spots throughout the region including the nearby town of Thompson Falls. And on Priscilla Peak, it's possible to survey a landscape that looks much the same as it did during Thompson's time.

EXTENDING YOUR TRIP
From just below the summit of Priscilla Peak, hikers can follow the Sundance Ridge Trail

some dozen miles as it wanders north to the Cube Iron–Silcox trail system.

21 Terrace Lake

RATING/ DIFFICULTY	ROUNDTRIP	ELEV GAIN/ HIGH POINT	SEASON
***/3	3.4 miles	1340 feet/ 5880 feet	Mid-June– Oct

Maps: USGS Vermilion Peak, MT; USGS Fishtrap Lake, MT; **Contact:** Lolo National Forest, Plains/Thompson Falls Ranger District; **Note:** Open to horses and bicycles; **GPS:** 47.7707°, -115.2404°

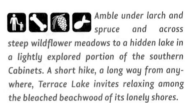 *Amble under larch and spruce and across steep wildflower meadows to a hidden lake in a lightly explored portion of the southern Cabinets. A short hike, a long way from anywhere, Terrace Lake invites relaxing among the bleached beachwood of its lonely shores.*

GETTING THERE
From Thompson Falls, drive east on Montana Highway 200 for 5 miles. At milepost 56, just before the bridge over the Thompson River, turn left (north) on Thompson River Road (County Road 556, which turns into Forest Road 56). It's paved the first 4 miles, then good gravel thereafter. At 14.8 miles, turn left onto Fishtrap Creek Road (FR 516). Drive 9.8 miles, then bear left onto West Fork Fishtrap Creek Road (FR 7609). Bear left at 3.1 miles across a bridge, and at 6.3 miles reach a switchback in the road and the trailhead (elev. 4740 feet).

ON THE TRAIL
Although an unauthorized user-constructed path has accessed this lake—little known

Haze from late summer wildfires settles in to the basin of Terrace Lake.

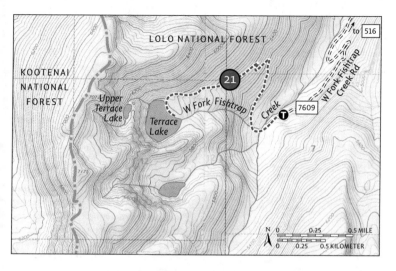

outside the communities of Plains and Thompson Falls—for years, the Forest Service recently constructed a great trail to Terrace Lake. And because this new trail was specifically built for recreation—unlike historic trails that accessed lookouts or mining claims as quickly as possible—users benefit from such trail pleasantries as the occasional switchback and boot-friendly tread. But make no mistake: the hike to Terrace Lake is far from flat.

In thick fir forest, the trail winds through huckleberry, thimbleberry, and maple before making a slight descent to cross Terrace Lake's outlet stream. Cross another small rivulet and begin a gradual sidehill ascent through an interesting mix of huckleberry, fir, larch, and lots of yew, a shrub usually more at home in inland temperate rain forest than the dry clime of the southern Cabinets.

After nearly three-quarters of a mile, make the first switchback. Raspberry, rose, and currant crowd under centuries-old larch. Thick, fire-resistant plating keeps these beauties standing long after they've died; notice the holes both man- and creature-made carved in many of the snags, the former cut by fur trappers for marten trapping.

At 1.3 miles (elev. 5680 feet), enter a steep, moist meadow and follow the trail straight up the fall line under the drooping canopies of some surprisingly large Engelmann spruce. A quarter mile farther, the trail crests the rim of the lake basin and descends through dense fool's huckleberry to the lake.

Sitting in a deep bowl, steep-sided meadows on its north end and the craggy crenellations common to the southern Cabinets wrapping around its west face, Terrace Lake might better be named "Hidden Lake." For the best water access, continue along the steep east side of the lake to a large dispersed campsite on the broad outlet plain. Low late-summer water levels reveal a beach of sorts here, and idle campers have arranged several driftwood shelters. Anglers will find room for a backcast and plenty of attention-starved fish.

EXTENDING YOUR TRIP

Tiny Upper Terrace Lake sits on a bench overlooking the main lake. A steep, off-camber—though never exposed—quarter mile of off-trail travel will deliver you to this true terrace tarn.

Sunrise highlights the alpine wildflowers at Big Hole Lookout.

22 Big Hole Lookout

RATING/ DIFFICULTY	ROUNDTRIP	ELEV GAIN/ HIGH POINT	SEASON
****/3	5.4 miles	1460 feet/ 6919 feet	Mid-June– Oct

Map: USGS Big Hole Peak, MT; **Contact:** Lolo National Forest, Plains/Thompson Falls Ranger District; **Note:** Open to horses and bicycles; **GPS:** 47.5858°, -115.0472°

The 2.7-mile hike to Big Hole Lookout, near the town of Plains, won't get your heart rate up, but the view will. From the recently restored lookout cabin, peer over the sheer sides of a sedimentary cliff into the lightly explored forests of the southern Cabinets.

GETTING THERE

From downtown Plains, drive northwest on Montana Highway 200 for 7.6 miles to Weeksville Creek Road (Forest Road 887). Turn right (north) and drive 2.1 miles, then bear left on FR 5587. Continue 9.6 miles on this steep, narrow, switchbacking mountain road to a gate beyond which it's closed to vehicles (elev. 5500 feet). A parking area on the shoulder accommodates two vehicles.

ON THE TRAIL

An open burn area and fire-loving flora—larch, huckleberry, lupine—greet hikers at the trailhead for Big Hole Lookout Trail 368. Traverse a sidehill, first through open lodgepole forest, then into an airy Douglas-fir parkland. The tree canopy blocks any views down into the Clark Fork Valley, but the immediate surroundings are sublime. Hikers are likely to see black bear, elk, and moose in this open forest.

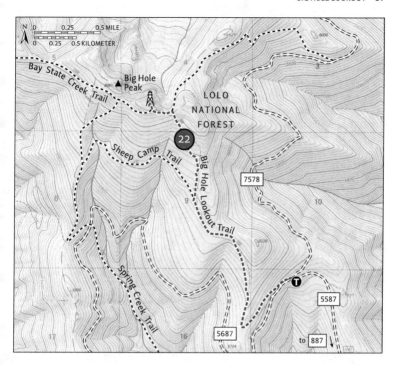

In a third of a mile, the trail hairpins right and the grade picks up slightly. The canopy gradually thickens, now a uniform phalanx of lodgepole pine, the signature forest of the Intermountain West. Aside from a blink-and-you'll-miss-it glimpse of Big Hole Lookout's barren summit, there's little but the creak of swaying snags to take your mind off the trail ahead. That's not to say there isn't a quiet, orderly beauty to row after endless row of lodgepole—for one thing, it masks all evidence of the outside world.

At 2 miles (elev. 6340 feet), as the horizon to the right begins to open, bear right at a junction with the Sheep Camp Trail. Nearly a half mile later, in a flat saddle, continue straight at a junction with the Bay State Creek Trail; immediately afterward, bear left and commence the quarter mile of only real climbing on the hike.

The trail finally emerges from the lodgepole forest onto Big Hole Lookout at 2.7 miles. The clapboard cabin, its white paint long flaked off, sat in lonely service from the 1930s to the 1960s on its perch upon the very edge of a small heather-clad bald, the steep front-door drop sure to cure any lookout's sleepwalking tendencies. The Lolo National Forest and volunteers are in the process of restoring the lookout, with the hope of adding it to the lookout rental system (they've installed a privy in the trees twenty yards downhill from the cabin). The view transfixes: to the northwest, Big Hole Peak, which was overlooked for a lookout location in favor of this more suitable spot; the rolling, forested foothills of the Little Thompson River drainage to the northeast; and to the east, Baldy Mountain and its distinctive heart-shaped snowfield and beyond it the dry massif of the Mission Mountains.

23 Baldy Mountain and Baldy Lake

RATING/ DIFFICULTY	ROUNDTRIP	ELEV GAIN/ HIGH POINT	SEASON
****/3	5 miles	2280 feet/ 7464 feet	Late June–Oct

Maps: USGS Coney Peak, MT; USGS Baldy Lake, MT; **Contact:** Lolo National Forest, Plains/Thompson Falls Ranger District; **Note:** Open to horses and bicycles; **GPS:** 47.6280°, -114.8470°

Bald is beautiful on this "island" peak that stands head and shoulders above the surrounding valleys. The southernmost trail-accessible peak of the Cabinets, Baldy bears more in common with its granite-complected kin to the north than its grassy southern Cabinets' neighbors.

GETTING THERE
From downtown Plains, drive northwest on Montana Highway 200 for 0.5 mile to Kruger Road (signed for the hospital). Turn right and proceed to a T-junction with Clayton Street. Turn left and drive 8.3 miles, then bear left onto Cedar Creek Road (Forest Road 1025). Drive 4.2 miles, then turn right onto FR 886 and continue 3.9 miles to the road's end and trailhead (elev. 5910 feet).

ON THE TRAIL
The Baldy Mountain Trail has two trailheads, the lower of which connects one stretch of forest road to another and is of interest only

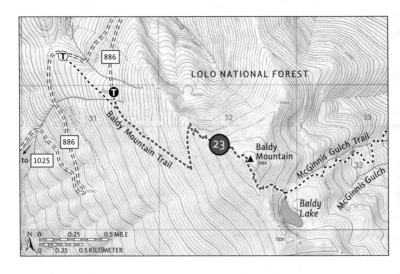

Baldy Lake reflects the sheer cirque above it.

to trail completists. Begin this hike from the upper trailhead on an old roadbed flanked by larch, purple vetch, and colonnades of beargrass. An old Plum Creek clear-cut on the downhill side of the trail permits a view of the "big bend" of the Clark Fork River.

Join the trail coming from the lower trailhead and ascend through an increasingly open forest of larch and subalpine fir. The squat square form of Big Hole Lookout is visible to the west; to the south stand the prominent peaks of the Coeur d'Alene Divide: Eddy Peak and its lookout on the right, Penrose Peak on the left. Underfoot, shiny-leaved kinnikinnick clambers on old stumps.

At 0.8 mile (elev. 6540 feet) the trail breaks out of the trees and onto a steep talus slope. Switchback up the packed-talus path, enjoying some of the best subalpine walking in the area. In a quarter mile, round a

switchback where a short spur trail accesses a rock knob with views over talus slopes of Thompson and Little Thompson Peaks.

At 1.9 miles (elev. 7464 feet) reach the flat summit of Baldy. A drystone-fitted rock foundation and old concrete pilings are all that remain of the fire lookout structure that stood sentinel here. Elsewhere on the broad summit stand rock structures that are surely the result of idle fire lookouts. A small ski area, Corona Divide, used to operate on Baldy, but its tow bars have gone the way of the lookout structures nearby. Listen for the whistle-squeak of pikas among the ground-hugging purple blooms of penstemon. Walk to the east side of the summit for an aerial view of the arid Hot Springs Valley and the Missions beyond. Kidney-shaped Baldy Lake lies almost directly below. Although part of the larger Cabinet Mountains range, Baldy

Mountain is an island of sorts; the nearly vertical mile of elevation separating its summit from the valleys below makes it the thirteenth-highest prominence in Montana. It's also at the heart of another "island"—a pristine 16,000-acre roadless area in a sea of clear-cuts.

From the old lookout structure, the trail descends 0.6 mile, first through wind-twisted whitebark pines, then a beargrass meadow, to a well-used outfitters' camp on the shore of Baldy Lake, where it connects with the McGinnis Gulch Trail. Snow lingers late on the steep, shaded rock face above the west side of the lake. Hunks of sharp-cornered granite compose the lakeshore and lakebed, so barefoot wading in Baldy's icy waters is not recommended.

Opposite: *Evening sun highlights the bedrock-flecked bald of McGuire Mountain (Hike 26).*

upper kootenai river

Snags wave in the breeze atop Flagstaff Mountain.

Nearly twenty miles upstream of Libby, the 422-foot-high Libby Dam impounds the dual-citizen Kootenai River in the deep waters of Lake Koocanusa. The 90-mile-long shoreline of Koocanusa (the name is a portmanteau of the first three letters from "Kootenai," "Canada," and "USA") dominates a landscape of low, lodgepole-forested ridges and rocky meadows, the rounded, glacier-ground purview of the Purcell Mountains. Despite the presence of some unfortunately placed clear-cuts, the Upper Kootenai River country rewards hikers with doorstep views of the Cabinet Mountains and the crazed peaks of Glacier National Park to the east.

Map: USGS Scenery Mountain, MT; **Contact:** Kootenai National Forest, Libby Ranger District; **Note:** Open to horses and bicycles; **GPS:** 48.4707°, -115.6797°

The story goes that returning World War I vets set a flagpole on this Libby-area landmark nearly a century ago. The flag no longer flies, but abundant wildflowers unfurl every spring. And the views across the Kootenai River to the Cabinet Mountains Wilderness should have a salutary effect all summer long.

GETTING THERE

From Libby, drive north on Montana Highway 37, across the Kootenai River. Approximately 1 mile from downtown, turn left on Kootenai River Road. Drive 4.7 miles, then turn right onto Quartz Creek Road (Forest Road 600). Drive 5.1 miles, then bear left onto West Fork Road (FR 4690). Cross the bridge over Quartz Creek and bear left at the Y-intersection, then

24 Flagstaff Mountain

RATING/ DIFFICULTY	ROUNDTRIP	ELEV GAIN/ HIGH POINT	SEASON
****/3	4 miles	1660 feet/ 6075 feet	Late May–Oct

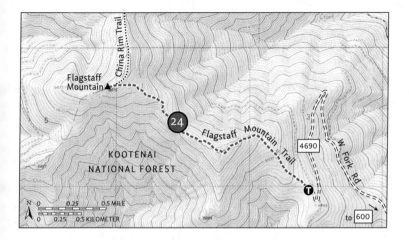

at 1.6 miles, turn left to continue on FR 4690. Drive this rocky, washboarded road 6.8 miles to the trailhead (elev. 4720 feet). A pullout next to the trailhead on the left side of the road accommodates two vehicles.

ON THE TRAIL

From a flat, forested saddle ascend Flagstaff Mountain Trail 446 through an open forest of larch, pine, and fir. This is black bear and cougar country—in fact, it is the only trail in western Montana on which I have seen the elusive cat. Flowers flank the steep, straight, faded tread; throughout the spring and summer, red and gold paintbrush, arnica, cat's ears, coral bells, meadow death camas, prairie smoke, and hawkweed all bloom in profusion. Make sure to look up, though, for an aerial view of Libby and, across the Kootenai River, the steep spire of Scenery Mountain at the north end of the Cabinet Mountains Wilderness. The trail occasionally grows faint in thick foliage; keep to the spine of the ridge.

At 0.9 mile (elev. 5580 feet), crest a small knob, and then descend into a draw thick with willows. The infrequently maintained tread makes several brisk dips in and out of dry creek drainages before curving around to the east side of the ridge. At 1.4 miles (elev. 5540 feet), the tread leaves the trees and essentially disappears. The occasional cairn marks the way, but if in doubt head straight up. As you near the top of the ridge, spot an old "Flagstaff Mountain" sign, then, shortly after, the wooden summit marker at 2 miles (elev. 6075 feet).

A 1994 wildfire scorched Flagstaff Mountain, leaving behind thousands of snags and even more wildflowers. No flag remains, but there's plenty of red huckleberry, blue lupine, and white yarrow to be found. And there's a front-row view of Scenery Mountain straight across the river and, to the east, the low, forested Purcells. The exposed rock and thousands of snags should make it clear that Flagstaff is also a lightning rod; stay off this peak if thunderstorms are in the forecast.

EXTENDING YOUR TRIP

Maps show a trail from the summit of Flagstaff Mountain along the ridgeline to

China Rim, but it's even less visible on the ground than the last half mile of tread to the Flagstaff summit. Hikers experienced in off-travel navigation may wish to make the 3-mile ridge run, but be forewarned: most of the way plods through tangled deadfall or thick, trackless timber.

25 Boulder Lakes

RATING/ DIFFICULTY	ROUNDTRIP	ELEV GAIN/ HIGH POINT	SEASON
****/3	4.8 miles	1050 feet/ 6140 feet	Mid-June– Oct

Map: USGS Boulder Lakes, MT; **Contact:** Kootenai National Forest, Rexford Ranger District; **Note:** Open to horses and bicycles; **GPS:** 48.8288°, -115.4095°

Moose and the reclusive grizzly are known to frequent this far-off-the-beaten-path pair of lakes. But few humans do, save for the occa-sional thru-hiker. It's a shame, because Boulder Lakes boast perhaps the easiest trail-accessible subalpine pools in northwest Montana.

GETTING THERE
From Montana Highway 37 about 13 miles south of Eureka, turn right (west) across the Lake Koocanusa Bridge. Across the bridge, turn right onto Forest Road 92. Drive 2.6 miles, then turn left on Boulder Creek Road (FR 337). Drive 8.7 miles, then continue straight onto FR 7183. Continue 1.3 miles to the signed pullout on the right, which has room for a handful of vehicles.

ON THE TRAIL
From its gated-road beginnings, Boulder Lakes Trail—a segment of the Pacific Northwest Trail (see "Crown to Coast" sidebar in the Yaak Valley section)—follows an old roadbed that is quickly being reclaimed by encroaching alder. This road used to continue another mile or so to the original Boulder Lakes trailhead, but the Forest

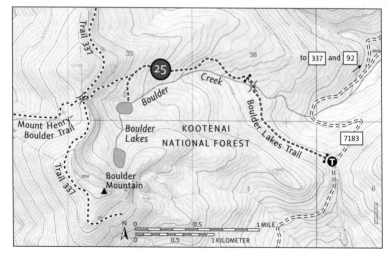

Service gated it to protect core grizzly habitat. Fortunately, even with the additional mile of "road" walking each way, Boulder Lakes are among the easiest-to-reach trail-accessible lakes in northwest Montana.

After a mile, the path comes to the road's end, where Boulder Creek crashes through a culvert under the road. From here, continue uphill a short distance on another segment of road before reaching the original

The shallow, grass-bottomed waters of Boulder Lake reflect the shoulder of Boulder Mountain.

trailhead. Pass an out-of-place gate; please close it behind you (assuming you find it closed) to prevent errant cows from fouling the lake—this is open-range country. Continue, now on the original trail, where larch and lodgepole overhead effectively limit views of the immediate surroundings, which fortunately consist of copious huckleberries.

Now heading west, the trail gently ascends a south-facing slope above the Boulder Lakes' outlet stream. At 2.1 miles (elev. 6120 feet), bear left onto a short spur trail to the lower of the two Boulder Lakes.

A dense forest of subalpine fir spires circles the lower lake; beargrass and huckleberry shrubs flank the shore, which has surprisingly few level spots to sit or stake a tent given the short distance of the hike. Above, glacier lilies carpet the rocky slope of a shoulder of Boulder Mountain, a worthwhile destination for backpackers and ambitious day hikers. Aquatic vegetation carpets most of the shallow, silt-bottomed lake; the grasses hide active trout, which reveal themselves in flashing belly-slaps of the surface. Should you choose to stay put, you can take your chances on catching dinner. Keep an eye out for larger critters: odds are you won't see a bruin, but moose are regular residents of this lake basin.

EXTENDING YOUR TRIP
From the trail junction, the Boulder Lakes Trail climbs 700 feet in 0.6 mile to a low pass north of Boulder Mountain. From this wooded defile, hikers can head south for 1 mile to Boulder Mountain's blocky mass, where a surprisingly large log lookout cabin molders. (Topographical maps show this trail continuing down to FR 7183, but that connector has disappeared entirely.) Meanwhile, the main trail continues northwest

2 miles to the marshy, moose-frequented woodlands of Purcell Summit and then beyond to Mount Henry's lookout tower.

26 McGuire Mountain

RATING/ DIFFICULTY	ROUNDTRIP	ELEV GAIN/ HIGH POINT	SEASON
***/2	4.6 miles	980 feet/ 6991 feet	June–Oct

Map: USGS McGuire Mountain, MT; **Contact:** Kootenai National Forest, Rexford Ranger District; **Note:** Open to horses and bicycles; **GPS:** 48.6718°, -115.1711°

Nearly level tread and a short climb accesses a historic ridgetop lookout, with a second life as a Forest Service rental cabin. The furnishings are rustic, but the views are first-rate: the Cabinets to the southeast, the Purcells and Lake Koocanusa to the north, and the Whitefish Range— and beyond, Glacier National Park—to the east.

GETTING THERE
From the south end of Eureka, drive west on Tobacco Road 0.6 mile to Othorp Lake Road (which becomes Forest Road 854). Turn right and drive 14 miles, then turn right on West Pinkham Road (FR 856). At 7.5 miles, bear far right at a three-way intersection onto FR 494. At 2.8 miles, bear right to continue on FR 494 another 1.3 miles to the trailhead parking area on the right, where there is room for a few vehicles (elev. 6390 feet). Privy available at McGuire Mountain Lookout.

ON THE TRAIL
Lookout trails tend to be steep, switchback-eschewing affairs. Not this one—there is negligible climbing until the last 0.3 mile.

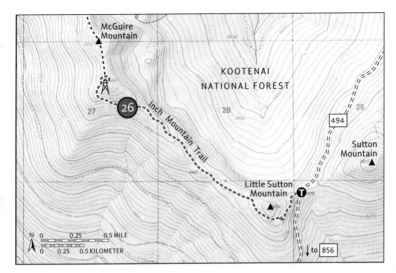

From the edge of the road, the trail splits at one hundred yards, both paths reuniting in a few hundred yards. Traversing an open, burnt lodgepole parkland, the trail remains almost completely level; the only legwork involved might be high-stepping it over horse manure.

Huckleberry and lupine, both sun-loving post-fire colonists, enliven the surroundings. The tread picks up the grade slightly, and at 1.5 miles (elev. 6640 feet) deposits hikers onto an expansive, grassy ridge. Aster, lupine, yarrow, harebell, and heather provide early- and midsummer color.

Numerous rock outcroppings flank the trail as it bends around the west side of the ridge. A trickle of water from a small spring at 1.9 miles provides a good place for lookout guests to top off bottles. Shortly after, the trail makes its only real climb as it crests the ridge. Bear right at the ridgeline and reach the lookout at 2.3 miles.

Built in 1923, McGuire Mountain Lookout saw active fire service for just over twenty years before being abandoned. Now it's available as an overnight rental. A pyramid-shaped cupola sits atop a 12-foot-by-12-foot white clapboard cabin wrapped in windows. Outside, white-painted stones in front of the cabin spell out "McGuire," an aid for aerial spotters. Inside, the scents

A snowshoe hare tries to blend in among the bare branches of late spring.

of old woodsmoke and bacon fat permeate the spare furnishings. Pull open the cupola shutters for a million-dollar view: the long pickets of the Whitefish Range and the Cabinets form the east and west horizons, respectively, and the horseshoe curve of the Kootenai River and its impoundment at Lake Koocanusa sprawl to the north.

EXTENDING YOUR TRIP

Consider arranging a shuttle to make a one-way ridge run north on the McGuire Mountain Trail. From the lookout, it's a steady 3.4-mile descent to a trailhead on FR 7993; from there, it's another 6 miles up and over Inch Mountain to Montana Highway 37 along Lake Koocanusa. If nothing else, enjoy the half mile of hiking just beyond the junction to the lookout, a pure parkland of widely spaced Douglas-fir and expansive wildflowers.

Opposite: *A hiker and her trail pup take in Bluebird Lake on the Ten Lakes Loop (Hike 27).*

whitefish range

Ten Lakes Scenic Area

Overshadowed by its famous neighbor to the east, Glacier National Park, 40,000-acre Ten Lakes Scenic Area, just shy of the Canadian border, boasts an abundance of shallow, grass-fringed lakes suited for foot-soaking amid rocky spires and wildflowers. Proposed for wilderness designation by the Forest Service for more than thirty years, the Ten Lakes Scenic Area remains a wild island amid a sea of timber activity. Acres of intact old-growth forest and expansive alpine meadows make for some of the best bruin habitat in western Montana. While hikers are unlikely to spot a grizzly, wildlife is plentiful in the area, including deer, moose, and the by turns wary and gregarious grouse. Two-legged locals also revere the area for its bumper crops of huckleberries, but visitors willing to walk can easily get their fill.

27 Ten Lakes Loop

RATING/ DIFFICULTY	LOOP	ELEV GAIN/ HIGH POINT	SEASON
*****/4	10 miles	2370 feet/ 7390 feet	July–early Oct

Map: USGS Ksanka Peak, MT; **Contact:** Kootenai National Forest, Rexford Ranger District; **Note:** Open to horses and bicycles; **GPS:** 48.9435°, -114.9013°

Hikers interested in a daylong trek in the locally revered Ten Lakes Scenic Area can sample a handful of picturesque lakes—with plenty of huckleberries as an appetizer—on the 10-mile Ten Lakes Loop.

GETTING THERE

From Eureka, drive south on US Highway 93 for 9 miles and turn left on Graves Creek Road (Forest Road 114). Continue 14 miles (pavement ends at 10 miles) to where it merges with FR 319. Continue straight on FR 319 for 14 miles to FR 7085 and Little Therriault Lake Campground. From the campground, continue 0.6 mile to the road's end and trailhead (elev. 5740 feet).

ON THE TRAIL

From the trailhead for Bluebird Basin Trail 83 near Little Therriault Lake, climb through huckleberry-laden forest 1.7 miles to shallow—and aptly named—Paradise Lake (elev. 6710 feet). Continue around its grassy shores for another tenth of a mile, then bear right at two junctions in quick succession. Shortly afterward, reach the boulder-strewn shores of Bluebird Lake at 2.1 miles (elev. 6840 feet). Well-used tent pads front the lake, which sits at the base of a sheer sedimentary headwall. Many hikers—and this is a surprisingly popular hike, given its long drive time from pretty much anywhere—turn around here for a kid- and dog-friendly 4.2-mile hike.

However, it's worth continuing the loop, which continues through a corridor of subalpine trees before tackling a series of switchbacks to near the crest of the Galton Range at 3.4 miles (elev. 7390 feet). To the north, Green Mountain rises above a sea of spruce and larch. Descend into a charming parkland of alpine larch—one of the best such stands of trees in western Montana—and grassy tarns, and then bear right at a junction at 3.7 miles (elev. 7300 feet). Continue descending to reach the first of the Wolverine Lakes on Wolverine Flat at 4.5 miles (elev. 6910). Trout crowd the

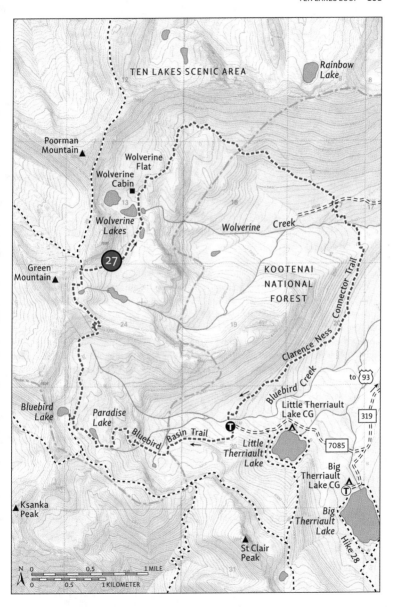

Enjoying a nightcap—and the scenery—in the cupola of Stahl Peak Lookout

larch-fronted lawns of these shallow lakes, next to which sits the Wolverine Cabin, which is open to the public (and, unfortunately, to pack rats). In recent years, the Border Patrol has also used this cabin owing to its close proximity to the Canadian border.

From Wolverine Flat, continue northward for a short time before curving east into the thick spruce bottomland of the Wolverine Creek drainage. At 7.3 miles, cross a forest road, and, now on the Clarence Ness Connector Trail—named for a well-loved backcountry horseman—cross Wolverine Creek before settling into several miles of uninspiring walking on a disused roadbed. Return to the trailhead at 10 miles to complete the loop.

28 Stahl Peak

RATING/ DIFFICULTY	ROUNDTRIP	ELEV GAIN/ HIGH POINT	SEASON
*****/4	6.2 miles	2130 feet/ 7435 feet	July–early Oct

Maps: USGS Ksanka Peak, MT; USGS Stahl Peak, MT; **Contact:** Kootenai National Forest, Fortine Ranger District; **Note:** Open to horses and bicycles; **GPS:** 48.9360°, -114.8778°

Short, sweet, and a tad steep, the hike to Stahl Peak surveys the sprawl of the Ten Lakes Scenic Area and its wilderness-worthy lakes and lawns. Open to the public on a first-come, first-served basis, the lookout on Stahl Peak's summit invites a night under the starry spread of Big Sky country.

GETTING THERE

From Eureka, drive south on US Highway 93 for 9 miles and turn left on Graves Creek Road (Forest Road 114). Continue 14 miles (pavement ends at 10 miles) to where it merges with FR 319. Continue straight on FR 319 for 14 miles, then bear left at the junction with FR 7085 and continue 0.5 mile to Big Therriault Lake Campground. The trail begins from just beyond the campground entrance. Privy available.

ON THE TRAIL

Departing from the surprisingly busy Big Therriault Lake Campground, curve around the west shore of the lake. The level walking invites lingering in the spruce-shaded huckleberry patches here; filling an empty water bottle with these treats should take little time. After a half mile, cross two small creeks in quick succession, then border a large meadow at the foot of St. Clair Peak; this stream-bisected meadow is a reliable spot to watch for moose and bruins.

At 0.7 mile (elev. 5600 feet), reach a junction with the Highline Trail; go right and begin climbing through shade-cooled forest to Therriault Pass at 1.7 miles (elev. 6390 feet). Turn left to continue south on the Highline Trail; the way right connects Little Therriault Lake and the Ten Lakes Loop to the north on a segment of the Pacific Northwest Trail.

In a half mile, bear right on the Stahl Lookout Trail (elev. 6750 feet) and commence a steep sidehill ascent through thinning tree cover to the south face of Stahl Peak. Reaching hummocky subalpine parkland littered with whitebark pine skeletons, the trail takes a straight-line course, passing a junction at 3 miles (elev. 7380 feet) and reaching Stahl's summit shortly after.

A clapboard lookout cabin sits at the crest of Stahl Peak's broad summit, below which the sheer north face drops into a shallow pond at the head of Clarence Creek's U-shaped valley. Complete with sleeping platforms and a woodstove, Stahl Peak Lookout is available on a first-come, first-served basis. Even if you choose not to stay the night, climb into the cupola. From its large windows sprawls the Ten Lakes Scenic Area below; the blocky massifs of Glacier are arrayed to the east, while the Cabinets cap the western horizon. The matching cabin at Mount Wam stands out to the northeast.

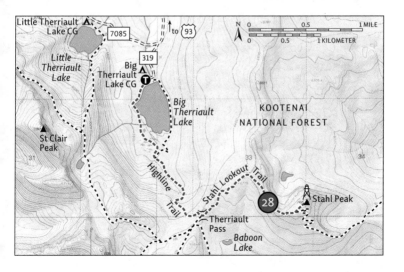

North Fork Wildlands

The grand landscape of Glacier National Park doesn't stop at the park border. The Whitefish Range, separated from its more famous neighbor by the slow sweep of the North Fork Flathead River, boasts wild, wilderness-worthy forests and dozens of tiny subalpine tarns, albeit on a smaller scale than the park. Here, in the area known locally as "up the North Fork," wildflowers flank faded trails on which grizzly tracks—the range harbors one of North America's highest concentrations of the reclusive bruins—often outnumber bootprints. From the rounded, subtly imposing summits of the Whitefish Divide, the green scrum of Glacier's North Fork region seems so close you can reach it.

Maps: USGS Tuchuck Mountain, MT; USGS Mount Hefty, MT; **Contact:** Flathead National Forest, Glacier View Ranger District; **Note:** Open to horses and bicycles; **GPS:** 48.9559°, -114.5792°

Sticking out like a tundra-clad thumb, Tuchuck Mountain marks the high point of the northern Whitefish Range. A long way from anywhere, Tuchuck's summit makes visitors feel as if they can reach out and touch the summits of Glacier National Park to the east.

GETTING THERE

From US Highway 2 in Columbia Falls, head north on Nucleus Avenue for 0.6 mile, then bear right, now on Railroad Street East, which becomes Outer North Fork Road after 0.6 mile. Continue on this road, a combination of pavement and dusty, washboarded gravel, for 49 miles, past the Polebridge turnoff, to Trail Creek Road (Forest Road 114). Turn left, and drive 4.9 miles, then turn right onto Frozen Lake Road (FR 114-A) for 6 bumpy miles to the trailhead (elev. 5160 feet).

29 Tuchuck Mountain

RATING/ DIFFICULTY	ROUNDTRIP	ELEV GAIN/ HIGH POINT	SEASON
****/5	11.6 miles	4170 feet/ 7736 feet	July–early Oct

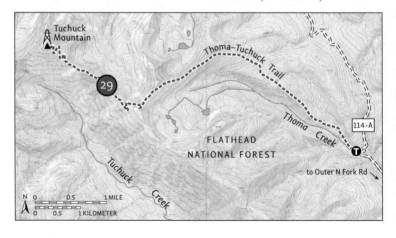

A hiker harvests western Montana's signature crop: huckleberries.

ON THE TRAIL

All trails seemingly lead to Tuchuck, which hikers can reach by nearly a half dozen trails, a number out of proportion to the peak's proximity to anywhere. This hike, from Frozen Lake Road, represents the best approach to Tuchuck—and one of the most scenic hikes in the Whitefish Range.

From the road's end, immediately head left down a disused Forest Service road. After two hundred yards, bear right onto true trail in a small clearing and commence climbing up a shallow, south-facing spine. Decreasing cover affords views of the tangle of timbered ridges that make up the Whitefish Range.

At 3 miles (elev. 6770 feet), gain an east-west ridge and bear west. Huckleberries grow abundantly here; below, an unnamed lake hides in the timber. After a mile of fine ridgetop hiking, signs guide the trail off the north side of the ridge, Tuchuck's tundra-like

summit coming into view. The steep switchbacks angling up the southeast face of the mountain will be your destination soon enough.

From here, the trail begins to descend off the west side of an unnamed high point, seemingly in defiance of your destination to the north. Keep on the trail, though, as it bears north to a saddle at the base of Tuchuck Mountain at 5 miles (elev. 6570 feet). Here, wildflowers speckle the sedimentary rocks; keep an eye out for signs of disturbed rocks, evidence of hungry bears hunting for grubs. Moose frequent the area as well.

From here the trail bends west around a low ridgetop before mounting the switchbacks that have seemed out of reach the last several miles. In a mere half mile of climbing, the trail rounds a bend and gains the summit at 5.8 miles.

Detritus from an old lookout site litters the summit; built in 1930, the lookout tower stood guard over the North Fork forests for nearly thirty years before the Forest Service destroyed it in its zeal to embrace aerial fire-spotting. In the Kootenai language, *Tuchuck* means "thumb"; from on top, it's difficult to determine whether this appellation is apt, but it does mark the high point of the entire 1200-mile Pacific Northwest Trail.

30 Mount Thompson-Seton

RATING/ DIFFICULTY	ROUNDTRIP	ELEV GAIN/ HIGH POINT	SEASON
****/5	10 miles	3350 feet/ 7820 feet	July–early Oct

Map: USGS Mount Thompson-Seton, MT; **Contact:** Flathead National Forest, Glacier View Ranger District; **Note:** Open to horses and bicycles; **GPS:** 48.8421°, -114.6433°

Named for nineteenth-century naturalist Ernest Thompson-Seton, who situated many of his beloved children's books in the region, this peak surveys from its summit a landscape that looks much the same as when Krag the Kootenai Ram scampered through Montana.

GETTING THERE

From US Highway 2 in Columbia Falls, head north on Nucleus Avenue for 0.6 mile, then bear right, now on Railroad Street East, which becomes Outer North Fork Road after 0.6 mile. Continue on this road, a combination of pavement and dusty, washboarded gravel, for 44 miles, past the Polebridge turnoff, to Whale Creek Road (Forest Road 318). Turn left, and drive 11 miles, then bear right onto FR 1674. Continue 2.5 miles to the road's end and trailhead (elev. 4730 feet).

ON THE TRAIL

Beginning on the Whale Creek Trail, an old roadbed, cross Inuya Creek, which early in the season can be daunting. After several hundred yards, turn right at a signed junction onto Inuya Pass Trail 92.

The remnants of Mount Thompson-Seton Lookout make for sparse accommodations.

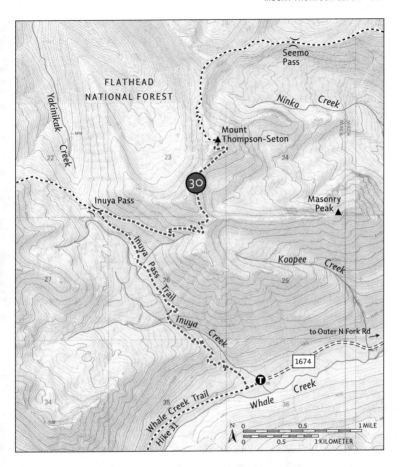

Heavy vegetation threatens to overtake the lightly used tread; after a mile or so of climbing, the trail bears north to parallel Inuya Creek, crossing this clear stream at 1.6 miles and again a tenth of a mile later. Thinning forest cover transitions to thickets of huckleberry and beargrass, the latter's cream-colored spires dusting passing hikers with pollen.

At 2.6 miles (elev. 6280 feet), reach the forested defile of Inuya Pass. From here, the trail bends east across the steep, scree-covered flank of Mount Thompson-Seton's south face. Switchback into a forested saddle at the head of a steep, shaded canyon that forms the north face of Masonry Peak. Curve northward, tracing the contour of Mount Thompson-Seton's steep east face,

OUR WILDERNESS HERITAGE

On September 3, 1964, President Lyndon B. Johnson signed the Wilderness Act. That enduring and popular piece of legislation is now more than fifty years old, but its ideals are as old as the nation itself. Like our country's other landmark pieces of legislation, the Wilderness Act is firm yet flexible, protecting the entire spectrum of our nation's natural habitats. Simply put, "wilderness" refers to those places truly free and untrammeled or unrestrained—land that, according to the Wilderness Act, "generally appears to have been affected primarily by the forces of nature, with the imprint of man's work substantially unnoticeable."

Wilderness connects us to our past—an American frontier that helped to shape our values of freedom, self-reliance, and perseverance. It helps preserve for future generations important reminders of this heritage, from ancient Native American trade routes to lonely peak-top lookouts. Wilderness designation also serves to protect critical habitat for fish and wildlife, providing refuges from the modern world and quality, undeveloped habitat in which to seek shelter and thrive. Ultimately, wilderness offers a sanctuary from the pressures of a rapidly growing and changing world, imparting an enduring legacy of recreational activities and adventure.

Chances are if you've hiked in western Montana, you've hiked in wilderness, or lands that qualify for protection. Wilderness calls to adventurers with the allure of recreation, inspiration, solitude, and physical challenge. It preserves the public's ability to enjoy hiking, backpacking, hunting, fishing, camping, bird watching, berry picking, horseback riding, skiing, and snowshoeing. Many of our state's premier hiking trails can be found in wilderness or potential wilderness areas. In these places, carrying all we need on our backs, we focus on the core necessities for living—food, water, shelter—and we learn what we can live without.

Wilderness can even be appreciated without walking within its boundaries. Wild places form the rugged horizons of many communities, the backdrop for scenic drives, the canvas on which to create dreams of future adventures. Even if we never once set foot in a wilderness, we benefit from its crisp, clean air and fresh, clear water.

In all, wilderness connects us to a healthy future. As our population increases and becomes more urbanized, our remaining backcountry lands become even more valuable as remnants of our once-vast wilderness heritage. More importantly, the wilderness provides a wide-open space for us to experience the intangible values that form the core of the American spirit.

the alpine larch grove here is one of the best in the Whitefish Range, if not all of western Montana. The trail gains the tundra-covered ridge at 4.4 miles (elev. 7400 feet) before following it north through scattered copses of trees to reach the summit at 5 miles.

A larch parkland spans the rocky summit of Mount Thompson-Seton, as does the detritus of a derelict fire lookout tower, complete with a set of bedsprings and an old stove. Named for the famed 19th-century naturalist Ernest Thompson-Seton, the peak—crown of some 84,000 acres of pristine wilderness-quality land—overlooks nearby jagged Krag and Krinklehorn Peaks, named for characters from his popular children's story "Krag the Kootenai Ram," which takes place in the area.

Steep canyons and gentle rolling moraines skirt the rounded forms of Mount Thompson-Seton's Whitefish Range neighbors, their forms less imposing than their kin across the North Fork Flathead River in Glacier National Park. But it is no less wild: here elk summer in shaded basins and one of North America's densest concentrations of grizzlies waits for protection of this wild country.

31 Whale Lake and Huntsberger Lake

Whale Lake

RATING/ DIFFICULTY	ROUNDTRIP	ELEV GAIN/ HIGH POINT	SEASON
****/4	10.4 miles	1510 feet/ 6100 feet	July–early Oct

Huntsberger Lake

RATING/ DIFFICULTY	ROUNDTRIP	ELEV GAIN/ HIGH POINT	SEASON
****/4	8.2 miles	1880 feet/ 6450 feet	July–early Oct

Map: USGS Mount Thompson-Seton, MT; **Contact:** Flathead National Forest, Glacier View Ranger District; **Note:** Open to horses and bicycles; **GPS:** 48.8411°, -114.6457°

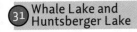 *Explore two tiny, glaciated lakes in the high hanging valleys in the lee of the Whitefish Divide. You'll find little competition—of the two-legged kind, at least—for some of the best berry picking for miles.*

Purple-stained fingers are a fashionable look in late summer.

GETTING THERE

From US Highway 2 in Columbia Falls, head north on Nucleus Avenue for 0.6 mile, then bear right, now on Railroad Street East, which becomes Outer North Fork Road after 0.6 mile. Continue on this road, a combination of pavement and dusty, washboarded gravel, for 44 miles, past the Polebridge turnoff, to Whale Creek Road (Forest Road 318). Turn left, and drive 11 miles, then bear right onto FR 1674. Continue 2.5 miles to the road's end and trailhead (elev. 4730 feet).

ON THE TRAIL

From the tank-trap trailhead for Whale Creek Trail 11, follow a derelict roadbed through a thick corridor of spruce and subalpine fir, the sere scree of the Whitefish Divide occasionally visible. Wayward stream channels cross the trail, watering alder and wildflowers as the route maintains a nearly level course.

At 1.6 miles (elev. 5190 feet), reach a signed junction. The left trail heads to Huntsberger Lake; the way straight leads to Whale Lake.

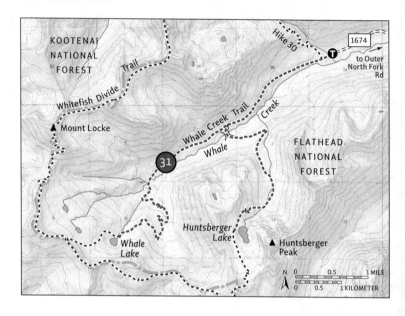

Whale Lake

For Whale Lake, continue on the roadbed as it ascends, with little elevation gain, upstream toward the Whitefish Divide. At 3 miles (elev. 5390 feet), make the first of several stream crossings in quick succession as the trail enters the hanging valleys that pour into the Whale Creek drainage. The trail then initiates a steep, seemingly aimless ascent through thinning forest cover toward the Whitefish Divide. Finally, at 5.2 miles (elev. 6100 feet), reach the tiny, timbered bowl of your destination.

The emerald waters of Whale Lake reflect the subalpine fir and spruce that encircle its shallow shoreline. Windfallen logs welter at the lake's outlet, but access elsewhere on the shore is easy. A well-used horse camp provides a picnic spot. Stunted, hungry stocked trout do little to live up to the lake's name.

Huntsberger Lake

From the junction, follow the left trail as it dives into a thick understory of thimbleberry, which will soak clothes on the frequent wet days that visit the Whitefish Range. Cross a split-log footbridge with handrail over Whale Creek at 1.8 miles (5180 feet) and continue uphill, still on old roadbed. Numerous brooks and seepages combine with the dense brush to ensure you will not remain dry.

Sweet subalpine huckleberries and currants crowd the trail as it gains elevation, now on true singletrack. The timber-clad hogbacks and steep, glaciated cirques of the Whitefish Range start to seem closer.

Subalpine hummocks, dotted with pockets of old-growth spruce that escaped a series of 1920s fires, surround the trail as you enter the cirque north of Huntsberger Peak's horn-like summit before descending to the grassy

Leaping into late autumn at Link Lake

shores of Huntsberger Lake at 4.1 miles (elev. 6450 feet). Steep couloirs descend to the far shore of the lake, one of some dozen or so subalpine tarns in the area—a testament to past glaciation. Frozen most of the year, Huntsberger harbors tiny, albeit hungry, trout.

EXTENDING YOUR TRIP

From Whale Lake, continue uphill a steep half mile through a high hanging valley to reach the Whitefish Divide Trail. From here, head south about three miles to reach the terminus of the Huntsberger Lake Trail;

descend to the latter lake for a nearly 15-mile loop.

32 Link Lake and Nasukoin Mountain

RATING/ DIFFICULTY	ROUNDTRIP	ELEV GAIN/ HIGH POINT	SEASON
*****/5	10.2 miles	3720 feet/ 8086 feet	July–early Oct

Map: USGS Red Meadow Lake, MT;
Contact: Flathead National Forest, Glacier

The uppermost of the Chain Lakes below Link Mountain

View Ranger District; **Note:** Open to horses and bicycles; **GPS:** 48.7617°, -114.5925°

🦴 🏠 🌸 🐾 *Its name derived from the Kootenai word for "chief," Nasukoin Mountain stands tall as the highest peak in the Whitefish Range, ruling over its subjects—some half dozen subalpine tarns and pure stands of alpine larch.*

GETTING THERE

From US Highway 2 in Columbia Falls, head north on Nucleus Avenue for 0.6 mile, then bear right, now on Railroad Street East, which becomes Outer North Fork Road after 0.6 mile. Continue on this road, a combination of pavement and dusty, washboarded gravel for 39 miles, past the Polebridge turnoff, to Red Meadow Road (Forest Road 115). Turn

left and drive 11.6 miles, past Red Meadow Lake Campground, to FR 589. Turn right and proceed 1.7 miles to the large trailhead parking area (elev. 6030 feet). (The trailhead is also accessible from US 93 via a considerably rougher continuation of FR 115.)

ON THE TRAIL

Beginning in spruce and subalpine fir, switchback out of the narrow valley containing the Link Lake Trail 372 trailhead. At 0.7 mile (elev. 6590 feet), reach a signed junction. From here, it's a short half-mile side trip through thick spruce to Link Lake. Take it. The imposing east face of Lake Mountain shades a lake that sees a very short summer. The Forest Service stocks Link Lake with cutthroat trout; small and starved of much of the summer growing season, these are

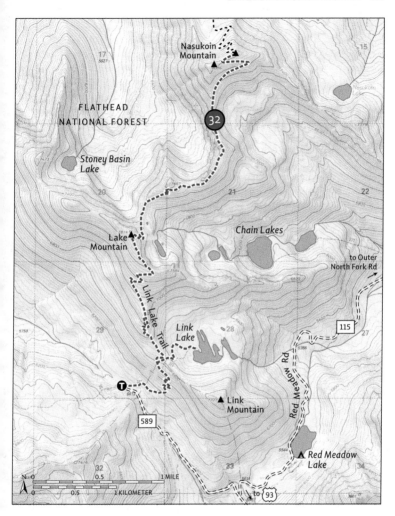

panfish only if you have a small pan. But it's a gorgeous spot, the many wooded islets and peninsulas inviting exploration.

To continue to Nasukoin Mountain, climb back to the main trail, then turn right. Glacier

lilies and beargrass gild alpine larch in its various twisted forms as the trail ascends Lake Mountain, reaching its grassy summit at 3.2 miles (elev. 7814 feet). Directly below lies the uppermost of the Chain Lakes, which sit, strung out like bobbers on a fishing line, in steep, stairstepped hanging valleys. Like Link Lake, the Chain Lakes see a very short snow-free season; snow that begins accumulating in September may stay on the ground until July. Hungry stocked trout reside in the Chain Lakes, their tiny size incommensurate with the effort needed to reach them.

From Lake Mountain, descend a dozen or so switchbacks on faint, cairn-aided tread to reach a long ridgeline of larch-lined parkland. Tiny Stoney Basin Lake lies below to your left; to the right are several basins for foraging bears. Round a nameless 7700-foot high point to reveal Nasukoin Mountain to the north; continue with your destination in full view as you ascend a dry subalpine ridge to reach Nasukoin's shoulder at nearly 5 miles (elev. 7580 feet). From here, it's a pleasant half mile or so of huckleberry-lined switchbacks to the top of Nasukoin.

With a name derived from the Kootenai word for "chief," 8086-foot Nasukoin Mountain crowns the Whitefish Range. Sagging bedsprings and old fire-finding tools mark the remains of an old fire lookout, the keeper of which would have had an enviable view of Glacier National Park to the east and as far as the Cabinet Mountains to the west.

Opposite: *Autumn sunlight shines on the Swan River (Hike 36).*

flathead valley

Whitefish Area

On the edge of Whitefish Lake and under the shadow of the ski runs of Whitefish Mountain Resort, the town of Whitefish bustles as a gateway to Glacier National Park. But while most tourists are content to cruise the cafes and curio shops of Baker Avenue, locals in this active community make use of a trail system—protected and promoted by and for human-powered sport enthusiasts—that belies the town's size.

33 Danny On Trail

RATING/ DIFFICULTY	ROUNDTRIP	ELEV GAIN/ HIGH POINT	SEASON
***/4	8.4 miles	2420 feet/ 6760 feet	Mid-June– Oct

Maps: USGS Skookoleel Creek, MT; USGS Whitefish, MT; **Contact:** Flathead National Forest, Tally Lake Ranger District; **Notes:** Dogs permitted on leash. Whitefish Mountain Resort sells lift tickets for both uphill and downhill travel of the mountain, but hiking is free; **GPS:** 48.4845°, -114.3557°

Better known for its lift-served, gravity-fueled descents during ski and biking seasons, Whitefish Mountain Resort boasts a sizable network of boots-only trails. Because the resort leases Forest Service land, the trails are free to the public, provided you don't pay for a lift ticket to access them from the top—and being the owner of a hiking guidebook, you wouldn't do that, would you?

GETTING THERE

From US Highway 93 in downtown Whitefish, drive north on Baker Avenue, which turns into Wisconsin Avenue, and, after 1.4 miles, into East Lakeshore Drive. Continue 0.8 mile, then bear right onto Big Mountain Road. Continue 4.1 miles, then turn right on Glades Drive and follow the signs to the base area of Whitefish Mountain Resort. The trail starts behind the base area (elev. 4740 feet). Privy inside the base area.

ON THE TRAIL

Some fifteen thousand hikers a year set foot on Danny On Memorial Trail, but few hike its full length, and fewer still hike it from the bottom. Thus, there's surprisingly good huckleberry picking for such a popular trail. From the base area of Whitefish Mountain Resort, the Danny On Trail ascends the south-facing slopes of Big Mountain (the name for the landmass itself, and the former name of the resort) through open Douglas-fir parkland. The waters of Whitefish Lake are a constant companion to the south. The Middle Fork Flathead River, the western portal to Glacier National Park, slips past the phalanx of the Swans to the east.

The white colonnades of beargrass bloom when climatic conditions are ideal. Each rosette blooms once in the plant's lifetime.

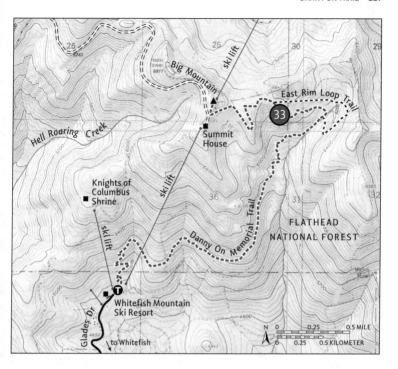

After about 2 miles of pleasant sidehill hiking, a steeper ascent ensues up a steep, spruce-shaded southwest-facing draw. The head of the draw, at nearly 3 miles, boasts the best berry picking of the hike. Be aware, though, that despite its haute resort status, the mountain is very much wildlands, and bears frequent the area.

Thinning subalpine forest gives way to beautiful beargrass meadows as the trail contours toward the summit. Boats ply Whitefish Lake below; the Whitefish Range, of which this peak is the southernmost, stretches to the north, its spruce-clad summit ridges hosting only a fraction of the visitors of Big Mountain.

Dedicated as a memorial to Danny On, a well-loved Forest Service silviculturist and avid skier who died in a ski accident on Big Mountain, the trail continues his work to inspire and educate. Be sure to stop in the Summit House to visit the Forest Service's Summit Nature Center. This award-winning exhibit details the flora and fauna of the Flathead National Forest and is staffed by naturalists who can answer questions about the area.

EXTENDING YOUR TRIP

Near the summit, the short East Rim Loop adds another 0.4 mile of subalpine huckleberry picking.

34 Whitefish Trail to Smith Lake

RATING/ DIFFICULTY	ROUNDTRIP	ELEV GAIN/ HIGH POINT	SEASON
***/3	5.5 miles	690 feet/ 3360 feet	May–Nov

Maps: USGS Beaver Lake, MT; USGS Werner Peak, MT; **Contacts:** Whitefish Legacy Partners; Stillwater State Forest; **Notes:** Dogs permitted on leash. Open to—and popular with—bicycles; **GPS:** 48.4920°, -114.4336°

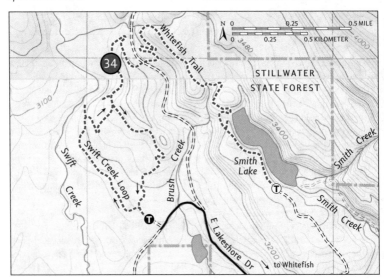

Wander along the sweep of Swift Creek en route to Smith Lake, a serene showpiece of the community-funded Whitefish Trail system. Away from the bustle of the boat launches and boutiques of Whitefish and its namesake lake, Swift Creek makes for a great morning jog or after-dinner stroll.

GETTING THERE
From US Highway 93 in downtown Whitefish, drive north on Baker Avenue, which turns into Wisconsin Avenue, and, after 1.4 miles, into East Lakeshore Drive. Continue, passing the turn to Whitefish Mountain Resort at 0.8 mile, for 6 miles to the signed Swift Creek trailhead on the right (elev. 3070 feet). Privy available.

ON THE TRAIL
At the trailhead kiosk, check out the map of the Swift Creek–Smith Lake unit of the Whitefish Trail system. Comprising nearly 40 miles of nonmotorized trail accessed from ten trailheads around Whitefish Lake, the Whitefish Trail is truly a community effort—funded by donors and planned by citizens. Valuable because it protects for public use a low-elevation forested landscape in a rapidly growing area, the Whitefish Trail is worthwhile on its own merits.

Begin on the Swift Creek Loop, following the ADA-accessible path clockwise. The wide, buffed, and brush-free tread is suitable for trail-running toddlers and jogging strollers. In a half mile, reach the first of two short spurs to viewpoints over the steep stream-cut of Swift Creek. In addition to preserving recreational opportunities such as this one, the Swift Creek area protects drinking water for the city of Whitefish.

In a quarter mile, bear left off the loop and follow a tight singletrack—keep an eye out for two-wheelers—as the trail parallels the watercourse before entering an old timber harvest unit. The surrounding forest is hardly unaltered, but isolated stands of old growth remain, and the rest is pleasant second- and third-growth timber.

Cross a gravel road, climb several steeply bermed switchbacks, and, now on a low ridge, travel south through the shade-free harvest area. The route gently descends to the north shore of Smith Lake at 2.4 miles (elev. 3300 feet). An 18-acre lake occupying state trust lands, Smith is a quiet spot for a picnic or evening bird watching. From the north end of the lake, the trail continues south above the west shore for another 0.4 mile to its terminus at a second trailhead. Shoreline access is limited, but this small pond is best enjoyed from underneath the shade of an evergreen anyway.

Return the way you came, bearing left at 4.8 miles (elev. 3150 feet) to close the Swift Creek Loop.

Kalispell Area

Kalispell sprawls at the peak of the Flathead Valley, the largest community in the northern tier of western Montana. Although the town serves as the primary jumping-off point for

Late summer foliage reflects in Smith Lake.

tourists cruising the winding roads of Glacier National Park or the waves of Flathead Lake—the largest natural freshwater lake west of the Mississippi—Kalispell and the surrounding Flathead Valley communities beckon hikers with their own trail systems. Urban in name only, these hikes boast wildlife and wildflowers in abundance.

35 Lone Pine State Park

RATING/ DIFFICULTY	LOOP	ELEV GAIN/ HIGH POINT	SEASON
***/2	2.6 miles	910 feet/ 3640 feet	May–Nov

Maps: USGS Kalispell, MT; Lone Pine State Park trail map; **Contact:** Lone Pine State Park; **Notes:** Montana State Parks pass required. Open to horses and bicycles; **GPS:** 48.1744°, -114.3373°

Lone Pine State Park perches on a pine-dotted knob west of Kalispell, its open forest affording sweeping views of the Flathead Valley below. Open year-round, the park's best showing is in mid-spring,

Lone Pine State Park provides a remarkable vista of Kalispell and the Flathead Valley.

when colorful blooms contrast with the Swans, swathed in snow, across the valley.

GETTING THERE

From the intersection of US Highway 2 and US 93 in downtown Kalispell, drive west on US 2 for 1 mile, then turn left onto US 93 Alternate. Continue 0.7 mile, and, at the roundabout, take the first right onto Foys Lake Road. Drive 2.7 miles, then turn left on Lone Pine Road and continue 1.2 miles to the park entrance. The trail begins from the Lone Pine State Park Visitor Center parking lot (elev. 3610 feet).

ON THE TRAIL

The secluded stacked loops of the Lone Pine State Park trail system belie the small size of this park perched on a pine-dotted knoll above Kalispell. At nearly 3 miles, this loop captures the highlights.

From the visitor center parking lot, cross the footbridge onto the Ernest and Hazel White Memorial Loop, leaving the paved path in a hundred yards to climb a set of rough stone steps to an overlook. A few firs guard a grassy knob garlanded with lupine, lomatium, and larkspur. But the view is the main attraction: the sweeping panorama stretches south to Flathead Lake and east to the Swan Crest, still swathed in snow when Lone Pine is at its floral peak. At the far side of the overlook, continue downhill through a pleasing interior Douglas-fir parkland; the cheery yellow of low-growing arnica carpets the forest come mid-May.

At 0.3 mile, bear right on the Lone Pine Trail. Descend in airy forest of Douglas-fir and larch, where songbirds make use of the many snags. Pass a nice viewpoint as the trail curves behind a neighborhood, and at 1.4 miles, take a sharp right uphill on the Cliff Trail. Immediately afterward, go straight at the next junction. Newly constructed tread climbs a lush draw lined with ferns and fairy orchids.

At 1.7 miles, bear left at a junction onto Raptor's Rest Trail. The tread rolls through thick timber and then breaks out onto a parklike meadow with incredible views. In another 0.2 mile, bear left at a Y-junction. Switchbacks descend to yet another junction; go right on Bearly There, a narrow ribbon of trail that truly feels like wilderness. Climbing under rocks hung with moss, bear left at the next two junctions, returning to the bridge on which you began.

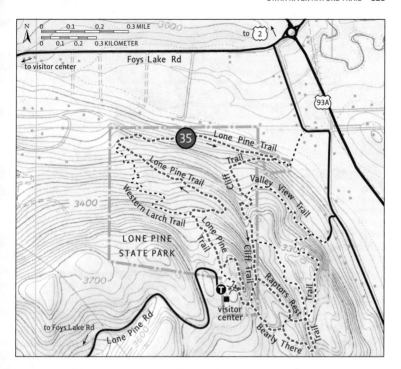

EXTENDING YOUR TRIP
Nearly 8 miles of trail, all well signed, lace Lone Pine. Myriad loops can be made from the main trailhead.

36 Swan River Nature Trail

RATING/ DIFFICULTY	ROUNDTRIP	ELEV GAIN/ HIGH POINT	SEASON
***/2	4 miles	370 feet/ 3060 feet	Apr–Nov

Map: USGS Bigfork, MT; **Contact:** PacifiCorp; **Note:** Open to bicycles; **GPS:** 48.0637°, -114.0698°

Walk a reclaimed roadbed within earshot of the "Wild Mile" of the Swan River on the edge of downtown Bigfork, its rapids a more serene experience for hikers than kayakers. Enveloped by the churn of the river and the call of songbirds, it is easy to forget you are minutes from one of Glacier Country's busiest tourist communities.

GETTING THERE
From Montana Highway 35 in Bigfork, head east on Grand Avenue toward downtown. Continue 0.6 mile, past Electric Avenue, and up the hill to the road's end and trailhead (elev. 3000 feet).

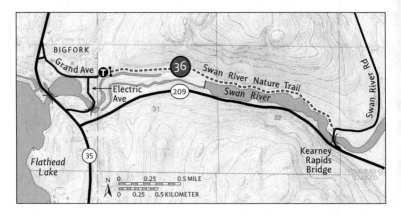

ON THE TRAIL

Built in 1914 as the primary thoroughfare between Bigfork and the Swan Valley to the east, this unmaintained county road became too treacherous for vehicle use and was converted to a nonmotorized trail in 1995. Bicyclists, birders, dog-walkers, and joggers make use of this nearly level path, which is characterized as much by sound as by what you see: trilling songbirds, crashing rapids, and the throaty bleat of deer.

Beyond the gated trailhead, sedimentary canyon walls speckled with wildflowers—balsamroot, purple penstemon, and tritelia—rise above the left side of the trail, reflecting the cacophony of the Swan River on the right. This first part of the trail parallels the aptly named "Wild Mile" of the Swan; its rapids, undimmed by the Bigfork Dam above, are a renowned whitewater kayaking destination.

In a little more than half a mile, leave the steep canyon walls behind; Douglas maple, ocean spray, and other fragrant shrubs flank the path. Pass a bike rack and bench opposite a side trail to the river through open forest. This is a good opportunity to view the "Wild Mile" up close, but be careful: the combination of slick rocks and the insistent Swan River can be treacherous.

Back on the trail, pass a privy at 0.8 mile; a side trail heads down to the Bigfork Dam. Upstream of here, the character of the river changes: the flow is slower, and it no longer obscures road noise. But it's a nice walk. Birds like it, and you will too, especially as the forest cover opens up to reveal the Swan Range to the east.

At 2 miles, reach the trail's end at Kearney Rapids Bridge on Swan River Road. Return the way you came.

EXTENDING YOUR TRIP

In 2017, a Bigfork-based community group proposed a trail plan that would connect the Swan River Nature Trail with new and existing paths on the south shore of the Swan River and downtown, which would add 6 miles to the trail system.

Opposite: A mountain goat forages above Hidden Lake (Hike 44).

glacier national park

North Fork

The North Fork Flathead River forms the northwest boundary of Glacier National Park and separates it from the wild Whitefish Range to the west. Owing to its relative remoteness, the North Fork region has remained quieter than elsewhere in the park, but savvy park travelers know the hiking here is some of the region's best. Plan on an hour to make the roughly thirty-mile drive from the West Glacier entrance to the community of Polebridge via the Outer North Fork Road, an occasionally paved but mostly potholed road that is suitable, if slow, for low-clearance vehicles. Fortunately, there's no hurry, as crowds beyond the campgrounds are nonexistent.

A quartet of glaciated peaks stands above the head of Bowman Lake.

37 Bowman Lake

RATING/ DIFFICULTY	ROUNDTRIP	ELEV GAIN/ HIGH POINT	SEASON
*****/4	13.6 miles	920 feet/ 4100 feet	May–Oct

Maps: USGS Quartz Ridge, MT; USGS Kintla Peak, MT; **Contact:** Glacier National Park Visitor Information; **Notes:** Park entrance fee required. Dogs prohibited; **GPS:** 48.8280°, -114.2008°

Bowman Lake is the showpiece of the lightly traveled North Fork area; the shore-hugging Bowman Lake Trail provides showstopping scenery. The head of the lake is a worthwhile destination, but the trail's up-close views of Glacier's peaks reward hiking as little or as long as you like.

GETTING THERE

From Apgar Visitor Center, drive 11.3 miles on Camas Road. Turn right on Outer North Fork Road, a combination of pavement and wash-boarded gravel, and drive 12.7 miles, turning right at the sign for Polebridge. In 0.4 mile, turn left at Polebridge Mercantile. Cross the North Fork Flathead River, and enter Glacier National Park at the Polebridge entrance at 1.4 miles. Once you're through the entrance, turn left on Inside North Fork Road and continue 0.5 mile. Bear right and, on a narrow, not-suitable-for-trailers Bowman Lake Road, proceed 5.5 miles to the campground. Park in the backcountry or picnic area. The trail begins near the boat launch (elev. 4040 feet). Privy available.

ON THE TRAIL

The scene from the foot of Bowman Lake is a classic, its shores of wave-smoothed red

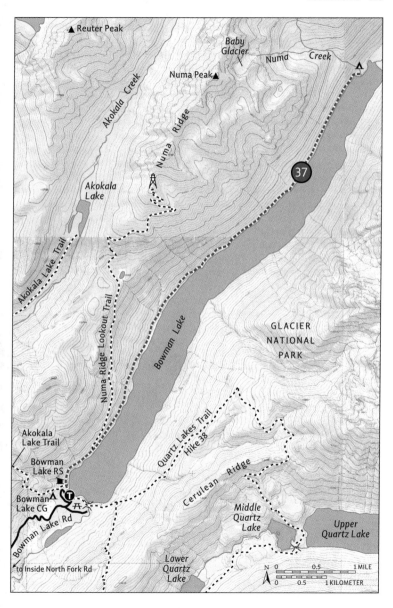

▲ Reuter Peak

Baby Glacier

Numa Creek

Akokala Creek

Numa Peak ▲

Numa Ridge

37

Akokala Lake

GLACIER NATIONAL PARK

Akokala Lake Trail

Numa Ridge Lookout Trail

Bowman Lake

Quartz Lakes Trail Hike 38

Cerulean Ridge

Akokala Lake Trail

Bowman Lake RS

Bowman Lake CG

T

Middle Quartz Lake

Upper Quartz Lake

Bowman Lake Rd

to Inside North Fork Rd

Lower Quartz Lake

N

0   0.5   1 MILE

0   0.5   1 KILOMETER

argillite stones framing a phalanx of peaks in the northern section of the park. Most visitors enjoy the view from the day-use area at the foot of the lake. But the 14-mile roundtrip hike to the head of Bowman Lake—nearly level, never far from shore—puts on a nonstop show. Although the hike is popular with tent-campers and picnickers as a post-meal stroll, few make it to the head of the lake and its backcountry campground. Although gaining in popularity, the North Fork is still relatively quiet, a long unpaved drive on the North Fork Road steering many visitors away; odds are, should you make it more than a mile or two from the trailhead, you'll have the shore to yourself.

Departing the boat launch, hike behind the log Bowman Lake Ranger Station—formerly part of a summer-camp complex for military-school cadets—and begin tracing Bowman's shore. Lodgepole pine provides constant shade for the nearly level tread. In three-quarters of a mile, pass the junction for Numa Ridge Lookout, an active fire lookout some five miles and 3000 vertical feet away. Continue along lake level, stepping over numerous wayward rivulets that flow toward Bowman.

In 4 miles (elev. 4060 feet), reach a large boulder on a sunny stretch of shore. Bowman Lake's wind-lashed waters imperfectly reflect a scene typical of the North Fork region of the park, the topography of which is characterized by breadth rather than depth—long, low valleys of lodgepole pine, the blocky massifs of the Continental Divide beyond. This is a great turnaround spot for an 8-mile hike; otherwise, continue toward the head of the lake, reaching Bowman's backcountry campground in 6.8 miles (elev. 4060 feet). Here, next to where a large stream flows into the lake, open shoreline grants views of several

high, glaciated peaks guarding the southeast skyline, including 9843-foot Thunderbird Mountain, 9843-foot Mount Carter, and 9891-foot Rainbow Peak.

Bowman Lake makes for excellent shoulder-season hiking. In springtime, when the higher reaches of the park's interior lie encased in snow, the lake provides a scenic conditioning hike. And the image of a becalmed Bowman Lake, framed by golden larches on the sides and snowcapped peaks above, is quickly becoming one of the quintessential views of autumn in Glacier. Try to hike this one in the morning, when Bowman's famed downlake whitecap waves are calm.

EXTENDING YOUR TRIP

Hike the 9-mile roundtrip Numa Ridge Lookout Trail to chat with the occupant of a working fire lookout; its history alone recommends it as an essential side trip, but so do the subalpine views—they are some of the best, and most easily accessible, on the west side of the park.

38 Quartz Lakes Loop

RATING/ DIFFICULTY	LOOP	ELEV GAIN/ HIGH POINT	SEASON
****/4	12.7 miles	2710 feet/ 5450 feet	Late May–Oct

Maps: USGS Quartz Ridge, MT; USGS Vulture Peak, MT; **Contact:** Glacier National Park Visitor Information; **Notes:** Park entrance fee required. Dogs prohibited; **GPS:** 48.8287°, -114.2001°

One of the few on-trail loop hikes in the park, the Quartz Lakes Trail strings together a trio of lakes typical of the North Fork. You won't find sprawling subalpine

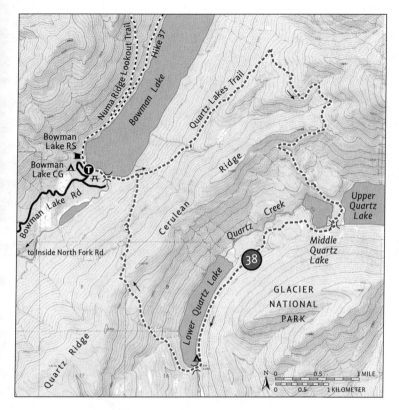

floral displays or sky-scraping summit scrambles here, but you will find quietude, rare in a park that sees some 2.5 million visitors a year. A good shoulder-season hike when high elevations are inaccessible and autumn larch are incandescent, this loop is quiet all season long, except for the haunting call of loons.

GETTING THERE

From Apgar Visitor Center, drive 11.3 miles on Camas Road. Turn right on Outer North Fork Road, a combination of pavement and washboarded gravel, and drive 12.7 miles, turning right at the sign for Polebridge. In 0.4 mile, turn left at Polebridge Mercantile. Cross the North Fork Flathead River, and enter Glacier National Park through the Polebridge entrance at 1.4 miles.

Once you're through the entrance, turn left on Inside North Fork Road and continue 0.5 mile. Bear right and, on narrow, not-suitable-for-trailers Bowman Lake Road, proceed 5.5 miles to the campground. Park in the backcountry or picnic area. The trail begins near the boat launch (elev. 4040 feet). Privy available.

Enjoying a mid-hike beverage at Upper Quartz Lake

ON THE TRAIL

From the Bowman Lake boat launch, head right on the Quartz Lakes Trail. Shortly afterward, bear left and cross a sturdy footbridge over the lake's outlet. Pass a ranger station and begin ascending in a shady forest scattered with dogwood blooms. At 0.6 mile (elev. 4200 feet), bear left at junction; to the right is your return route. Continue climbing the long sidehill, Bowman Lake intermittently visible and huckleberries occasionally available.

Quartz Lakes Trail capriciously cedes its elevation gains as it twice climbs and descends Cerulean Ridge south of Bowman Lake. Crest Cerulean Ridge for the first time at 4.4 miles (elev. 5420 feet). The recent wildfire on the south side of this ridge changed the character of the surrounding forest and also allows you the first views of the Quartz Lakes. Early in the season, windfallen snags might make this section

an agonizing affair. Descend the shadeless slope and, at 6.2 miles (elev. 4440 feet), reach the wooded moraine separating Upper and Middle Quartz Lakes. Upper Quartz Lake is the prettiest of the three, its cobbled shoreline reflecting Redhorn and Vulture Peaks above the timbered moraines enclosing the far shore. It's one of the more peaceful spots in the park.

Depart Upper Quartz Lake, cross a large bridge, and head southwest as the trail cups Middle Quartz Lake. Listen for loons at Middle Quartz, their call mournful even on a summer day. Several miles of unremarkable forest hiking ensue, Lower Quartz Lake frustratingly out of sight. At 9 miles (elev. 4230 feet), reach the backcountry campsites at Lower Quartz Lake. Surrounded by timber and lacking dramatic peaks on its skyline, Lower Quartz Lake is best enjoyed for the fish that stipple its surface and the moose that frequent its shore.

Cross the bridge at the lake's outlet and climb the ridge for the second time. At 10.8 miles (elev. 5120 feet), crest the ridge; from here, it's just over a mile to the junction you passed earlier on a soft, shallow incline.

39 Logging Lake

RATING/ DIFFICULTY	ROUNDTRIP	ELEV GAIN/ HIGH POINT	SEASON
****/3	10 miles	1120 feet/ 3900 feet	May–Oct

Maps: USGS Demers Ridge, MT; USGS Camas Ridge West, MT; USGS Vulture Peak, MT; **Contact:** Glacier National Park Visitor Information; **Notes:** Park entrance fee

required. Dogs prohibited; **GPS:** 48.6993°, -114.1938°

 *Lightly traveled even by the standards of its North Fork neighbors, Logging Lake's 7-mile-long shoreline invites quiet contemplation. Survey the effects of the 1988 Red Bench Fire on the broad Logging Creek drainage, which opened up distant vistas of Livingston Range peaks, and closer at hand, excellent wildlife habitat.*

GETTING THERE

From Apgar Visitor Center, drive 11.3 miles on Camas Road. Turn right on Outer North Fork Road, a combination of pavement and washboarded gravel, and drive 12.7 miles, turning

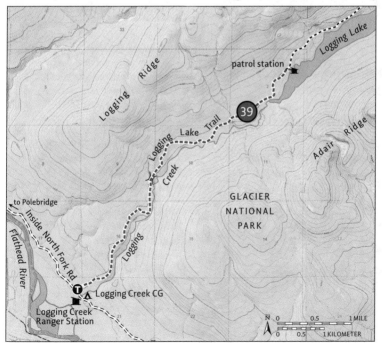

right at the sign for Polebridge. In 0.4 mile, turn left at Polebridge Mercantile. Cross the North Fork Flathead River, and enter Glacier National Park through the Polebridge entrance at 1.4 miles. Once you're through the entrance, turn right on Inside North Fork Road and drive 7.6 miles to the trailhead on the left (elev. 3440 feet), which has space for a handful of vehicles. Additional parking and a privy are located across the Logging Creek bridge at Logging Creek Ranger Station, Glacier National Park's oldest.

The grass-fringed and wind-whipped shore of Logging Lake

ON THE TRAIL

Ask a local if they've hiked Logging Lake, and the answer is likely to be "Where?" Unlike the east side of the park, where peaks stack atop one another and lakes huddle in high cirques, the North Fork sprawls, with lodgepole-thick valleys and long, timbered lakes. Loons and moose call this area home, and springtime sees a fair number of bears.

Departing from Logging Creek, the trail ascends through an open forest of larch, Douglas-fir, and spruce; woodland flowers spangle the slopes high above the creek. Gaining an open bench, witness the effects of the 1988 Red Bench Fire, which burned 38,000 acres of the park and surrounding areas, leaving hillsides bristling with snags. Alternating between snags and stands of forest spared the fire, the trail heads steadily upstream. Cross a footbridge at 2.2 miles (elev. 3690 feet) and then pass the first of several willow meadows and wetlands interspersed with cool spruce forest.

At 4.9 miles (3850 feet), bear right (straight continues up-lake) to reach the small ranger patrol station on Logging Lake's shores. Grass shadows the shore of the 7-mile-long lake, which occupies a narrow valley between Logging Ridge to the north and Adair Ridge to the south. Anaconda Peak and Mount Geduhn guard the skyline to the east; Grace Lake is tucked even more tightly at the head of the valley.

EXTENDING YOUR TRIP

The Logging Lake Trail continues another 7 miles up the shoreline, eventually reaching Grace Lake a mile or so beyond the head of Logging Lake. Both offer backcountry campsites and are mainly of interest to backpackers.

Lake McDonald and its surrounding glacier-scraped peaks, as viewed from Apgar Lookout

Going-to-the-Sun Road

The 50-mile Going-to-the-Sun Road is perhaps the most well-known activity in Glacier National Park, its hairpin turns and high-mountain vistas wowing—and occasionally terrifying—millions of visitors each year. But the road also accesses some of the park's best—and most popular—hiking as it traverses the marked contrasts between the west and east sides of the park. Beginning at West Glacier, drivers enjoy the wet, fog-enshrouded forest of the west side of the park, where larch garland Lake McDonald. As the road climbs out of the McDonald Creek drainage toward Logan Pass, the road's high point, cool birch forests transition to flower-flecked avalanche slopes and weeping rock walls high on Going-to-the-Sun Road. East of Logan Pass, aspen begin to take over as the road passes Saint Mary Lake and Two Dog Flats, a broad, aspen-framed prairie. These vistas are typical of the Rocky Mountain Front, where the escarpments of the Continental Divide sweep into Great Plains prairie.

To ensure you can park at your hike of choice, plan on being at the trailhead early in the morning. Better yet, make use of the park's hiker-friendly shuttle system and let someone else drive while you enjoy the scenery.

40 Apgar Lookout

RATING/ DIFFICULTY	ROUNDTRIP	ELEV GAIN/ HIGH POINT	SEASON
***/4	7 miles	2010 feet/ 5236 feet	May–Nov

Map: USGS McGee Meadow, MT; **Contact:** Glacier National Park Visitor Information; **Notes:** Park entrance fee required. Dogs prohibited. Open to horses; **GPS:** 48.5045°, -114.0212°

Amble to Apgar Lookout and its commanding views of Lake McDonald. One of the first trails at elevation to melt out in the spring, thanks to its south-facing aspect and relatively low summit, Apgar is a boot-breaking-in hike; avoid this in summer, when the shadeless slopes swelter and subalpine hikes elsewhere beckon.

131

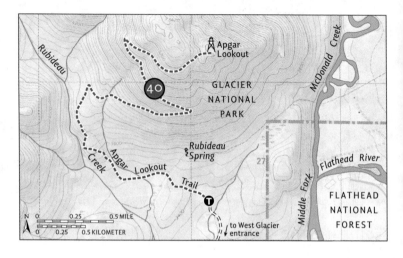

GETTING THERE

From the West Glacier entrance of the park, drive 0.3 mile on the Going-to-the-Sun Road. Turn left at the side road signed for Apgar Lookout. Drive 0.3 mile, then bear right (left goes to Glacier Institute), continuing 1.8 miles on good gravel to the trailhead (elev. 3370 feet).

ON THE TRAIL

Apgar Lookout Trail begins on old road, heading west through a lush lowland forest of larch, aspen, birch, and cedar. Bears frequent this area, so make plenty of noise. Bottom-lands quickly give way to burnt-over slopes as the trail, now on singletrack, swings north to parallel Rubideau Creek. At 1.4 miles (elev. 3840 feet), leave the stream drainage as the trail swings east to begin its steady, switchbacking ascent of the shadeless mountain. Peaks of the Great Bear Wilderness stand out on the southern skyline.

Nearing the lookout, the trail dips into and out of a shallow drainage before cresting

the ridge at 3.4 miles (elev. 5210 feet) in a cool, north-facing grove of trees; snowdrifts may linger here early in the summer. Pass a privy and horse-hitching rail and reach the lookout shortly after.

Named after Maine transplant Milo Apgar, who homesteaded in the area in 1892, after crossing Marias Pass (on what is today US Highway 2) in a two-wheeled cart, Apgar Lookout offers 360-degree vistas from the wraparound deck of its lookout cabin. The showpiece, though, is the wet, fog-enshrouded forest of the west side of the park, where larch garland Lake McDonald.

41 Sperry Chalet

RATING/ DIFFICULTY	ROUNDTRIP	ELEV GAIN/ HIGH POINT	SEASON
****/5	12 miles	3640 feet/ 6590 feet	July–Sept

Map: USGS Lake McDonald East, MT;
Contact: Glacier National Park Visitor Infor-

Looking down on Lake Ellen Wilson from the warming cabin at Gunsight Pass

mation; **Notes:** Park entrance fee required. Dogs prohibited. Open to horses; **GPS:** 48.6165°, -113.8754°

🏠 *Climb to the site of a century-old chalet on Glacier National Park's first officially sanctioned trail. It's a charming view into the park's history. And the views of Lake McDonald from this rocky redoubt are, to this day, some of the best in the park west of the Continental Divide.*

GETTING THERE
From the West Glacier entrance of the park, drive 10.5 miles on Going-to-the-Sun Road to Lake McDonald Lodge (elev. 3230 feet). This trail begins across the road from the lodge; parking is available near the road. Privy available.

ON THE TRAIL
From the trailhead near Lake McDonald Lodge, Gunsight Pass Trail immediately retreats into a cool forest of cedar, hemlock, and larch, which let in little in the way of sunlight. This trail to Sperry Glacier was the first official trail constructed in Glacier National Park, built by University of Minnesota professor Lyman Sperry and a group of his students in 1902. It stands strong to this day, ably handling the stamping of horse parties en route to Sperry Chalet.

Having gained 900 feet in 1.4 miles, bypass the trail to Mount Brown Lookout (the steepness of which makes the preceding ascent feel leisurely) and, in quick succession, the trail to Snyder Lake. Shortly after, make a quick descent into a crossing of Snyder Creek at Crystal Ford. Bear left at a junction (the way right goes to Fish Lake) then resume climbing, this time above Sprague Creek.

As thick hemlock gradually gives way to subalpine spruce-fir forest, keep an eye out for Beaver Medicine Falls splashing down the Sprague Creek drainage to your right. Beyond here, the trail begins to bend more northerly as it climbs steeply toward Glacier Basin at 5.6 miles (elev. 6300 feet). Some half dozen cascades pour down the steep limestone cliff walls above the basin, which occupies a high hanging valley of subalpine fir and beargrass.

The trail swings south out of the basin and, shortly afterward, comes to a junction. The way left climbs to the Sperry Glacier observation point, nearly four miles away; it's a worthy excursion for those staying over at the Sperry Chalet. To reach the chalet, bear right, ascending a slick-rock trail to the chalet at 6 miles (elev. 6590 feet).

Built in 1913 by the "Empire Builder," James J. Hill, of the Great Northern Railway,

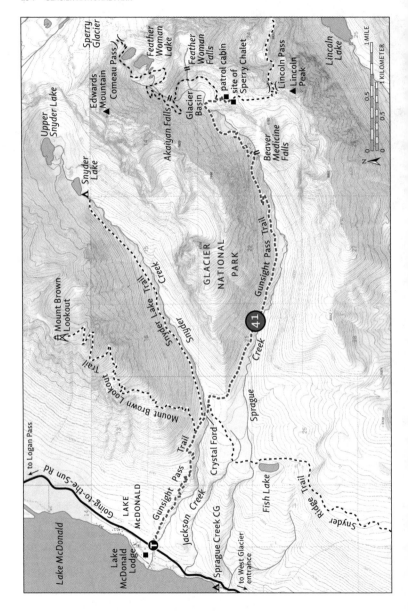

JAMMIN' IN THE PARK

Since 1936, Glacier's fleet of thirty-three iconic open-topped Red Buses have been shuttling sightseers up Going-to-the-Sun Road and the park's other less hair-raising roads. Considered to be the oldest fleet of touring vehicles anywhere, the buses earned their drivers the nickname "Jammers" because the gearshifts of the manual transmissions had to be constantly jammed from one gear to another while negotiating the steep curves of Going-to-the-Sun Road. The park recently refurbished the buses to run on gas and clean-burning propane, and while the Jammers no longer have to mash the gears, the ride is no less breathtaking. Hikers accessing trails via Going-to-the-Sun Road who are simply looking for hop-on, hop-off service rather than a guided excursion should consider using the park's free shuttle service, which runs roughly every half hour in both directions between Apgar Visitor Center on the west side and St. Mary Visitor Center on the east side.

As the park grows in popularity—recent years have seen one record-shattering season after another—park administrators will likely have to look at traffic-abatement options, including shuttles, to maintain the park's primary mission of wildlife and habitat preservation. But it is not too early to hop on the shuttle bandwagon; you will keep your car off the congested road and your eyes on the scenery.

---

the rustic two-story chalet offered hostel-style accommodations, prix fixe meals, and prime views before a fast-moving wildfire gutted it in 2017. With any luck, site-stabilization and restoration efforts will allow the chalet to see a second century of use.

EXTENDING YOUR TRIP

Ambitious day hikers—or backpackers lucky enough to snag a permit—can connect Sperry Chalet to Gunsight Lake via Gunsight Pass on a 19-mile life-list-worthy open loop. From Sperry Chalet, descend through rocky notches and spires of subalpine fir to Lake Ellen Wilson, which occupies a high, heathered cirque just below Gunsight Pass. The views from the slopes above the backcountry campground at Lake McDonald astound. From the campground, a mile or so of climbing gains Gunsight Pass and its tiny warming shelter. From here, descend to Gunsight Lake (Hike 46).

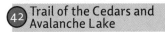

42 Trail of the Cedars and Avalanche Lake

Trail of the Cedars

RATING/ DIFFICULTY	ROUNDTRIP	ELEV GAIN/ HIGH POINT	SEASON
****/1	1 mile	120 feet/ 3460 feet	Early June– early Oct

Avalanche Lake

RATING/ DIFFICULTY	ROUNDTRIP	ELEV GAIN/ HIGH POINT	SEASON
*****/3	5.4 miles	1290 feet/ 3990 feet	Early June– early Oct

Map: USGS Mount Cannon, MT; **Contact:** Glacier National Park Visitor Information; **Notes:** Park entrance fee required. Dogs prohibited; **GPS:** 48.6801°, -113.8189°

  Don't let the crowds deter you: this is one of the park's

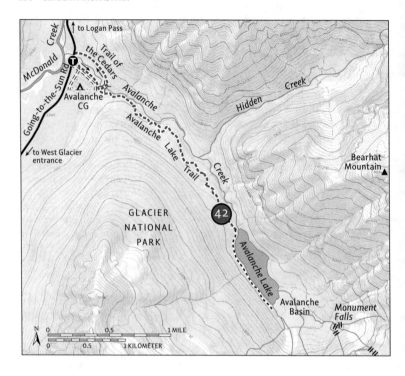

most popular hikes for good reason. Ascend alongside glacier-fed Avalanche Creek as it squeezes through a narrow canyon of red argillite rock, where dippers frequently flit about the rushing waters. Lunch on the shore of Avalanche Lake with scores of like-minded visitors—perhaps the prettiest subalpine lake setting on the west side of the park.

GETTING THERE

From the West Glacier entrance to the park, drive 16.5 miles on Going-to-the-Sun Road, past Lake McDonald Lodge, to the large trailhead parking area that occupies both sides of the road (elev. 3410 feet).

The trail begins on the south side of the road. Privy available.

ON THE TRAIL

From the trailhead, follow the ADA-accessible Trail of the Cedars as it winds southeast through a mature western hemlock and western redcedar forest, some specimens of which sprouted shortly after Columbus set sail for the East Indies. Although this grove grows on the extreme eastern edge of the Pacific Northwest maritime climate zone, the high humidity and deep snowpack have allowed some of the trees to reach diameters of seven feet.

Visitors from the wet west side of the Cascades will feel at home here.

At the apex of the loop, reach a footbridge over Avalanche Creek. Here, the creek squeezes through a narrow canyon of sculpted red argillite rock, where dippers frequently flit about the rushing waters.

To complete the Trail of the Cedars loop, continue counterclockwise on a raised boardwalk past the gnarled roots of cedars. To continue to Avalanche Lake, turn right onto Avalanche Lake Trail; a short, steep ascent deposits hikers at the banks of Avalanche Creek for an even better look at the sculpting powers of the water.

The trail loses sight of the creek as it continues up the drainage, but the water's flow, combined with the surrounding forest—western redcedar, western hemlock, and a dense understory of mountain maple—muffles the serenade of a parade of tinkling bear bells. The trail eventually departs the canyon and weaves through a tumble of downed trees from avalanches off Mount Cannon (northeast of the trail); this is a reliable spot to scope for the shaggy shapes of mountain goats high on the slopes.

Descend into a brushy corridor of willow and thimbleberry, past a privy, before reaching Avalanche Lake at 2.7 miles (elev. 3930 feet). Tree debris at the outlet, weathered by winter and thousands of hiker backsides, provides good spots to sit. Nearby Sperry Glacier provides much of the water that feeds the lake; depending on runoff, visitors might see up to five cascades tumbling off the surrounding cirques, a reminder of the power of water—in liquid or frozen form—to sculpt the park's famed contours.

EXTENDING YOUR TRIP

Avalanche Lake Trail continues another three-quarters of a mile to the head of the lake, where a sandy beach abuts brushy Avalanche Basin.

43 Highline Trail to Granite Park Chalet

RATING/ DIFFICULTY	ROUNDTRIP	ELEV GAIN/ HIGH POINT	SEASON
*****/4	14.8 miles	3210 feet/ 7280 feet	July–early Oct

Map: USGS Logan Pass, MT; **Contact:** Glacier National Park Visitor Information; **Notes:** Park entrance fee required. Dogs prohibited; **GPS:** 48.6966°, -113.7180°

Considered by many to be the park's premier trail, the trek to Granite Park Chalet along the Highline Trail is the hiking equivalent of Going-to-the-Sun Road: popular; narrow, although not as harrowing as it is made out to be; and worth the hype—and the hordes. Vast avalanche slopes of flowers and breathtaking vistas amply reward the scant effort of a hike that, for most of its length, gains little elevation.

GETTING THERE

From the West Glacier entrance, drive 32 miles on Going-to-the-Sun Road to the Logan Pass Visitor Center (elev. 6646 feet). The trail begins on the north side of the road across the pedestrian crosswalk from the parking lot entrance. During high season—from its opening until Labor Day weekend—the parking lot at Logan Pass Visitor Center is uniformly full. Plan on arriving before 9 AM or after 4 PM, or make use of the park's shuttle system.

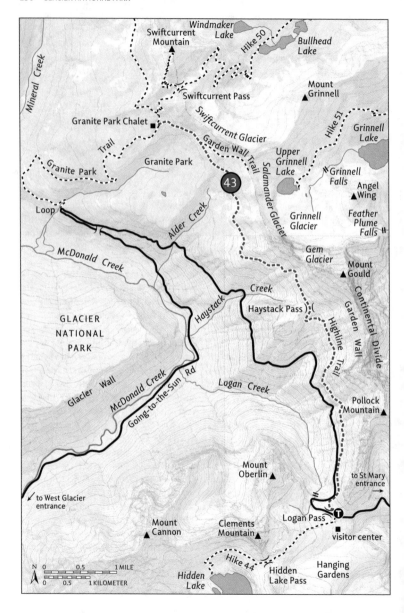

ON THE TRAIL

After crossing Going-to-the-Sun Road, follow the wide, well-tended, and well-traveled tread of the Highline Trail through a subalpine meadow a quarter mile before reaching the Garden Wall. Blasted out of the side of the striated limestone sediment, the 6- to 8-foot wide trail peers over a precipitous drop to Going-to-the-Sun Road. It truly feels narrow should you have to rub shoulders with one of the bears or goats that make use of this route. Fortunately, this section only lasts a quarter mile, and a cable handrail helps those with acrophobia.

Now with eyes in front of you rather than on your feet, enjoy the grand flower displays of the Garden Wall. The vistas inspire awe every step, with the heavily glaciated horns of Mounts Cannon and Oberlin overlooking Going-to-the-Sun Road to the south and Heavens Peak shining on the skyline to the west.

The trail gradually ascends as the Garden Wall recedes in steepness, and at 3 miles (elev. 6740 feet) you'll begin your only sustained climb of the hike: one long switchback that deposits you on Haystack Pass. This is a popular picnic spot, which is not lost on the resident mountain goats.

Continue climbing, reaching the high point of the hike at 3.9 miles (elev. 7280 feet); from here, the trail settles into a gradual descent above forested basins through which bruins frequently travel. At 6.9 miles (elev. 6610 feet), reach a junction with the Garden Wall Trail, which climbs 900 strength-sapping feet in 0.6 mile to an overlook on the crest of the Continental Divide, from which one can peer down on the Grinnell and Salamander Glaciers snugged into the high, east-facing basins.

Resting amid the high-wire Highline Trail

For the stone sleeping quarters of the Granite Park Chalet, continue straight another 0.4 mile. Built in 1914 and 1915 by the "Empire Builder," James J. Hill, of the Great Northern Railway, the chalet marked the last of nine such structures constructed by the railroad to draw tourists to the then-new park. Backpackers staying at Granite Park Chalet will find few amenities other than its twelve basic bunk-style rooms. Packaged foods and bottled water are available at the prices you'd expect to pay at such a remote setting; fortunately, there's a spring a quarter mile away. And the views are top-shelf.

EXTENDING YOUR TRIP

Rather than returning the way they came, many hikers choose to continue 4 miles down the Granite Park Trail, first through subalpine timber, then a shadeless burn area, to the loop on Going-to-the-Sun Road, where they can catch the shuttle or hitch a ride to Logan Pass.

44 Hidden Lake Overlook and Hidden Lake

RATING/ DIFFICULTY	ROUNDTRIP	ELEV GAIN/ HIGH POINT	SEASON
*****/3	4.8 miles	1480 feet/ 7180 feet	Mid-July– Sept

Maps: USGS Mount Cannon, MT; USGS Logan Pass, MT; **Contact:** Glacier National Park Visitor Information; **Notes:** Park entrance fee required. Dogs prohibited; **GPS:** 48.6951°, -113.7184°

Some three thousand sets of boots stamp the boardwalk to Hidden Lake Overlook during high season. The good news: alpine blooms on the broad terrace of Logan Pass's layer-cake bedrock benches outnumber boots by a large margin. The even better news: beyond Hidden Lake Overlook, mountain goats are likely to equal humans as the trail descends to Hidden Lake, which Bearhat Mountain caps in one of Glacier's most iconic scenes.

GETTING THERE

From the West Glacier entrance, drive 32 miles on Going-to-the-Sun Road to the Logan Pass Visitor Center (elev. 6646 feet). The trail begins behind the visitor center. During high season—from its opening until Labor Day weekend—the parking lot at Logan Pass Visitor Center is nearly always full. Plan on arriving before 9 AM or after 4 PM, or make use of the park's shuttle system.

ON THE TRAIL

From behind the Logan Pass Visitor Center, follow the Hidden Lake Trail south on wide boardwalk, which protects Logan Pass's fragile alpine landscape from thousands of feet. Hikers hunched over zoomed-out camera lenses take in the delicate daises and anemones that color the Hanging Gardens. Contour around Clements Mountain, where sun-cupped late-summer snowdrifts often linger. Reynolds Mountain, the green ramp across its north face a popular scrambling route to the summit, rises to the south; the striped limestone sides of Heavy Runner Mountain jut over the hanging valley to the southeast.

A series of steps exit the boardwalk a half mile from the trailhead. The jauntily tilted summit block of Bearhat Mountain soon comes into view as the trail gains a slight rise and then descends past a couple shallow meltwater ponds.

Cross to the Pacific Ocean side of the Continental Divide, and, at 1.3 miles (elev. 7150 feet), reach Hidden Lake Overlook. Bearhat Mountain caps the comma-shaped lake below; to the southeast, sunlight glints off Sperry Glacier and Gunsight Mountain. Mountain goats frequently wander the broad bench just below the overlook; please give them space. And please stay on the trail so as not to trample the alpine vegetation.

To continue to Hidden Lake, descend across the south slope of Clements Mountain, Mount Cannon directly ahead of you. The crowds will have thinned considerably by here, perhaps owing to the prospect of a return climb out of Hidden Lake on the long, loping switchbacks. At 2 miles (elev. 6870 feet), begin those switchbacks, which descend about 400 feet over the next 0.4 mile to the shore of Hidden Lake. Water-polished argillite makes up the bed of this bracingly cold lake, and scattered pockets of subalpine fir provide privacy. It's an appealing spot to rest, sans crowds, before the return climb to Hidden Lake Overlook.

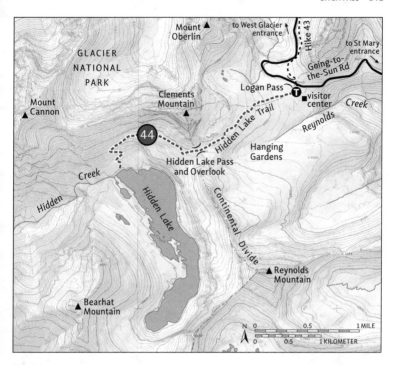

Mount ▲
Oberlin

to West Glacier
entrance

Hike 43

to St Mary
entrance

GLACIER
NATIONAL
PARK

Going-to-
the-Sun Rd

Logan Pass

Clements
Mountain

visitor
center

Creek

Mount
▲ Cannon

Reynolds

Hidden Lake Trail

44

Hanging
Gardens

Hidden Lake Pass
and Overlook

Creek

Continental Divide

Hidden

Hidden Lake

Hidden

▲ Reynolds
Mountain

Bearhat
▲ Mountain

N   0   0.5   1 MILE

0   0.5   1 KILOMETER

45 Siyeh Pass

RATING/ DIFFICULTY	ONE-WAY	ELEV GAIN/ HIGH POINT	SEASON
*****/4	9.5 miles	2320 feet/ 8110 feet	July–early Oct

Maps: USGS Logan Pass, MT; USGS Rising Sun, MT; **Contact:** Glacier National Park Visitor Information; **Notes:** Park entrance fee required. Dogs prohibited; **GPS:** 48.7015°, -113.6676°

*Stand atop one of the highest maintained trails in Glacier National Park, the wind-blown col of Siyeh Pass grant-*ing views into several glacier-scoured valleys. One of four historic sites of Alps-inspired locomotive bells, Siyeh once sang with the hammer strikes of passing hikers. Now it sings with the sigh of wind and the stamp of hiking boots.*

GETTING THERE

From the West Glacier entrance, drive 35 miles on Going-to-the-Sun Road, past the Logan Pass Visitor Center, to the Piegan Pass trailhead just east of Siyeh Bend, elev. 5850 feet. (From the St. Mary entrance, drive west 15.6 miles on the Going-to-the-Sun Road.) To complete the open loop as written using a second vehicle, continue east another 5 miles to the Sunrift Gorge trailhead.

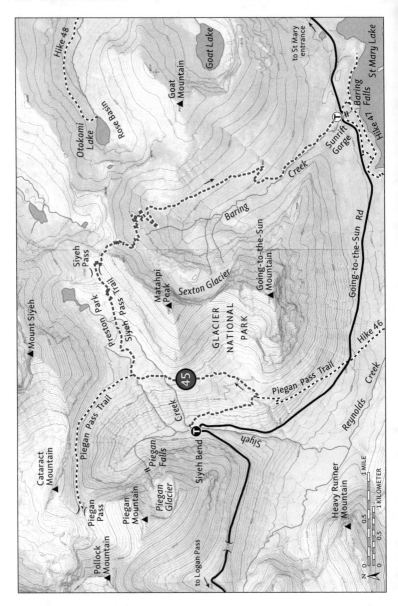

A hiker looks over the Baring Creek drainage from just below Siyeh Pass.

ON THE TRAIL

Although Siyeh Pass can be hiked as an out-and-back, the park's shuttle system allows for a much more appealing open loop that descends to Sunrift Gorge. If the shuttles aren't running and you're averse to thumbing, retrace your steps from the pass to the upper trailhead.

The Siyeh Pass Trail follows Siyeh Creek upstream a short distance before plunging into deep green forest. There's little of visual interest for the first mile as the trail ascends through thick spruce and fir forest at a stately stock-friendly grade. At 1.1 miles (elev. 6300 feet), reach a junction, and bear left for Siyeh Pass.

Increasing altitude shrinks the surrounding forest to ice-stunted shrubs and krummholz. At 2.7 miles (elev. 7000 feet), reach the junction with the trail to Piegan Pass; head right. Shortly beyond the junction, the trail enters the sprawling subalpine meadows of Preston Park, its panoply of alpine blooms one of the park's best. Low hedges of trees surround the meadows, which appear to pour down from Mount Siyeh to the left and 9365-foot Matahpi Peak to the right. The former is a nontechnical summit scramble objective, but the steeply terraced rock bands guard against easy approach. Cross Siyeh Creek downstream of where it flows from a meltwater tarn and climb to the windswept col of Siyeh Pass. For the best views, continue climbing as a series of rigorous switchbacks gain 900 feet in the next mile, a glance backward revealing the rough-hewn hulk of Heavy Runner Mountain.

A large cairn marks the high point of the trail at 4.6 miles (8110 feet). Naturalist George Bird Grinnell named the pass and peak after a Blackfoot Indian named "Sai-yeh," which in the Blackfoot language means "Crazy Dog" or "Mad Wolf." Siyeh Pass once hosted one of four locomotive bells in the park. A Swiss Alps tradition, borrowed by advertising agents for Great Northern Railway and Glacier Park Hotel

Company in the 1920s, allowed passing mountain travelers to ring the large bells. In 1943 the park donated the bells to a wartime scrap-metal drive, but the views still ring out: of the long shoulder of Mount Siyeh ahead, and the Baring Creek Valley, bulldozed by an ice-age glacier, below your feet.

Continue south on the trail as it contours around the northeast face of Matahpi Peak, Sexton Glacier snug in its shoulder. Steep, dusty switchbacks descend into the Baring Creek Valley, losing 1500 feet of elevation in the next 1.5 miles. At 6.3 miles, settle into a south-running sidehill descent above the burnt-over drainage of Baring Creek, which the Reynolds Creek Fire ravaged in 2015, before reaching the Sunrift Gorge trailhead at 9.5 miles.

Crossing the St. Mary River after the bridge at the foot of Gunsight Lake has been removed for the season.

46 Gunsight Lake

RATING/ DIFFICULTY	ROUNDTRIP	ELEV GAIN/ HIGH POINT	SEASON
****/4	12 miles	1870 feet/ 5370 feet	July–early Oct

Map: USGS Logan Pass, MT; **Contact:** Glacier National Park Visitor Information; **Notes:** Park entrance fee required. Dogs prohibited. Bridges over Reynolds Creek and the outlet of Gunsight Lake are installed at the beginning of summer and removed in early autumn. Crossing these waterways is possible, but cold, when the bridges have been removed; **GPS:** 48.6772°, -113.6524°

Gunsight Lake sees only a fraction of the traffic of some of its Logan Pass neighbors, thanks in large part to its length. But Gunsight Lake is one of the highlights of Going-to-the-Sun Road: set in a sere, glacier-scraped cirque, the large body of *water dutifully reflects the snowcapped Continental Divide.*

GETTING THERE

From the St. Mary entrance of Glacier National Park, drive west 12.6 miles on Going-to-the-Sun Road to the large trailhead parking area on the south side of the road (elev. 5260 feet). The parking area is signed for Jackson Glacier Overlook.

ON THE TRAIL

From Going-to-the-Sun Road, descend the southbound section of the Piegan Pass Trail, which thickets of thimbleberry threaten to overtake as it angles toward Reynolds Creek. At 1.1 miles, draw near Deadwood Falls on Reynolds Creek, where the water drops 10 feet into a clear pool below sculpted stone. Walk briefly downstream, bearing right at a junction for Gunsight Pass, then cross a long suspension bridge over Reynolds Creek. Just beyond the bridge is tiny Reynolds Creek Campground, its sites purely utilitarian.

Walk through open forest a short ways before reaching the St. Mary River, the marshy bottomlands of which harbor moose. Staying in the forest, the trail passes several mud-wallow meadows, and, at 2.7 miles (elev. 4660 feet), Mirror Pond,

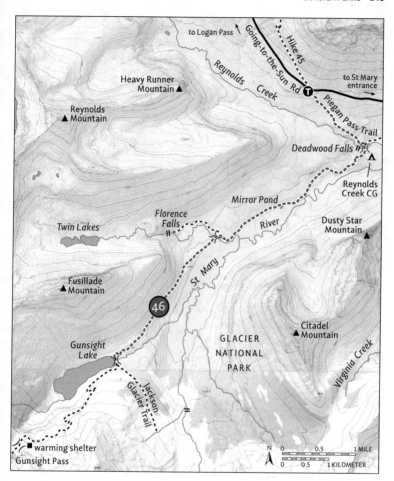

the grassy swale framing Mount Jackson, Gunsight Mountain, and Fusillade Mountain in the distance. From here, continue upstream, reaching a small set of cascades on an unnamed creek and a spur trail to Florence Falls at 3.8 miles (elev. 4740 feet).

Cross the creek on a bridge and continue upstream along a steadily ascending sidehill above the St. Mary River, with unruly brush bordering the trail. Shrinking tree cover reveals Mount Jackson, Blackfoot Mountain, and their respective glaciers, and Mount Logan. The trail levels out in a broad moraine swept clean of any trees of significance by massive avalanches. Pick your way through krummholz and shrubs before briefly

Enjoying the view—and the mist—of St. Mary Falls

descending to Gunsight Lake's east shore at 6 miles (elev. 5320 feet).

Wedge-shaped Gunsight Lake occupies a large basin of scalloped and striated bedrock, where numerous cascades tumble down nearly 4000 feet of vertical relief from Gunsight Mountain on the Continental Divide to lake level. Three trail miles distant (see Extending Your Trip), Gunsight Pass offers the only egress between Gunsight Mountain and Mount Jackson to the south.

For the best views of the lake, cross its shallow, slow-moving outlet on a footbridge and follow the path as it climbs through shoulder-high fool's huckleberry and flowers. Incidentally, this is a fairly common route for grizzlies commuting to and from the high country—make plenty of noise.

EXTENDING YOUR TRIP

The hike to the austere arête of Gunsight Pass is an essential side trip, one of the park's highlights. After crossing the suspension bridge at the outlet of Gunsight Lake, the trail traces the southern shore of Gunsight Lake as it climbs 1600 feet in just shy of 3 miles to the pass. Late-lingering snowfields and snowmelt sheeting over the upper parts of the trail, which have been blasted into the bedrock, may make the going treacherous. A simple warming shelter greets hikers upon reaching the pass, the views from its porch—of Gunsight Lake to the east and Lake Ellen Wilson to the west—unparalleled.

47 Three Falls Loop

RATING/ DIFFICULTY	LOOP	ELEV GAIN/ HIGH POINT	SEASON
***/3	5.1 miles	930 feet/ 4830 feet	May–Oct

Map: USGS Rising Sun, MT; **Contact:** Glacier National Park Visitor Information; **Notes:** Park entrance fee required. Dogs prohibited; **GPS:** 48.6748°, -113.6045°

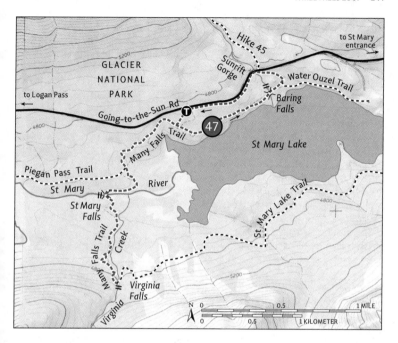

 A charming trio of trailside cascades, St. Mary Falls, Virginia Falls, and Baring Falls are each popular destinations, owing to their short hike lengths and scenic appeal. Connecting them via this 5.1-mile loop, which makes use of a short road walk, makes the wait for a trailhead parking spot worthwhile. Visit early in the season—before Going-to-the-Sun Road opens completely—when snowmelt swells these cascades and their mists turn into full-on showers.

GETTING THERE

From the St. Mary entrance of Glacier National Park, drive 11.6 miles west on Going-to-the-Sun Road to the St. Mary Falls parking lot (elev. 4730 feet). The lot, which can accommodate a dozen vehicles, fills up early; late arrivals may have to park in one of the nearby pullout parking areas.

ON THE TRAIL

From the St. Mary Falls trailhead, descend across open slopes above St. Mary Lake. Closed-canopy forest once encroached, but the 2015 Reynolds Creek Fire spurred a surfeit of pioneer flowers and opened up views of 8064-foot Dusty Star Mountain, 8922-foot Almost-a-Dog Mountain, and 9541-foot Little Chief Mountain. Nearly three-quarters of a mile from the trailhead, bear right, and shortly after, left, at junctions with the Piegan Pass Trail. Round a bend, revealing the St. Mary River, and reach St. Mary Falls at 1 mile (elev. 4520 feet). The three-tiered waterfall drops nearly forty feet through a tight cleft of angled bedrock just upstream of its junction with Virginia Creek. Late in the summer, low water levels invite wading, but be careful on the slick rock.

Cross the large footbridge below St. Mary Falls and follow Virginia Creek upstream, shady spruce forest replacing burnt boles of lodgepole. Pass a footbridge over Virginia Creek (this way leads first to a privy and then the St. Mary Lake Trail). Clamber up a couple stone steps to reach Virginia Falls at 1.8 miles (elev. 4830 feet). This 50-foot horsetail cascade produces an impressive spray most of the summer—"misting" is putting it mildly.

Stay in the spray as long as you're comfortable, then begin retracing your steps. At 3.5 miles (elev. 4650 feet), just before

An early-summer snowfield caps Rose Basin above Otokomi Lake

reaching the trailhead, continue straight along the contour rather than climbing back to the road. In three-quarters of a mile, reach Baring Falls. Named for London bankers who visited the park in the 1880s, Baring Falls spills out of a steeply angled cut some 25 feet before flowing into St. Mary Lake a short distance away.

To finish the loop, cross the footbridge over Baring Creek, bear left at the trail junction shortly after, then gently ascend a quarter mile to Going-to-the-Sun Road. From here it's a half mile back to your vehicle—closer if you had to park in an overflow area.

48 Otokomi Lake

RATING/ DIFFICULTY	ROUNDTRIP	ELEV GAIN/ HIGH POINT	SEASON
****/4	10.4 miles	2570 feet/ 6590 feet	Mid-June– early Oct

Map: USGS Rising Sun, MT; **Contact:** Glacier National Park Visitor Information; **Notes:** Park entrance fee required. Dogs prohibited. Open to horses; **GPS:** 48.6947°, -113.5198°

Named for a Blackfoot guide, oft-overlooked Otokomi Lake offers early-season access to clear waters. Along the way, Rose Creek's riffles and pools provide refreshment on shadeless summer days, and, thanks to the effects of the 2015 Reynolds Creek Fire, prime wildflower viewing.

GETTING THERE
From the St. Mary entrance of Glacier National Park, drive 5.3 miles west on Going-to-the-Sun Road to Rising Sun Motor Inn and general store. Turn right into the general store parking area. The trailhead is west

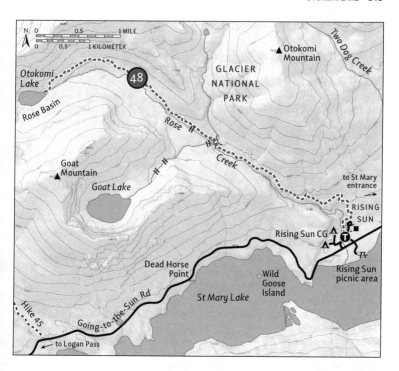

of the general store (elev. 4550 feet). Privy available at Rising Sun Campground.

ON THE TRAIL

Paralleling Rose Creek, pass prairie flowers: yellow cinquefoil, paintbrush, and Jacob's ladder. The Rose Creek drainage sits on the edge of where the Great Plains peel away from the Rocky Mountain Front. In a quarter mile, bear left to continue on the trail. Climb through forest burned by the 2015 Reynolds Creek Fire; the conflagration revealed views of St. Mary Lake and Curly Bear Mountain to the south.

As the trail retreats upstream, gain a ridge above Rose Creek, profuse post-fire pioneer flowers contrasting with burnt snags. As you enter patchy unburnt timber, the canyon walls close in as the trail dips into and out of forested swales. After having been high above Rose Creek, the trail once again draws near it; a series of small cascades at 2.4 miles (elev. 5520 feet) make a nice stopover spot. Cross a footbridge over an unnamed creek, then begin climbing through an area where the 2015 fire's devastation is more stark. However, the series of steep cascades known as Rose Falls is now more clearly visible.

Amid thinning tree cover, lose and regain elevation before a shallow, granite-aided creek crossing at 4.2 miles (6270 feet). Eventually liberated from timber, the route crosses an austere avalanche slope, the snow-crimped krummholz and stunted subalpine fir a testament to regular slides.

Curve southwest and descend off the scree fields to Otokomi Lake's outlet at 5.1 miles (elev. 6520 feet). Glass-clear and smooth-bottomed, Otokomi invites a summer swim. But the water is bracingly cold: snowmelt streaks the ruddy mudstone of Rose Basin's sheer amphitheater all summer long. The south shore offers the best views of the amphitheater's gray balustrades and meltwater cascades, provided you don't get cold feet in the crossing.

Many Glacier

For bear watching, berry picking, and big views of green-hued glacier lakes, many visitors favor the Many Glacier region of the park. Here, hikers can appreciate the long, grinding genesis that created the park's long U-shaped valleys and shadowed cirques high on the Continental Divide.

49 Iceberg Lake and Ptarmigan Tunnel

Iceberg Lake

RATING/ DIFFICULTY	ROUNDTRIP	ELEV GAIN/ HIGH POINT	SEASON
*****/4	9.4 miles	1810 feet/ 6160 feet	July–Sept

Ptarmigan Tunnel

RATING/ DIFFICULTY	ROUNDTRIP	ELEV GAIN/ HIGH POINT	SEASON
*****/5	10.4 miles	2980 feet/ 7330 feet	July–Sept

Map: USGS Many Glacier, MT; **Contact:** Glacier National Park Visitor Information; **Notes:**

Park entrance fee required. Dogs prohibited; **GPS:** 48.7994°, -113.6795°

These two treks, roughly 10 miles each, to Iceberg Lake and Ptarmigan Tunnel offer nearly nonstop views of the dramatic cirques and flower-draped slopes typical of the Many Glacier area. With the shallow, stock-grade climbs and soft, smooth tread, tourists are able to venture on longer hikes than they may be used to. Besides, the stunning destinations—an amphitheater of an ice-bath in which to soak sore legs and a cool, 240-foot mountaintop tunnel—will spur hikers onward.

GETTING THERE

From St. Mary, drive US Highway 89 north for 8.6 miles. Just before the community of Babb, turn left onto Montana Highway 3. Drive 12.4 miles, through the Many Glacier entrance to the park and past the Many Glacier Hotel, to the Swiftcurrent Motor Inn at road's end (elev. 4950 feet). Privy available at Swiftcurrent Motor Inn. The trailhead is at the west end of the expansive parking area.

ON THE TRAIL

Beginning in a landscape typical of the Many Glacier portion of the park, the Iceberg-Ptarmigan Trail retreats upstream through an arid understory of wild currant, serviceberries, and aspen. Low wildflowers provide unfettered views of 8851-foot Mount Grinnell and 8436-foot Swiftcurrent Mountain towards the southwest and 9321-foot Mount Wilbur to the west. Keep an eye out for grizzlies, though; this valley is a well-used bear thoroughfare, and rangers frequently close this trail due to bear activity. After a mile or so, enter more thickly shaded pine forest, and at 2.4 miles (elev. 5630 feet),

Making a midsummer polar bear plunge in Iceberg Lake

reach an overlook of Ptarmigan Falls; just beyond is a popular picnic spot in the cool of Ptarmigan Creek's downdraft. Cross a footbridge over Ptarmigan Creek, and at 2.7 miles (elev. 5760 feet), reach a junction; continue straight for Iceberg Lake, or turn right for Ptarmigan Tunnel.

Iceberg Lake

Shortly after you continue straight at the trail junction, the forest parts to reveal your destination in a steep cirque covered by snowfields, some two miles distant. Skirting the steep southern flank of the Ptarmigan Wall, tack southwest through low subalpine vegetation, views of Grinnell Point, Mount Grinnell, Mount Wilbur, and the snow-filled couloir Iceberg Notch filling your field of view. Below, keep an eye on the dense willows of Iceberg Creek's basin; moose, unfazed by the hiking hordes above, congregate here.

At 4.4 miles (elev. 6070 feet), descend to a crossing of Iceberg Creek. From here, the trail makes a slight climb among a stunning subalpine meadow at Iceberg Lake's outlet before descending to its shore a tenth of a mile later.

Glacier National Park derives its name not for any extant glaciers within its boundaries but for the ice-age glaciers that carved the park's many cirques and peaks. Iceberg Lake is one of the most striking locations in which to see the elemental power of ice and water still in action. Most summers, chunks of ice bob and weave in the wind-driven waters until early August, the occasional crack of a calving iceberg echoing across the high, nearly vertical walls of the cirque in which the lake sits. Care to take a midsummer polar bear plunge?

Ptarmigan Tunnel

From the junction just beyond Ptarmigan Falls, continue right as the trail proceeds

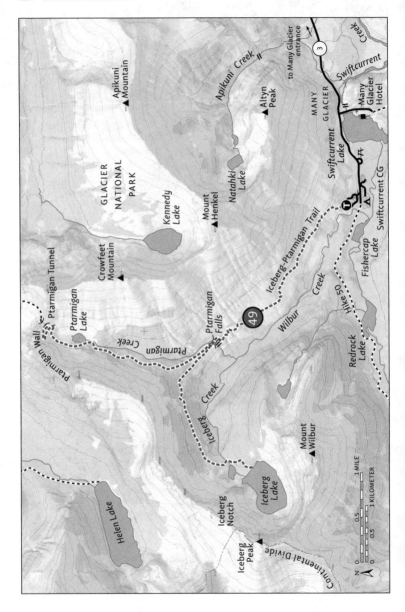

upstream along Ptarmigan Creek. Here, fool's huckleberry mingles with the real thing among the open subalpine fir canopy. Gaining elevation, leave tree cover behind, entering first a series of open meadows colored by shrubby penstemon, salsify, harebell, alpine forget-me-not, and nodding onion, and then austere scree fields. Curve around the tiny blue tarn of Ptarmigan Lake and view the objective in front of you: a half mile of steep, strength-sapping switchbacks over loose scree. Set to work, glancing down valley at Mount Wilbur in the far distance, and at 5.2 miles (elev. 7310 feet), complete the final switchback at the mouth of Ptarmigan Tunnel.

Blasted through the arête of the Ptarmigan Wall with jackhammers and dynamite as a make-work project in the 1930s by the Civilian Conservation Corps, the 240-foot tunnel connects the Many Glacier Valley with the Belly River Valley to the north. In 1975 the National Park Service added steel doors to either end of the tunnel, closing it seasonally from October to summer snowmelt. On the far side of the tunnel, behold the sweep of the Belly River as it connects to Elizabeth Lake. Walk one hundred yards past the tunnel opening to get a good view of Old Sun Glacier on Mount Merritt. Then, rest in the cool of the tunnel before proceeding back the way you came.

50 Swiftcurrent Valley

RATING/ DIFFICULTY	ROUNDTRIP	ELEV GAIN/ HIGH POINT	SEASON
****/3	7.2 miles	840 feet/ 5260 feet	Late May–Oct

Map: USGS Many Glacier, MT; **Contact:** Glacier National Park Visitor Information; **Notes:**

Park entrance fee required. Dogs prohibited; **GPS:** 48.7975°, -113.6785°

Lovely Swiftcurrent Valley offers good early-season access to Many Glacier for hikers and wildlife: scan the steep slopes of glacier lilies for grizzlies—the bulbs are a favorite snack of bruins—and scope the open meadows for bighorn sheep and mountain goats. The easy-going grade gains only about 100 feet a mile en route to three lakes of increasing scenic beauty. The easy walking allows hikers to focus on the vast views of Mount Grinnell, Swiftcurrent Mountain, and the Continental Divide.

GETTING THERE

From St. Mary, drive US Highway 89 north for 8.6 miles. Just before the community of Babb, turn left onto Montana Highway 3. Drive 12.4 miles, through the Many Glacier entrance to the park and past the Many Glacier Hotel, to the Swiftcurrent Motor Inn at road's end (elev. 4950 feet). Privy available at Swiftcurrent Motor Inn. The trailhead is at the west end of the expansive parking area.

ON THE TRAIL

In heavy lodgepole forest, immediately bear left onto the Continental Divide Trail, crossing a large footbridge over Swiftcurrent Creek. Aspen begin to mix with lodgepole as the main trail passes a horse trail coming in from the right, and at 460 yards a short spur trail to Fishercap Lake. The hundred-yard detour accesses shallow, tree-lined Fishercap Lake, Grinnell Point reflected in its green waters. The name "Fishercap" refers to the name the Blackfeet Indians gave to naturalist George Bird Grinnell, the father of Glacier National Park.

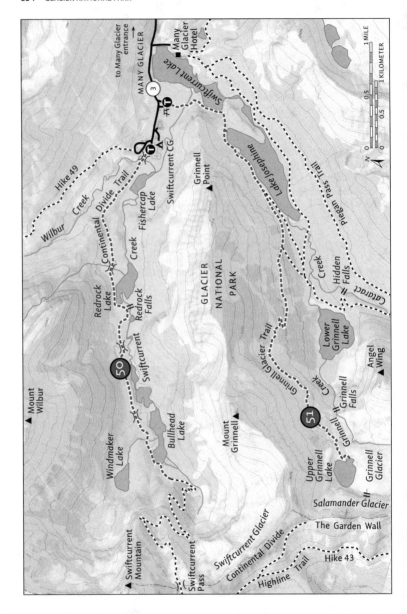

Early summer snow swells Redrock Falls.

Back on the main trail, keep climbing at a barely perceptible grade, keeping an eye out in the brief openings in the aspen-lined corridor for moose. At 1.3 miles (elev. 5090 feet), cross a small creek on a footbridge; open pocket meadows of paintbrush begin to intercede. Shortly after the bridge, reach Redrock Lake. Look up at the streaked lime-stone sheaves surrounding the lake; grass encircles much of the shore. At 1.8 miles, Redrock Falls cascades into a group of deep pools at the head of the lake. This is a popular turnaround point for many day hikers; beyond the falls, the crowds thin considerably.

Continue upstream, aspen gradually giving way to beargrass and mossy outcroppings. To the right, mountain goats and bighorn sheep frequently traverse the scalloped slopes of Mount Wilbur. Cross a small footbridge

at 2.2 miles (elev. 5180 feet) as thickets of snow-battered timber flank the trail. Soon, Bullhead Lake's extensive outlet marshes and pool come into view. Cross a short suspension bridge at 3.2 miles (elev. 5230 feet) and reach Bullhead Lake shortly afterward.

Beargrass and subalpine fir surround the near shore of Bullhead Lake; at the far end, above a headwall that rarely sees the sun, lies Swiftcurrent Glacier, and, above that, Swiftcurrent Mountain. Bullhead's blue-green waters beg for a dip before a return trip to the trailhead.

EXTENDING YOUR TRIP

Part of the Continental Divide Trail, the backpack to Swiftcurrent Pass is at the top of Glacier's many life-list treks. Past Bullhead Lake, the trail lunges a lung-scorching 1800 feet in the final 3-mile push to Swiftcurrent Pass, a good turnaround point or launchpad for miles of Crown-country wandering.

51 Grinnell Glacier

RATING/ DIFFICULTY	ROUNDTRIP	ELEV GAIN/ HIGH POINT	SEASON
*****/4	10 miles	2580 feet/ 6530 feet	July–early Oct

Map: USGS Many Glacier, MT; **Contact:** Glacier National Park Visitor Information; **Notes:** Park entrance fee required. Dogs prohibited. Open to horses; **GPS:** 48.7965°, -113.6680°

Grinnell Glacier, largest in the park, is but one of three glaciers on display on this hike that offers a highlight reel of Glacier's defining characteristics. Easy shoreline ambling leads to alpine meadows profuse with wildflowers. Mountain goats and bighorn sheep scramble on the steep surrounding slopes, and the trail passes through prime grizzly habitat. Grinnell Glacier Overlook grants hikers view of the 152-acre namesake glacier, the Garden Wall, and the Continental Divide.

GETTING THERE

From St. Mary, drive US Highway 89 north for 8.6 miles. Just before the community of Babb, turn left onto Montana Highway 3. Drive 12.1 miles, through the Many Glacier entrance to the park and past the Many Glacier Hotel, to the large, signed trailhead on the left (elev. 4900 feet). Privy available.

ON THE TRAIL

From the busy trailhead, head out on level tread through lodgepole forest, the serrated faces of Mount Siyeh and its neighbors frequently visible among their crowns. Cross

a sturdy bridge at three hundred yards, and shortly after reach the grass shore of Swiftcurrent Lake. Proceed up the shoreline, a glance back revealing Many Glacier Hotel and, if you're lucky, a moose in the lake's morning mist. Cross the little hump separating Swiftcurrent Lake from Lake Josephine.

At 1.6 miles (elev. 4950 feet) bear right at a junction (the way left goes to Lower Grinnell Lake). Above the boat dock and marshy inlet of Lake Josephine, begin climbing in earnest. As the trail ascends out of the valley, the hatchet-faced horn of Mount Gould looms, guarding the Garden Wall as it curves north along the Continental Divide. Notice the prominent banding on Mount Gould

Glacial ice floats in Upper Grinnell Lake.

GLACIER'S DISAPPEARING GLACIERS

Although Glacier National Park was named for the ice-age forces that shaped its distinctive saw-edged silhouette, its extant glaciers are stars of the park. And, within the century, they will have faded into memory.

When the National Park Service created Glacier National Park, the landscape harbored 150 glaciers. Today, 37 remain, and in the last half century some of those have shrunk by as much as 85 percent. Aside from the loss of their spectral allure, glacier recession can affect stream water volume, water temperature, and runoff timing. But perhaps more importantly, these disappearing glaciers are the most visible bellwether of anthropogenic climate change; their diminishing stature year after year is clear to anyone who visits the park.

and its glaciated neighbors. Near at hand, mountain goats clamber on the cliffs above Josephine's north shore.

Soon, stunted trees are all that screen an impressive view of Hidden Falls—which can be heard thundering for quite some distance—and the emerald pool of Lower Grinnell Lake. Making its way into a broad beargrass amphitheater, the path narrows where it's been blasted into the finely mortised mudstone. Rocky runnels of meltwater sluice down the trail, and early-summer snowfields can make travel treacherous. Climb above the level of the falls to reach a picnic area in a willow-edged moraine at 4.5 miles (elev. 6240 feet). From here, ascend on marbled mudstone a half mile before descending slightly to the shore of Upper Grinnell Lake at 5 miles (elev. 6470 feet).

A steep headwall streaked by meltwater hems milky-white Upper Grinnell Lake, in which free-floating, free-form sculptures of calved ice can persist all summer long. Above the lake sits Grinnell Glacier and the Salamander Glacier, once one and the same but now separated and slowly succumbing to climate change, the footprint shrinking each year.

EXTENDING YOUR TRIP

The hike to Lower Grinnell Lake gains little elevation en route to its deep green waters. It's a popular hike for families with children or passengers on the scenic boat tours across Swiftcurrent Lake.

52 Cracker Lake

RATING/ DIFFICULTY	ROUNDTRIP	ELEV GAIN/ HIGH POINT	SEASON
*****/4	12.6 miles	2210 feet/ 6060 feet	Late June– mid-Oct

Maps: USGS Many Glacier, MT; USGS Lake Sherburne, MT; USGS Logan Pass, MT; **Contact:** Glacier National Park Visitor Information; **Notes:** Park entrance fee required. Dogs prohibited; Open to horses; **GPS:** 48.7952°, -113.6561°

No, it's not Photoshop trickery: Cracker Lake's Technicolor cerulean hue is unique even among Glacier's pantheon of lakes. The wide, hoof-hammered trail to Cracker Lake stays in thick timber for most of its 6-mile approach to the lake, but the rewards once the trail reaches the basin more than make up for the preceding miles. The

Summer sun highlights the opaque, milky surface of Cracker Lake.

sheer summit block of Mount Siyeh and the opaque waters of the alpine lake invite lingering, if not swimming.

GETTING THERE

From St. Mary, drive US Highway 89 north for 8.6 miles. Just before the community of Babb, turn left onto Montana Highway 3. Drive 11.9 miles, through the Many Glacier entrance to the park, then turn left for the Many Glacier Hotel. Continue over the outlet for Swiftcurrent Lake for two hundred yards to the large parking area. Privy available in the Many Glacier Hotel.

ON THE TRAIL

A popular equestrian destination—one of the few in Glacier in which a concessionaire offers guided rides—the trail to Cracker Lake tends to get hammered with hooves, making it a bit of a wallow on wet days. The wide, well-tended tread follows a level grade as it rounds Lake Sherburne before beginning

to climb in earnest through thick timber. Before the damming of Lake Sherburne submerged it, the mining town of Altyn sat where Cracker Flats, near the start of the trail, is today; mining at the head of Cracker Lake operated for quite some time after.

Cross a bridge over Allen Creek—its source at tiny Falling Leaf and Snow Moon Lakes an intriguing off-trail destination—at 1.6 miles (elev. 4890 feet) before switchbacking up to a high bench over the broad cut of Canyon Creek. The trail crosses in and out of brushy avalanche chutes as it parallels the creek upstream, crossing a broad talus apron as the trail settles into the drainage.

At 3.6 miles (elev. 5470 feet), cross a long log bridge and reenter timber; thickets of thimbleberry carpet the snow-stunted subalpine forest. The long ridge of which Cracker Peak is the high point gradually comes into view as the trail opens up into the broad Cracker Lake basin, its steep meadows a reliable spot to watch for goats and grizzlies.

At 5.4 miles (elev. 6000 feet), reach the foot of Cracker Lake. Mount Siyeh's sheer summit block—nearly 4000 feet of vertical relief—crowns the lake with its steep shoulders. A series of high rock benches at the lake's outlet allow an aerial view of the lake, its Mediterranean blue the result of glacial flour and mine runoff. Direct sunlight highlights the tropical color of the lake, its depths unseen. For a lakeside view, continue past the established backcountry sites to the head of the lake, where low willow surrounds derelict mining equipment; as iridescent as the lake looks from above, its eerily impenetrable opacity really comes into focus at shore level. Save the swim for a different destination.

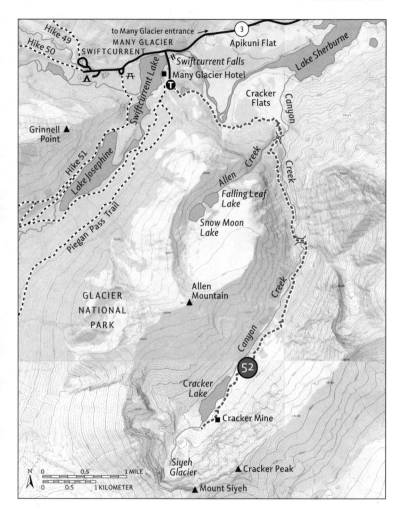

Goat Haunt

The border-crossing fjord of Waterton Lake spans Waterton-Glacier International Peace Park, its glacial-till green waters the jumping-off point for visitors to the Goat Haunt region in the northeast corner of Glacier. Most visitors to the Goat Haunt Ranger Station arrive via the MV *International* scenic cruise and depart some thirty minutes later, meaning that hikers are likely to have the lush bottomland forests—and four-legged fauna—to themselves.

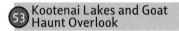 53 Kootenai Lakes and Goat Haunt Overlook

Kootenai Lakes

RATING/ DIFFICULTY	ROUNDTRIP	ELEV GAIN/ HIGH POINT	SEASON
***/3	5.6 miles	550 feet/ 4450 feet	June–Sept

Goat Haunt Overlook

RATING/ DIFFICULTY	ROUNDTRIP	ELEV GAIN/ HIGH POINT	SEASON
****/3	2 miles	870 feet/ 5070 feet	June–Sept

Map: USGS Porcupine Ridge, MT; **Contact:** Glacier National Park Visitor Information; **Notes:** Glacier National Park and Waterton Lakes National Park (Canada) entrance fees required. Dogs prohibited. Waterton Lake Ranger Station open seasonally, typically the first weekend of June through the last weekend of September, and accessible from Waterton, Alberta, by the 8-mile Waterton Lakeshore Trail or via the MV *International*. Contact the Waterton Shoreline Cruise Co., www.watertoncruise.com, for fares and times. Goat Haunt Ranger Station is a US Class B Port of Entry. Hikers must present a valid passport or equivalent identification; **GPS:** 48.9574°, -113.8920°

Nature knows no borders, and you're likely to see dual-citizen bruins, moose, and goats on these hikes in the quietest corner of the park. Kootenai Lakes accesses low-elevation lakes where you've a good chance of seeing moose; Goat Haunt Overlook grants a goat's-eye view of Waterton Lake's green, glacial-flour-speckled waters. Incidentally, mosquitoes ignore international borders, too, and they are notorious blood-smugglers here.

GETTING THERE
From the Chief Mountain Port of Entry north of Babb, follow AB-6 North for 24 miles to AB-5. Turn left (west) and drive 11 miles, entering Waterton Lakes National Park, to the lakeshore community of Waterton. The MV *International* departs from the boat docks just north of downtown. Take the MV *International* to Goat Haunt Ranger Station. Disembark and walk 0.25 mile to the ranger station and trailhead (elev. 4210 feet). Privy available at boat dock.

ON THE TRAIL
Beginning behind the Goat Haunt Ranger Station employee bunkhouse, head south, the inauspicious beginnings belying this trail's stature as the northern terminus of the Continental Divide Trail. Passing through dense forest, reach a junction in two hundred yards. Bear right for Kootenai Lakes, left for Goat Haunt Overlook.

Kootenai Lakes
A thicket of thimbleberries flanks the wide trail as it crosses a bridge at 0.6 mile (elev. 4320 feet). Ascend a low rise, then head south as the trail gains and loses little elevation. Pass a muddy moose wallow and, at 1.4 miles (elev. 4390 feet), cross a bridge over a shallow brook. Wet meadows to the right permit views of Olson Mountain to the north.

Continue south, crossing a small footbridge at 2.1 miles (elev. 4440 feet). A slightly thinning forest reveals to the north the gray crenellations of Cathedral Mountain, one of the most recognizable

WATERTON-GLACIER INTERNATIONAL PEACE PARK

The Canadian government established Waterton Lakes National Park in 1895, fifteen years before the formation of Glacier National Park. In 1932, the year that Going-to-the-Sun Road opened, Canada and the United States connected the two parks as the world's first International Peace Park.

Designated during the building tensions that gripped Europe in the run-up to World War II, Waterton-Glacier International Peace Park was intended to demonstrate that international neighbors could solve problems without resorting to violence. Since then, the parks have worked together on a variety of issues that resist international boundaries, such as wildlife monitoring, wildfire management, and climate change mitigation.

As the centerpiece of the transboundary Crown of the Continent, which spans the Northern Rockies from northwest Montana through Alberta, Waterton-Glacier International Peace Park protects some of the world's unique refugia for endangered flora and fauna.

It's said that "nature knows no borders." Visitors to Waterton-Glacier International Peace Park will no doubt see this dictum in action. But, perhaps more importantly, they will see that humans as well as wildlife thrive when the walls separating us are thrown down.

silhouettes on the scenic boat cruise to Goat Haunt. Cross another footbridge at 2.5 miles (elev. 4440 feet), this time over the crashing rapids of Camp Creek, and immediately bear right toward Kootenai Lakes Campground. A quarter mile of walking downstream deposits hikers at the thickly screened shore of the lowermost of the Kootenai Lakes. A welter of small, forested ponds, Kootenai Lakes don't easily reveal themselves. But moose just might, and ducks and other waterfowl frequent the slow-moving channel here. Fish dimple its surface, too, but if you plan to stay and cast a line, bring bug spray; the mosquitoes ignore international borders.

Goat Haunt Overlook

At the junction just behind the administrative quarters, continue east through lofty lodgepole before entering the first of numerous

The crags of Citadel Peaks over Camp Creek

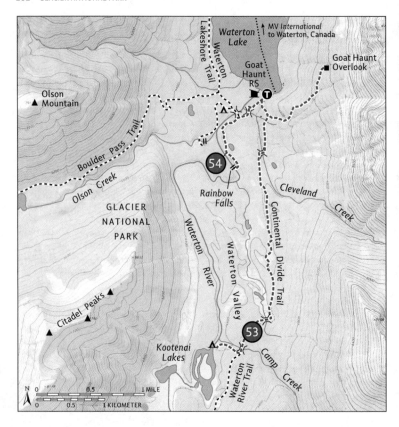

pocket meadows. The trail then bends left and begins steeply climbing. Beargrass bordering the corridor may leave your pant legs covered with cream-colored pollen. After a half mile of calf-cramping climbing, the trail bends to angle across the slope through rocky meadows of wildflowers, reaching trail's end at a set of simple benches at 1 mile (elev. 5070 feet).

From here, peer down onto Waterton Lake's wind-lashed waters—the lake endures some of Canada's strongest, most sustained winds. The striking turquoise color results from glacial sediment mixing into the lake during snowmelt, the color becoming more muted as summer wears on. Waterfalls tumble down the steep avalanche slopes of the serrated peaks on the lake's far shore, just above the cabin where the MV *International* resides during the winter as a stipulation of it being an American-christened ship.

EXTENDING YOUR TRIP

The Waterton River Trail continues for some ways into a lightly explored portion of the park and is the disembarkation point for open-loop trips over Stoney Indian Pass and out the Belly River drainage.

54 Rainbow Falls

RATING/ DIFFICULTY	ROUNDTRIP	ELEV GAIN/ HIGH POINT	SEASON
***/2	1.8 miles	250 feet/ 4320 feet	June–Sept

Map: USGS Porcupine Ridge, MT; **Contact:** Glacier National Park Visitor Information; **Notes:** Glacier National Park and Waterton Lakes National Park (Canada) entrance fees required. Dogs prohibited. Waterton Lake Ranger Station open seasonally, typically the first weekend of June through the last weekend of September, and accessible from Waterton, Alberta, by the 8-mile Waterton Lakeshore Trail or via the MV *International*. Contact the Waterton Shoreline Cruise Co., www.watertoncruise.com, for fares and times. Goat Haunt Ranger Station is a US Class B Port of Entry. Hikers must present a valid passport or equivalent identification; **GPS:** 48.9574°, -113.8920°

Stroll to a colorful cataract that catches sunlight in its spray on clear days. The rocky benches above the falls make a nice picnic spot for MV International boat passengers staying over at Goat Haunt, or a short scenic diversion for passengers with only limited time until the next scheduled departure.

GETTING THERE
From the Chief Mountain Port of Entry north of Babb, follow AB-6 North for 24 miles to AB-5. Turn left (west) and drive 11 miles, entering Waterton Lakes National Park, to the lakeshore community of Waterton. The MV *International*

departs from the boat docks just north of downtown. Take the MV *International* to Goat Haunt Ranger Station. Disembark and walk 0.25 mile to the ranger station and trailhead (elev. 4210 feet). Privy available at boat dock.

ON THE TRAIL
Depart the employee compound behind the ranger station, and soon cross a sturdy footbridge over a side channel of Waterton River. In less than half a mile, draw abreast of the large river, which flows opaquely early in the season. Scan the mud of the low-lying bottomlands for moose and deer prints; they frequent the area, attracted to the mineral-rich mud wallows visible from the trail.

At 0.6 mile (elev. 4240 feet) bear left at a junction, pass a large grass-ringed pond, and then parallel the river through a narrow forested channel upstream. A short climb ensues, ending on a lodgepole-covered bluff. From here, descend slightly to a large rock outcropping at the top of Rainbow Falls at 0.9 mile (elev. 4290 feet).

The MV International docked near the Goat Haunt port of entry on Waterton Lake

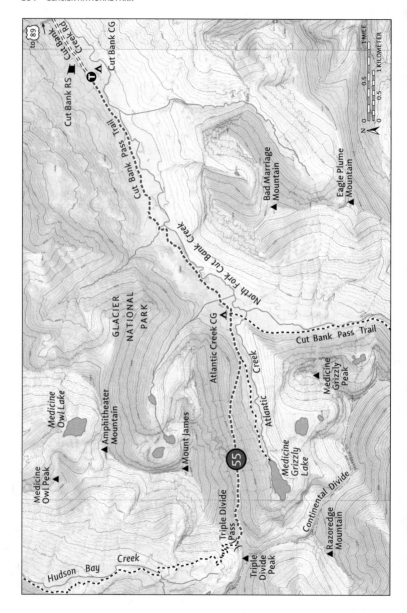

to 89

Cut Bank Creek Rd.

Cut Bank RS

Cut Bank CG

Cut Bank Pass Trail

Bad Marriage Mountain

Eagle Plume Mountain

North Fork Cut Bank Creek

GLACIER NATIONAL PARK

Atlantic Creek CG

Cut Bank Pass Trail

Medicine Owl Lake

Medicine Owl Peak

Amphitheater Mountain

Mount James

Atlantic Creek

Atlantic Creek

Medicine Grizzly Peak

Medicine Grizzly Lake

55

Triple Divide Pass

Triple Divide Peak

Continental Divide

Razoredge Mountain

Hudson Bay Creek

N

1 MILE

1 KILOMETER

0.5

0.5

More of a large cascade or cataract than a waterfall, Rainbow Falls nonetheless inspires with its early-season ferocity. Low subalpine trees on either side of the north-flowing watercourse allow sunlight to refract through the spray of the cascades, the kaleidoscopic result pairing with the colorful river cobbles.

EXTENDING YOUR TRIP

The Boulder Pass Trail is the jumping-off point for one of the most coveted backcountry permits in the park: a multiday trip over Boulder and Brown Passes to Kintla Lake in the North Fork region.

Two Medicine Area

Prior to the construction of Going-to-the-Sun Road, the Two Medicine area of Glacier was the preeminent east-side portal to park travelers; today, it's much quieter than its neighbor to the north, but the views are still as magnificent as they were to those early-20th-century tourists. Thanks to the open, windswept terrain on the edge of the Great Plains, the hiking here offers near-constant views of the snow-dusted upper reaches of the Rocky Mountain Front and the low, shrubby foothills below.

55 Triple Divide Pass

RATING/ DIFFICULTY	ROUNDTRIP	ELEV GAIN/ HIGH POINT	SEASON
*****/5	14 miles	2750 feet/ 7397 feet	July–early Oct

Maps: USGS Mount Stimson, MT; USGS Cut Bank Pass, MT; **Contact:** Glacier National Park Visitor Information; **Notes:** Park entrance fee required. Dogs prohibited; **GPS:** 48.6021°, -113.3838°

Raindrops that land mere inches away from one another on this mudstone summit, itself an ancient ocean floor, end up thousands of miles away in the Pacific, Atlantic, or Arctic Oceans—a phenomenon repeated in only one other place in North America. Fortunately, it's a much shorter trip there and back for hikers intent on reaching one of the centerpieces of the park, geographically and visually.

GETTING THERE

From US Highway 2 in East Glacier, drive north on Montana Highway 49 (Looking Glass Highway) for 11 slow, winding miles. Bear left onto US 89 and continue 5 miles to Cut Bank Creek Road. Turn left and drive 5 gravel miles, through the Cut Bank entrance to the park, to the trailhead parking area just before Cut Bank Campground (elev. 5170 feet). Privy available.

ON THE TRAIL

From the primitive trailhead, Cut Bank Pass Trail immediately retreats upstream near the coiling course of the North Fork Cut Bank Creek. The course gains almost no elevation as it passes through a wide, meadowed valley of willow and prairie wildflowers. Take the time on this easy section of trail to scan the willows for signs of wolf, moose, and grizzly: all make use of this wide, lightly traveled valley.

Alternating between open conifer forests and low-growing meadows, reach a trail junction at 3.8 miles (elev. 5390 feet). Keep right, and immediately pass through Atlantic Creek Campground, its densely shaded campsites serving a purely utilitarian purpose for hikers bound for Triple Divide or Pitamakan Passes. Atlantic Creek is a good spot to top off water bottles; the trail is dry beyond here.

Tiny alpine flowers carpet the high shoulder of Mount James.

Beyond the campground, the trail quickly departs the trees before passing the junction to Medicine Grizzly Lake at 4.4 miles, elev. 5510 feet (see Extending Your Trip). For the pass, keep right as the trail mounts a shadeless, switchback-free ascent across the sheer southern flanks of Mount James. Fruitful huckleberry picking aids the first mile or so before increasing elevation reduces the vegetation to low-growing mats of alpine plants.

With every step, the views increase in grandeur, Medicine Grizzly Peak standing above the green waters of Medicine Grizzly Lake below. A hanging valley some two thousand feet below the summit hides a small tarn that has doubtless seen no more than a few hiking boots on its shores.

Having gained nearly two thousand feet in the preceding 3 miles, reach 7397-foot

Triple Divide Pass at 7 miles. The triangular prow of Triple Divide Peak stands skyward to the immediate southwest; it's a strenuous Class 2-plus scramble to its summit. Mountain goats, attracted to the sweat-soaked strip of hikers' packs, frequently congregate near here. Relax, taking in the birthplace of three oceans, before returning the way you came.

EXTENDING YOUR TRIP
Medicine Grizzly Lake provides a short but scenic side trip to its green, grass-ringed waters. From the junction just past Atlantic Creek Campground, keep left, the trail gaining little elevation as it passes through stands of snow-cowed subalpine fir and colorful meadows. Pass a few willowy side channels of Atlantic Creek before reaching the lake 1.5 miles from the junction. Trout stalk its glassy surface.

56 Dawson-Pitamakan Loop

RATING/ DIFFICULTY	LOOP	ELEV GAIN/ HIGH POINT	SEASON
*****/5	18.2 miles	3690 feet/ 8050 feet	Mid-July– Sept

Map: USGS Cut Bank Pass, MT; **Contact:** Glacier National Park Visitor Information; **Notes:** Park entrance fee required. Dogs prohibited; **GPS:** 48.4910°, -113.3659°

Quite possibly the premier alpine traverse in the park, the 18-mile Dawson-Pitamakan loop is long but within the realm of done-in-a-day trips; hikers will encounter flatlanders and first-time visitors to the park over the course of this hike. Scale two wind-battered alpine passes while enjoying near-constant views of the tightly stacked summits of the park's interior. If Glacier National Park is the backbone of the world, this is the giant's skeleton laid bare.

GETTING THERE

From East Glacier, travel north on Montana Highway 49 for 3.6 miles to Two Medicine Road. Bear left, past Lower Two Medicine Lake and through the Two Medicine entrance, for 7.2 miles to the Two Medicine Campground. Turn right into the campground and continue to the trailhead parking area at the end of campground Loop A (elev. 5170 feet).

ON THE TRAIL

From Two Medicine Campground, cross a bridge over the outlet of Pray Lake and come to a junction. The way right is your return; continue left, following Two Medicine Lake's shoreline contours through conifer forest and wildflower meadows.

At 3 miles (elev. 5230 feet), keep right at a junction; the way left leads to a confusing tangle of trails to Upper Two Medicine Lake and south around Two Medicine's shore. Begin climbing in earnest, the 7620-foot Pumpelly Pillar coming into view directly ahead. This glacially carved, cone-shaped rock is named after Raphael Pumpelly, leader of the Northern Trans-continental Railway Survey party that crossed Pitamakan Pass in 1883. Crossing huckleberry-laden slopes before retreating back into the trees, the trail makes a steep ascent before leveling out in the narrow hanging valley of No Name Lake at 4.5 miles (5980 feet). Go left a short distance to check out the lake, which occupies the base of a steep, boomerang-shaped wall under Pumpelly Pillar.

Back on the main trail, resume climbing the south flank of Flinsch Peak, through an area appropriately known as Bighorn Basin. Leaving tree cover behind, make one final push to Dawson Pass at 7 miles (elev. 7940 feet).

Named after Thomas Dawson, a Blackfoot descendent and a guide during the early days of Glacier National Park, the exposed col is better known for its fierce and unceasing gales. The wind may make for a brief stop; sequester in one of the rock shelters, or join the hunched-over hikers clutching their hats on the pass. The stark form of Mount Phillips dominates the view to the west. More than 3000 feet below its summit are the remnants of the Lupfer Glacier. Due to considerable shrinkage in recent years, Lupfer is no longer a glacier, and is now considered a permanent snowfield. Directly below lies the U-shaped valley through which Nyack Creek flows. Follow its course to the south to spot the snowy cap of Saint

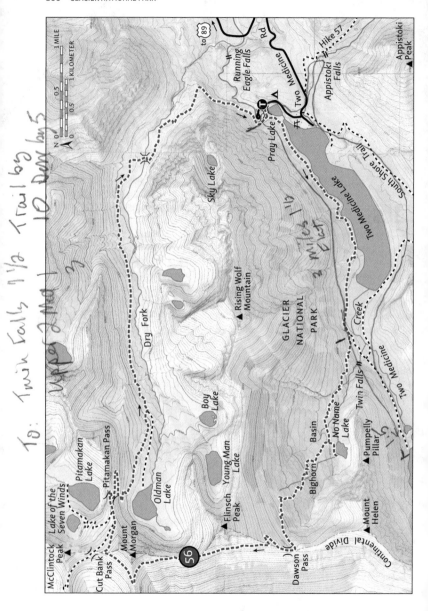

Hikers brace themselves against the incessant gales of Dawson Pass.

Nicholas, the most recognizable of Glacier National Park's horns.

Continuing north from Dawson Pass, trace the west aspect of Flinsch Peak on a narrow, packed-talus path high above Nyack Creek. The trail reaches a sere saddle between Flinsch Peak and Mount Morgan to the north; below lies the hanging valley occupied by Young Man Lake. Curve around the star-shaped summit block of Mount Morgan—side paths here lead to a set of photogenic pillars with views to the northwest of the stacked massifs of the Continental Divide—before making one last traverse on narrow tread near Cut Bank Pass at 9.4 miles (elev. 8050 feet). Here, begin a set of long, sheltered switchbacks, bearing right at two junctions in quick succession, to Pitamakan Pass at 10.1 miles (elev. 7540 feet).

Named for a female warrior leader of the Blackfeet in the early 18th century—the only Blackfoot female to lead raiding parties or take a male name—Pitamakan Pass stands proud over Pitamakan Lake and Lake of the Seven Winds to the north and Oldman Lake to the south. (The English translation of Pitamakan, "Running Eagle," has been bestowed upon a waterfall accessed via a short trail just east of Two Medicine Lake.)

From Pitamakan Pass, descend steeply, losing 1200 feet in 2 miles, to a junction at 12 miles (elev. 6340 feet). The way right continues a half mile to the cobbled, wind-whipped shoreline of Oldman Lake, which occupies a steep cirque on the east face of Mount Morgan. The backcountry campsites here are some of the park's best; day hikers will find a welcome respite from the sun in the lake's cold waters.

From the main trail, continue through airy lodgepole forest—and some of the park's premier huckleberry patches—as the trail proceeds east across the open south-facing slopes of the Dry Fork, the ragged silhouette of Rising Wolf Mountain occupying the skyline to the south. At 13.7 miles (elev. 5770 feet), pass a spur trail to a waterfall viewpoint, and at 15.1 miles reach a junction on the open gravel-bar bottomland of the Dry Fork. Bear right (the way straight goes to the Two Medicine park entrance). Cross a footbridge over a low creek and settle in for several miles of forested lowland hiking

A bighorn sheep ascends the shoulder of Scenic Point.

around the east face of Rising Wolf Mountain before reaching Pray Lake and the end of a life-list loop.

57 Appistoki Falls and Scenic Point

RATING/ DIFFICULTY	ROUNDTRIP	ELEV GAIN/ HIGH POINT	SEASON
****/4	7.4 miles	2540 feet/ 7522 feet	Late May– early Oct

Map: USGS Dancing Lady Mountain, MT; **Contact:** Glacier National Park Visitor Information; **Notes:** Park entrance fee required. Dogs prohibited; **GPS:** 48.4851°, -113.3617°

A spare, flower-specked summit surveys the peaks of the Two Medicine portion of the park and the prairie of central Montana. Scenic Point's shadeless climb is best done in spring, when wildflowers fleck windswept tundra and Glacier's full, snowy glory is on display.

GETTING THERE

From East Glacier, travel north on Montana Highway 49 for 3.6 miles to Two Medicine Road. Bear left, past Lower Two Medicine Lake and through the Two Medicine entrance, for 7 miles to the trailhead on the left (elev. 5270 feet). Privy available.

ON THE TRAIL

Beginning in shaded forest, head southeast on wide, nearly level tread, the Scenic Point Trail curving away from and then returning to Appistoki Creek. Begin ascending the steeply sloping drainage, and at 0.6 mile (elev. 5440 feet), reach a short spur trail to Appistoki Falls. A hundred-yard walk brings hikers to a viewpoint of the falls, which tumble out of

A hiker skirts a late-lingering snowfield on the final approach to Scenic Point.

the basin beneath Mount Henry and Appistoki Peak. Named for the Blackfoot deity who watches over everything, Appistoki Falls is frustratingly obscured by forest.

Back on the main trail, begin an ascent of long, rocky switchbacks up the west face of Scenic Point. Twisted whitebark pine skeletons add a desolate air to this landscape of low-growing lichen, where bighorn sheep can often be found.

Nearing a small knob on Scenic Point's Y-shaped ridge, proceed past a copse of

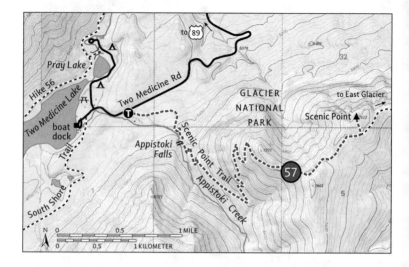

small subalpine fir before leaving tree cover behind entirely. At your feet is a fellfield, an alpine tundra slope where freeze-thaw cycles push rocks out of the soil and only mats of hardy cushion plants survive, their hairy leaves and low posture a defense against desiccating winds.

The striated limestone structure of Mount Henry's north face dominates the view directly ahead. At 2.8 miles (elev. 7260 feet), crest, then cross, the ridge; the shaded north-facing aspect can hold snow well into early summer, making crossing tricky.

Contour around the ridge, just below its top, to reach a spur trail to Scenic Point proper at 3.5 miles. From here, bear left for 150 feet of climbing to Scenic Point.

Constructed by the Great Northern Railway to ease transportation between its Glacier Park Lodge and Two Medicine

Chalet properties, the route to Scenic Point once hosted one of four locomotive bells in the park, a Swiss Alps tradition, borrowed by advertising agents for Great Northern Railway and Glacier Park Hotel Company in the 1920s, that allowed passing mountain travelers to ring the large bells. In 1943 the park donated the bells to a wartime scrap-metal drive. Although no longer a primary port of entry to the park, Scenic Point still inspires: the sheer prow of Sinopah Mountain stands proud at the far end of Two Medicine Lake; Rising Wolf's ragged silhouette dominates the view to the north.

EXTENDING YOUR TRIP

From Scenic Point, the trail continues down to East Glacier; the open terrain also allows for easy scrambles to Appistoki Peak and beyond.

Opposite: Hikers make the final scramble to the summit of Great Northern Mountain (Hike 58).

flathead range

Eyeing the final approach to the summit of Great Northern Mountain

The Flathead Range rises some four thousand vertical feet above the Middle Fork Flathead River, which forms the southern boundary of Glacier National Park. Although separated from the park by US Highway 2, this landscape, which is protected as the Great Bear Wilderness, part of the massive Bob Marshall Wilderness Complex, bears much in common with its northern neighbor: it's a lush, brushy landscape of green, glaciated valleys; the abundant snowfall and vegetation constantly threatens to swallow the steep trails that provide access. Bears, perhaps attracted by the lack of traffic, thrive here; so do self-reliant hikers.

Map: USGS Mt. Grant, MT; **Contact:** Flathead National Forest, Hungry Horse and Glacier View Ranger Districts; **Note:** Wilderness rules apply. **GPS:** 48.3337°, -113.8308°

Named after the northernmost of the transcontinental railroads, and the one that facilitated much of Glacier National Park's early tourism, Great Northern Mountain will require legs, lungs, and nerves of steel to reach its lofty summit. A successful summit attempt on what is without a doubt the hardest hike in the book is a fast track toward serious trail cred among the locals.

GETTING THERE

From Columbia Falls, drive east on US Highway 2 through Hungry Horse. At 0.9 mile past Hungry Horse, turn right (south) on East Side Hungry Horse Road (Forest Road 38). Drive 0.5 mile, bearing right onto North Fork Road in "downtown" Martin City, and continue another 14.7 miles, the first 1.5

58 Great Northern Mountain

RATING/ DIFFICULTY	ROUNDTRIP	ELEV GAIN/ HIGH POINT	SEASON
*****/5	7.2 miles	5190 feet/ 8705 feet	Late July–Sept

FLATHEAD NATIONAL FOREST

to (2)

38

1048

GREAT BEAR WILDERNESS

58

Stanton Glacier

Great Northern Mountain

Dudley Creek

T to Hungry Horse Reservoir

N 0 0.5 1 MILE

0 0.5 1 KILOMETER

miles on pavement, the remainder on good gravel, making a sharp left onto Forest Road 1048. (If you reach a T-junction with FR 3818, you've gone about fifty feet too far.) Drive 1 mile, crossing the small bridge, to the road's end (abandoned past here) and trailhead (elev. 4250 feet).

ON THE TRAIL

Several climbers' routes, none of them on Forest Service trails, tackle Great Northern, but the approach described here is the most popular, with an "unofficial" route that's in better shape than many system trails. The trail departs from the north side of the unnamed creek and immediately proceeds straight up a calf-cramping, lung-searing 1700 feet in the first three-quarters of a mile. Put the idea of switchbacks out of your mind; there aren't any. While your heels won't make acquaintance with the ground for quite some time, you'll be well acquainted with those of the person in front of you.

The steepest of the climbing behind you, reach a beargrass-clad saddle at 1.2

miles; here, the seemingly sheer west face of Great Northern's summit block is in full view. From here the trail runs east along the crest of Great Northern's spur ridge, its tread remarkably well tended for an unofficial climbers' path. The trail descends to follow the lip of a cirque, small subalpine trees providing handholds. Here the trail begins to braid across the scree-scattered west face of the narrow arête; follow the path that feels most comfortable. All gain elevation in great bursts. On the west side of the ridge is loose scree; the other side is a sheer drop. As the route makes its way toward the false summit, enjoy the views of Hungry Horse Reservoir to the west and the crenellated crags of Glacier to the north.

Nearing the summit, hikers must navigate several tricky spots with moderate exposure; the rock here is a mix of solid and rotten, so make sure your handholds are trustworthy before committing. The final approach to the summit block presents a dilemma: to the left a series of rock perches with moderate exposure but good hand- and footholds, and

Great Northern Mountain towers above Stanton Lake.

to the right a goat path dips into and steeply out of loose dirt. Either way, a final fifty feet of four-points-of-contact scrambling over dicey rock is all that stands between you and

a few hundred yards of easy walking to the summit at 3.6 miles.

Congrats! The 360-degree views—of receding Stanton Glacier and Stanton Lake below, pyramidal Mount Stimson and its Glacier kin to the north, Hungry Horse Reservoir and the scalloped east-facing cirques of the Swan Range to the west, and the glacier-clad cirques of the Flathead Range to the south—are worth the effort. Bragging rights await in the valley.

EXTENDING YOUR TRIP

You've just completed the hardest hike in the book. Take a break. May I suggest the Great Northern Bar & Grill in Whitefish?

59 Stanton Lake

RATING/ DIFFICULTY	ROUNDTRIP	ELEV GAIN/ HIGH POINT	SEASON
***/3	3.6 miles	880 feet/ 3960 feet	May–Nov

Map: USGS Stanton Lake, MT; **Contact:** Flathead National Forest, Hungry Horse Ranger District; **Notes:** Wilderness rules apply. Open to horses; **GPS:** 48.3996°, -113.7158°

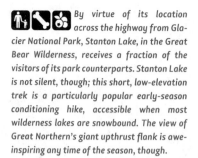 *By virtue of its location across the highway from Glacier National Park, Stanton Lake, in the Great Bear Wilderness, receives a fraction of the visitors of its park counterparts. Stanton Lake is not silent, though; this short, low-elevation trek is a particularly popular early-season conditioning hike, accessible when most wilderness lakes are snowbound. The view of Great Northern's giant upthrust flank is awe-inspiring any time of the season, though.*

GETTING THERE

From West Glacier, drive US Highway 2 for 16 miles. Just past the Stanton Creek Lodge, turn right into the large parking area (elev. 3590 feet).

ON THE TRAIL

Following a streamside course but not a stream gradient, the short trail to Stanton Lake gets the bulk of its elevation gain in the first half mile, eschewing switchbacks

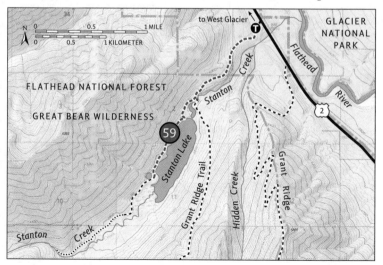

Early autumn snowfall coats the shores of Marion Lake.

in favor of straight, steep stair-like climbing. Enter a patch of forest where young subalpine fir and spruce have begun to crowd out the old boles of fire-dependent larch. A bevy of berry-bearing shrubs—serviceberry, thimbleberry, black elderberry—suggests the popularity of this drainage with both four- and two-legged locals. A backward glance reveals Wolftail Mountain and its neighbors in the Coal Creek area of Glacier National Park, all little-visited denizens of the park's family of peaks.

A half mile in, well above the rushing waters of Stanton Creek, the trail completes another short, steep climb and most of its elevation gain. Now on narrow tread above the creek, enter the Great Bear Wilderness at 0.6 mile; just beyond the wooden wilderness sign is an excellent vista of the Stanton

Creek drainage and Mount Grant to the south. Continue right, descending, steeply at times, through an open forest of larch and beargrass. At 0.9 mile, bear right at the junction (the way left goes to Grant Ridge).

Pass the broad, slow-moving outlet of Stanton Lake, and, at 1.2 miles, bear left down to the lake's foot, where well-used, willow-shaded tent sites flank its pebbled shore. The head of the lake reflects a succession of forested ridges, towered over by the awe-inspiring 8705-foot Great Northern Mountain, its chipped-granite summit massif tilted like a sinking steamship. The long, glacier-carved cirque hints at the presence of extant glaciers on Great Northern Mountain and its glacier-clad kin in the Flathead Range. From the foot of the lake, continue another 0.6 mile through birch, bracken

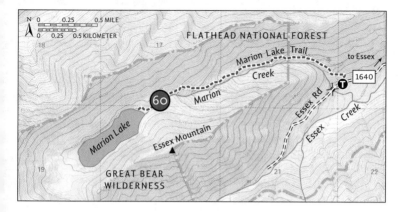

fern, and thimbleberry—a late-summer snack for hikers and grizzlies alike—to the thickly timbered inlet, which offers several slightly less popular tent sites.

EXTENDING YOUR TRIP

From the inlet of Stanton Lake, the trail continues a half mile or so through brushy bottomland of cow parsnip and bracken fern before petering out. It's possible to take this route as an alternate approach to Great Northern Mountain (Hike 58), though I recommend solid map and compass skills and a detailed map.

60 Marion Lake

RATING/ DIFFICULTY	ROUNDTRIP	ELEV GAIN/ HIGH POINT	SEASON
****/3	4.2 miles	2010 feet/ 5950 feet	Late June–Oct

Map: USGS Pinnacle, MT; **Contact:** Flathead National Forest, Hungry Horse Ranger District; **Notes:** Wilderness rules apply. Open to horses; **GPS:** 48.2722°, -113.6333°

A short, at times steep, ascent through brushy bear forage leads to a quiet lake in the Great Bear Wilderness. Although popular with Nordic skiers in the winter, Marion Lake sees but a handful of summer visitors if the grassy tread and untouched berries are any indication.

GETTING THERE

From West Glacier, drive east on US Highway 2 for 26.2 miles to Dickey Creek Road. Turn right (south), cross the railroad tracks, then bear left onto Essex Road (Forest Road 1640). Continue for 2.5 miles to the trailhead on the right (elev. 4100 feet). If you reach a small bridge, you've gone about one hundred yards too far. A small shoulder pullout accommodates two vehicles.

ON THE TRAIL

From the unremarkable Marion Lake Trail 150 trailhead, immediately begin a steep, switchbacking ascent through a sun-dappled canopy of Douglas-fir and larch. Thimbleberry and other open-shade forest plants thrive underneath. The trail bends west, retreating upstream above Marion Creek through yew and huckleberry, Essex Mountain forming the far side of the narrow valley. Enter the Great Bear Wilderness as thick alder and brush begin to obscure the trail, and thimbleberries and mountain ash berries provide a late-summer snack for bruins. This is a good spot to work on your "Hey bear!" call.

Drawing near Marion Creek, the trail mounts an ascent of several steep, root-snarled switchbacks, the creek's various side channels occasionally assuming the path of the trail. Leveling out in a broad outwash plain,

hike through cool spruce forest to Marion Lake's outlet at 2.1 miles (elev. 5920 feet).

A nameless, nearly eight-thousand-foot peak rises above the head of the lake, its tiered amphitheater of almost perfectly circular sheets of rock an excellent example of rock exfoliation. To the north, orderly avalanche slopes descend all the way to the water. Well-used tent sites sit back in the trees, and, despite the lake's popularity, access to the water is tricky, with tall spruce growing right up to the shoreline, while a log boom effectively bisects the foot of the lake.

Opposite: *Fall colors swaddle Holland Lake (Hike 67).*

swan range

Forming the westernmost buttress of the broad expanse of peaks that comprises the Bob Marshall Wilderness Complex, the Swans lie within an hour's drive of both Missoula and Kalispell but somewhat off the beaten path of the hiking masses. Here, stream-bottom trailheads access great swatches of subalpine meadows and dozens of tree-shaded tarns high above the Flathead and Seeley-Swan Valleys. Aside from the justifiably popular Jewel Basin Hiking Area, the Swans promise solitude.

61 Columbia Mountain

RATING/ DIFFICULTY	ROUNDTRIP	ELEV GAIN/ HIGH POINT	SEASON
****/5	11 miles	5140 feet/ 7234 feet	Early June–Oct

Maps: USGS Hungry Horse, MT; USGS Columbia Falls South, MT; USGS Doris Mountain, MT; **Contact:** Flathead National Forest, Hungry Horse Ranger District; **Note:** Open to horses and bicycles; **GPS:** 48.3811°, -114.1143°

Often overlooked even by local hikers in favor of its more famous neighbors, Columbia Mountain offers commanding views of the Flathead Valley and the forested shores of Hungry Horse Reservoir to the east. But it comes at a cost: an eye-popping—or, more accurately, knee-popping—5140 feet of elevation gain!

GETTING THERE
From Columbia Falls, drive east on US Highway 2 for 4 miles, and, just past the House of Mystery, turn right (south) onto unmarked Berne Road. Drive 0.5 mile to the large trailhead on the left (elev. 3100 feet).

ON THE TRAIL
Thanks to its west-facing aspect on the edge of the Flathead Valley, Columbia Mountain melts out earlier than many of its neighbors. It's a test piece for local trail runners, whom you're more likely to encounter than hikers.

Beginning in a lush forest cover of thimbleberry and fir, ascend the west slope of Columbia Mountain. Although never so steep that your heels don't touch the tread, Columbia Mountain Trail 51 is always climbing. Or descending: after gaining 900 feet of elevation in the initial 1.2 miles, the trail levels out—then loses half that hard-won elevation.

Having squandered its gains, the trail surges upslope at 1.9 miles (elev. 3750 feet) in pursuit of the unseen summit. Continue steeply uphill through dense forest cover, the occasional small rock prominence

Alpine daisies dot the top of Columbia Mountain.

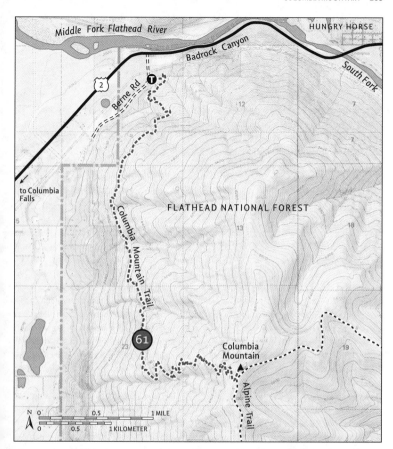

offering a stop-off spot with views of the Flathead Valley.

After wandering like a rudderless boat upslope for nearly two miles, the trail attacks a series of steep switchbacks, gradually leaving tree cover (and shade) behind in favor of low lithosol plants underfoot.

Finally, at 5.3 miles (elev. 7150 feet), the trail reaches Alpine Trail 7 on Swan Crest in a low wooded saddle; snow may hold on here well after melting off the rest of the peak. Bear left and ascend some two hundred yards up the south aspect of Columbia Mountain's screen-strewn summit.

The northernmost peak of the Swan Range, Columbia Mountain boasts a commanding view of the Flathead Valley to the west. To the east, Great Northern's distinctive plow-shaped prominence towers over the inlets and bays of Hungry Horse Reservoir. To the south runs the gentle undulation of the Swan Crest, the forested bulwark of the Bob Marshall Wilderness Complex.

EXTENDING YOUR TRIP
Columbia Mountain forms the northern terminus of Alpine Trail 7, which runs nearly 25 ridge-riding miles south along the Swan Crest. Tiny Strawberry Lake, just south of Columbia Mountain, is within the reach of day hikers.

62 Birch Lake

RATING/ DIFFICULTY	ROUNDTRIP	ELEV GAIN/ HIGH POINT	SEASON
*****/3	6 miles	1660 feet/ 6380 feet	July–Oct

Map: USGS Jewel Basin, MT; **Contact:** Flathead National Forest, Hungry Horse Ranger District; **Note:** Dogs permitted on leash; **GPS:** 48.1606°, -113.9482°

 *Southeast of Kalispell, the Jewel Basin Hiking Area has a lake for every preference. Like lounging on the grassy lawn of a shallow tarn? Pick Picnic Lakes. How about plunging into a deep, granite-set pool? Choose Crater Lake. For an easy introduction to the calling cards of the Jewel Basin—quiet pools and copious flowers— hike the 6-mile roundtrip to Birch Lake.*

GETTING THERE
From the junction of Montana Highways 35 and 83 north of Bigfork, head east on MT 83 for 2.7 miles to the community of Echo Lake. Turn left (north) on Echo Lake Road and proceed for 2.2 miles, then turn right onto Foothill Road. After 1.1 miles, continue straight on Jewel Basin Road and follow this

steep, washboarded road for 6.3 miles to the road's end and trailhead (elev. 5750 feet). Privy available.

ON THE TRAIL
Aside from a brief ascent out of the trailhead, most of the 3-mile hike to Birch Lake follows a nearly level course as it sidehills across steep slopes awash in color from purple penstemon, lupine, aster, and more. The wildflowers thrive thanks to the copious snowfall of the Swans, the long north-south bulwark against the Bob Marshall Wilderness.

From the busy parking area, follow the old closed-to-motors road past the trailhead sign as it swings through brushy bottomland before angling upslope, accompanied by views to the north of Swan Crest. Soon the trail hairpins and begins a level walk through old snags, fireweed, aster, and beargrass. Nearly nonstop views showcase the expansive Flathead Valley below. At 1 mile, reach "malfunction junction," a confusing tangle of trails; bear hardest right onto Alpine Trail 7.

The trail soon turns into singletrack flanked by a stunning array of alpine wildflowers on the steep southwest slope of Mount Aeneas. Pass by rockbound Martha Lake far below and, at 2.9 miles (elev. 6210 feet), reach a short spur trail to Birch Lake.

Birch Lake occupies a broad, flat bench on the Swan Crest, its numerous spits and inlets sheltering semiprivate swimming and tenting spots. A backcountry pit toilet sits back a hundred or so yards from the shallow shore.

EXTENDING YOUR TRIP
Ambitious hikers can continue another 3 miles—with blooms and berries as added motivation—to the granite tub of Crater Lake. Rock outcroppings plunge immediately

A hiker and her trail dog bask in the sun at Birch Lake.

into cold, chest-deep water below; you'd be hard-pressed to find a better shore from which to cannonball.

63 Jewel Basin Loop

RATING/ DIFFICULTY	LOOP	ELEV GAIN/ HIGH POINT	SEASON
*****/4	9.9 miles	2360 feet/ 6780 feet	July–Oct

Map: USGS Jewel Basin, MT; **Contact:** Flathead National Forest, Hungry Horse Ranger District; **Note:** Dogs permitted on leash; **GPS:** 48.1607°, -113.9477°

Take in a tour of the Jewel Basin's subalpine tarns, from grassy lawns to deep lakes set under massive shadowed peaks, on this 10-mile highlight reel of the Swan Range.

GETTING THERE

From the junction of Montana Highways 35 and 83 north of Bigfork, head east on MT 83 for 2.7 miles to the community of Echo Lake. Turn left (north) on Echo Lake Road and proceed for 2.2 miles, then turn right onto Foothill Road. After 1.1 miles, continue straight on Jewel Basin Road and follow this steep, washboarded road for 6.3 miles to the road's end and trailhead (elev. 5750 feet). Privy available.

ON THE TRAIL

From the ranger cabin, switchback up through a moist, steep meadow of angelica, aster, and cow parsnip. Bear right at a junction (the way left is your return route) and begin switchbacking in a southeasterly direction through open-timbered meadows to reach a second junction at 1.2 miles (elev. 6370 feet). Turn left and climb to a narrow notch in the

Traversing the wildflower fields above Twin Lakes

ridgeline, the Flathead Valley spread out to the west.

Passing onto the east side of the Swan Crest, bear right at a junction, crossing a meadow of prairie crocus, lilies, and late-lingering snow to descend to the shallow pair of Picnic Lakes, which sprawl out below a large cirque, at 2.2 miles (elev. 6650 feet). As their name implies, both lakes are an ideal spot for foot-soaking. Cross a log bridge at the lakes' clear-running connecting stream, then bear left at a Y-junction. Cross the lake's outlet and parallel this stream through a sprawling meadow, views of distant peaks in the Bob Marshall Wilderness Complex towering over Hungry Horse Reservoir far below to the east.

Now in open spruce forest, turn right at a junction at 2.9 miles (elev. 6470 feet) and descend to Black Lake. Black Lake's blue-green waters sprawl at the base of a glacier-scoured cirque below the craggy buttresses of Mount Aeneas; several large campsites cluster near the log-clogged outlet. Through midsummer, "Black Fly Lake" might be a more appropriate name.

Shortly past Black Lake, bear left at an easy-to-miss junction (turn around to see the sign on a spruce) to reach the first of the Jewel Lakes at 3.8 miles (6040 feet). Shallow and grassy, all four lakes support healthy populations of blood-sucking black flies; the North and South Lakes also support trout.

To continue the loop, pass the northernmost lake and cross its outlet pond before making a northeasterly descent through heavy brush and craggy spruce. At 5.3 miles (elev. 5600 feet), cross the outlet of Blackfoot Lake. Burnt snags and brush sprawl out from this shallow lake, lending it an eerie feeling at odds with its Jewel Basin neighbors.

From the north shore of the lake, begin a meandering ascent of the south face of Tongue Mountain, brush ceding to beargrass as you gain elevation. At 7.2 miles (elev. 6540 feet), at a timbered junction, bear left, now following a flat, meadowy pass southward through snowbanks and glacier lilies. At 7.8 miles (elev. 6500 feet), reach a junction with the short trail to shallow Twin Lakes below. Immediately afterward, bear right and climb through the Noisy Creek notch, entering a broad talus apron above Noisy Creek. Beargrass and views of the Flathead Valley accompany your descent back to the junction you passed upon leaving the trailhead. Here, at 9.3 miles, bear right to complete your loop.

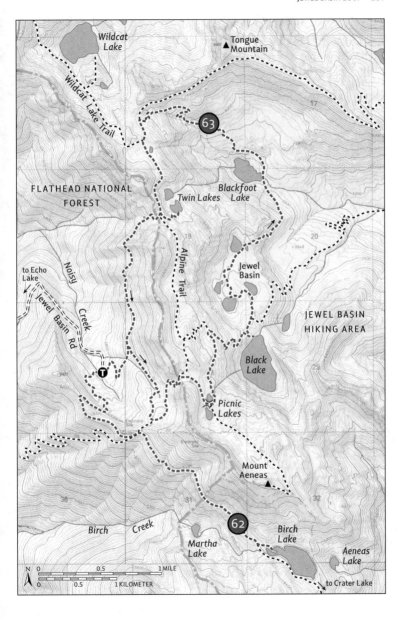

CROWN OF THE CONTINENT

For some two hundred fifty miles in western Montana and Alberta, the Northern Rockies run themselves ragged in a final swell of razor-edge peaks and steep, shadowed glacial cirques. The mountains here form the northern terminus of the Continental Divide, the hydrological high point that separates the waters that drain into the Pacific Ocean from those that drain into the Atlantic and, farther north, the Arctic. The 18-million-acre area known as the Crown of the Continent embraces Waterton-Glacier International Peace Park, the Bob Marshall Wilderness Complex, and the headwaters of three of North America's great rivers of the Pacific, Atlantic, and Hudson Bay.

Sacred to the Blackfeet Indians for millenia, this landscape is also essential to the survival of wildlife found nowhere else on the continent, from grizzly bear and wolverine to woodland caribou; it's the largest intact ecosystem in the United States. Climate change and suburban sprawl claw at the edges of the Crown of the Continent. But a diverse group of stakeholders, from cattle ranchers to conservationists, tribal members to dyed-in-the-wool wheat farmers, have come together to protect this special place. Set foot in Glacier National Park, the Missions, the Swans, or the Whitefish Range and you will have benefitted from efforts to conserve the Crown.

Diving into Hall Lake

64 Hall Lake

RATING/ DIFFICULTY	ROUNDTRIP	ELEV GAIN/ HIGH POINT	SEASON
****/4	8 miles	2570 feet/ 5310 feet	June–Oct

Map: USGS Swan Lake; **Contact:** Flathead National Forest, Swan Lake Ranger District; **Note:** Open to horses and bicycles; **GPS:** 47.9363°, -113.8240°

Hemmed in by high ridges, Hall Lake harbors eager trout that taunt anglers on its tightly forested shore. Although the steep-walled, north-south basin limits big-mountain views, the high valley side slopes offer abundant alpine wildflowers in the rocky outcroppings of the Swan Crest. Owing to its relatively low-elevation destination, Hall Lake makes a great early-season high-country trek.

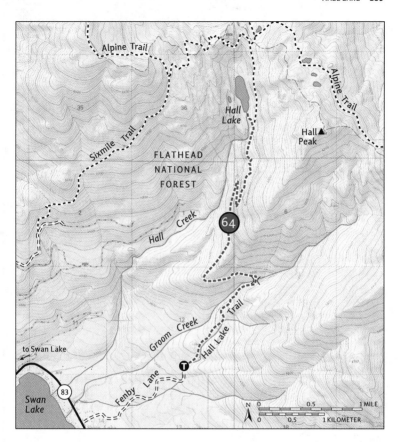

GETTING THERE

From Montana Highway 83 in the community of Swan Lake (between mileposts 71 and 72), turn east on Fenby Lane. Pass the Laughing Horse Lodge, and proceed 1.1 miles to the trailhead (elev. 3530 feet).

ON THE TRAIL

Hall Lake Trail 61 immediately retreats into the lush reach of the Groom Creek drainage, paper birch and pathfinder—so named because their overturned leaves indicate whether someone or something has brushed by—flanking the trail. Once open to trailbikes, the trail to Hall Lake was closed to motors to protect prime grizzly habitat, although it still lacks the wilderness designation it deserves. At 1.2 miles (elev. 4140 feet) cross the creek on a log jam with a rope "handhold"; continuing through dense forest, climb out of the Groom Creek drainage, over a shallow toe ridge, and onto a steep sidehill above Hall Creek.

Fly-casting for panfish in Bond Lake

Now shadowing Hall Creek upstream, switchback across talus slopes and under Douglas-firs; the occasional outcroppings provide views of Swan Lake to the west and the slopes of pyramidal Hall Peak to the north. Small huckleberries share space with thimbleberries alongside the trail, but they lack the sweet taste of high-elevation specimens.

Just shy of 4 miles (elev. 5270 feet), bear left at a junction (the way right climbs a mile to the Swan Crest) and elbow aside thick brush for a quarter mile to reach the log-jammed lake outlet.

Westslope cutthroat trout trawl the turquoise hue of Hall Lake, but, aside from one campsite, there's little open ground here; it's one of very few trails in the region with no anglers' trail around the shore. A little bushwhacking on the rocky bench above the west shore will reveal a few choice swimming spots, where a shallow shoreline quickly gives way to rock drop-offs. Anglers will need a short backcast to work this one.

EXTENDING YOUR TRIP
Hall Lake sits just below Alpine Trail 7, which runs the length of the northern Swan Crest. Backpackers with multiple vehicles could easily connect an open loop between Hall Lake and Bond and Trinkus Lakes to the south.

65 Bond and Trinkus Lakes

RATING/ DIFFICULTY	ROUNDTRIP	ELEV GAIN/ HIGH POINT	SEASON
****/4	11.4 miles	3300 feet/ 6130 feet	July–Oct

Maps: USGS Swan Lake, MT; USGS Connor Creek, MT; **Contact:** Flathead National Forest, Swan Lake Ranger District; **Note:** Open to horses and bicycles; **GPS:** 47.9175°, -113.8163°

Border Bond Creek's meander to the green waters of Bond and Trinkus Lakes, tucked high on the meadowed slopes of the Swan Crest. You're likely to encounter a steady stream of pack strings on the way to Bond Lake, owing to its fishing-

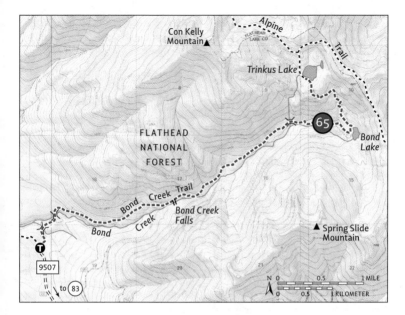

friendly reputation. But abundant huckleber-
ries and the far-quieter shores of Trinkus Lake
should persuade hikers.

GETTING THERE

Two miles south of Swan Lake on Montana Highway 83 (milepost 70), immediately south of the lower Bond-Trinkus trailhead, turn east onto Lost Creek Road (Forest Road 680). Drive 1.5 miles, then bear left onto FR 9507, continuing for 0.7 mile to the road's end and trailhead (elev. 3350 feet). The large parking area can accommodate a half dozen vehicles.

ON THE TRAIL

From the trailhead, immediately join Bond Creek Trail 21 as it comes in from the left. In a dappled larch, hemlock, and birch forest, cross a small bridged stream and, at 0.5 mile (elev. 3340 feet), a long bridge over Bond Creek.

The trail, nearly level to this point, sets to work climbing in earnest, the well-constructed tread ably withstanding the demands of hordes of horse hooves en route to fishing and hunting camps on Bond Lake.

At 1.9 mile (elev. 3960 feet), reach a short side trail to Bond Creek Falls, which tumbles 20 feet through a narrow crack before disappearing into the timber. Continue ascending, the sounds of busy Bond Creek a constant accompaniment to the airy forest. Huckleberries begin flanking the trail, which may stall forward progress.

The trail crosses a small, easily hoppable rivulet before traversing the first of several talus incursions. Brushy meadows of head-high hollyhock and hyssop replace thick tree canopy. At 3.8 miles (elev. 5000 feet), cross a wooden footbridge, and at 4.6 miles (elev. 5440 feet) reach the north shore of Bond Lake, which sits in a slide-scoured cirque. The northwest shore of the lake offers horse-trampled campsites amid a lush meadow of high fireweed, false hellebore, fool's huckleberry, and cow parsnip. Fish dimple the lake's surface.

To reach Trinkus Lake, continue on the trail as it retreats northward into a lush creek drainage. Ascend a series of switchbacks under the shady bower of cow parsnip, then reach level ground just above Trinkus Lake. A quick descent reaches its wooded south shore at 5.7 miles (elev. 6050 feet).

Its wind-driven surface a kaleidoscope of color reflecting off the steep brush fields above, Trinkus Lake occupies a high hanging valley just below the flowered defile of the Swan Crest. Conservationists (myself included) would like to see this portion of the Swan Crest set aside as wilderness.

EXTENDING YOUR TRIP
Trinkus Lake makes an easy staging point for trips on the Swan Crest, which runs just above the lake. Backpackers with multiple

shuttles could easily make an open-loop trip connecting this hike with Hall Lake to the north.

66 Inspiration Point

RATING/ DIFFICULTY	ROUNDTRIP	ELEV GAIN/ HIGH POINT	SEASON
****/5	10.8 miles	3520 feet/ 7628 feet	Late June– early Oct

Map: USGS Thunderbolt Mountain, MT; **Contact:** Flathead National Forest, Swan Lake Ranger District; **Note:** Open to horses and bicycles; **GPS:** 47.7864°, -113.7334°

Survey the snow-covered shoulders of Swan Peak from this former lookout site on the tundra-clad hummocks of the Swan Crest. Although you may be inspired to choose this hike for its high-elevation trailhead, be warned: Inspiration Point manages to sneak in the Swan Range climbing quota between its beginning and end.

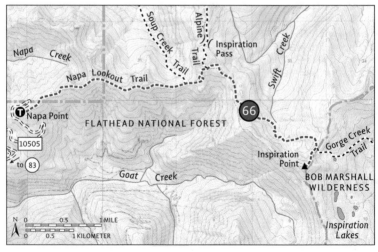

GETTING THERE

From Montana Highway 83, 13 miles south of Swan Lake (between mileposts 58 and 59), turn left (east) onto Goat Creek Road (Forest Road 554). Drive 3.6 miles, keeping left at a signed junction at 1.6 miles, then turn left onto Napa Point Road (FR 554). Continue 1 mile, then turn right onto FR 10505 and drive 6.9 switchbacking, occasionally rough miles to the road's end at Napa Point and trailhead (elev. 6423 feet).

ON THE TRAIL

Eschewing the stream-bottom beginnings of many Swan Range hikes, the hike to Inspiration Point starts and ends high. But don't be fooled: this hike gains—and loses, and gains again—several times its share of elevation.

From the wooded Napa Lookout Trail 31 entrance, a half mile of hiking leaves thick fir forest for a tundra-covered subsidiary ridge of the Swan Crest. Spangling the slopes is the early-summer color of glacier lilies, which begin blooming before the snow cover melts completely. To the south, the pyramidal form of Swan Peak soars over the surrounding ridgeline. Climb steeply to just below the crest of the ridge, then descend into the head of a shallow draw. From here, make a second, shallower climb before dropping sharply into a wooded saddle. Occasional openings in the trees reveal a waterfall to the north.

Begin climbing out of the saddle, and at 2.5 miles (elev. 6540 feet), bear right at a junction with a trail climbing out of the Soup Creek drainage. Continue climbing in steep, spruce-shaded forest to the forested defile of Inspiration Pass at 2.9 miles (elev. 6960 feet). Here the trail meets the Alpine Trail, which runs north-south; turn right (south) and continue through low

The hike to Inspiration Point traverses miles of alpine tundra.

subalpine parkland. The trail gradually slips off the ridgeline into Swift Creek drainage, the talus-strewn slopes of Inspiration Point now in view. Descend steep, rocky tread into old-growth spruce at the base of the avalanche-scraped north face of Inspiration Point; snow lingers here well into summer.

Ascend several switchbacks to a series of flat benches on Inspiration Point's shoulder, and at 4.5 miles (elev. 7000 feet), reach a marked trail junction. The progressively rougher-looking trail to Gorge Creek heads left; instead, take the Inspiration Point Trail as it ascends a wooded saddle and scattered snags, flirting with Inspiration Point's summit as it circles first to the south face before mounting the last summit bench on its east face at 5.4 miles.

A former lookout site, 7628-foot Inspiration Point surveys the western Bob Marshall Wilderness and the White River Syncline to the east. Below, the Inspiration Lakes might provide the impetus for an overnight trip. You may just be inspired to voice your support for wilderness efforts for this area, which deserves to be added to the neighboring Bob Marshall Wilderness Complex.

EXTENDING YOUR TRIP

Inspiration Pass is the ingress for a south-to-north ridge run along the Alpine Trail, which continues all the way to Columbia Mountain past charming wooded tarns and flower-draped slopes.

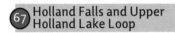

67 Holland Falls and Upper Holland Lake Loop

Holland Falls

RATING/ DIFFICULTY	ROUNDTRIP	ELEV GAIN/ HIGH POINT	SEASON
****/2	3 miles	950 feet/ 4440 feet	July–Oct

Upper Holland Lake

RATING/ DIFFICULTY	LOOP	ELEV GAIN/ HIGH POINT	SEASON
*****/5	12.1 miles	3970 feet/ 7440 feet	July–Oct

Map: USGS Holland Lake, MT; **Contact:** Flathead National Forest, Swan Lake Ranger District; **Note:** Open to horses and bicycles; **GPS:** 47.4529°, -113.6033°

The fjord-like shoreline of Holland Lake in the Seeley-Swan Valley north of Missoula is the departure point for a family-friendly waterfall hike just above the popular lake, or a classic 12-mile loop high into the Swan Crest, where Upper Holland Lake is but one of a panoply of subalpine pools high on the crest.

GETTING THERE

From Montana Highway 83 about 20 miles north of Seeley Lake (just past milepost 35), turn east on Holland Lake Road. Drive this good gravel road 3.9 miles, past the Holland Lake day-use area and Holland Lake Lodge, to the road's end and trailhead (elev. 4060 feet). Privy available.

ON THE TRAIL

Hiking through open ponderosa forest on the wide, boot- and hoof-beaten Holland Falls Trail 416, immediately come to a signed junction. Bear right for Holland Falls, left for Upper Holland Lake.

Holland Falls

Tracing the pine-shaded shoreline of Holland Lake, the trail gains little elevation as it goes past several inlets and bays along the lake. About a mile in (elev. 4140 feet), round the head of the lake and enter an aspen-choked gully, and cross a brook on a small bridge. Crossing broad, aspen-studded talus incursions, begin climbing in earnest as the trail curves high above the marshy inlet of the lake before reaching the falls at 1.5 miles (elev. 4400 feet).

Holland Falls plunges some thirty feet into a broad basin, where large rocks and storm-felled logs provide picnic perches. A tangle of user-created paths climb the steep walls of the catch-basin, but spray from the falls and loose soil make the going treacherous. Several rock outcroppings afford aerial views of the lake, where you may see osprey clawing cutthroat out of the lake's blue depths.

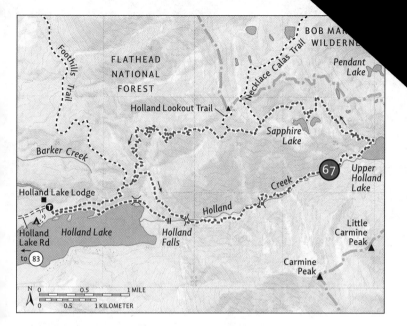

Upper Holland Lake Loop

From the junction with the falls trail, begin climbing through thick, view-scarce forest, passing a junction at 1.2 miles with the East Foothills Trail and shortly after a junction with the Holland Lookout Trail (elev. 4690 feet). Keep right at both junctions; you will return from the way to the left on the latter, which climbs unrelentingly to Holland Lookout.

Curving around the talus slopes at the head of Holland Lake, cross a log bridge over Holland Creek above a small rushing cascade at 2.3 miles (elev. 4680 feet). Immediately after, bear left at unsigned junction by a pretty plunge pool (the trail to the right is an alternate route that climbs higher above the creek drainage). Continuing upstream of the falls, parallel the crooks and cascades of Holland Creek; backward glances reveal

Holland Lake below and the snow-clad panorama of the Mission Mountains to the west.

In less than a mile, rejoin the alternate trail just before crossing a footbridge to the north side of the creek (elev. 5630 feet). Entering oft-saturated subalpine bottomland, reach the horse-trampled camps at Upper Holland Lake at 5.1 miles (elev. 6170 feet).

Upper Holland Lake is a miniature version of its low-elevation kin, a wooded pool with a moose-friendly marsh at the inlet. But the star is Sapphire Lake, actually a pair of pretty infinity-pool tarns perched on stacked bedrock benches a mile or so beyond Upper Holland Lake. To reach them, bear left at a junction just past the campsites nestled in a rock bench. Begin climbing, now in hummocky subalpine parkland, to the signed junction for the Sapphire Lakes spur trail at

Holland Falls mists hikers in its broad plunge pool.

6.5 miles (elev. 7060 feet). Head left and, in a few hundred feet, reach the high bedrock bowl of the upper Sapphire Lake.

The lakes mirror the layer-cake pyramid of Little Carmine Peak directly across the Holland Creek drainage; to the east unfurl the endless bastions of the Bob Marshall Wilderness. A few tent sites flank these infinity-pool jewels, which make much more desirable backpacking destinations than Upper Holland Lake.

To continue the loop, head back to the main trail, which angles west across the beargrass-lined hanging valley above the upper lake. Upon reaching a signed junction in a rocky draw, head uphill; a handful of switchbacks will deposit you in a narrow notch in the rock. The view upon stepping through this grass-floored defile stuns, with Holland Lake below and the jagged roof of the Missions beyond.

From this point at 7.6 miles (elev. 7440 feet), settle into a series of steep switchbacks

that descend, first through an elk-friendly forest of fire-killed snags, and then into thick, featureless forest with limited views of Holland Lake. At 10.7 miles, upon reaching the junction you passed earlier, bear right to return to the trailhead.

A popular horse-packing portal into the Bob Marshall Wilderness, the Upper Holland Lake loop can get crowded on summer weekends; plan on departing the trailhead early to ensure a desirable tent spot. Finish up your trip with a meal at the log-cabin grandeur of Holland Lake Lodge.

68 Morrell Falls

RATING/ DIFFICULTY	ROUNDTRIP	ELEV GAIN/ HIGH POINT	SEASON
****/3	5.4 miles	990 feet/ 4930 feet	May–Oct

Map: USGS Morrell Lake, MT; **Contact:** Lolo National Forest, Seeley Lake Ranger District;

Note: Open to horses and bicycles; **GPS:** 47.2736°, -113.4516°

🚶 🐴 🚲 *Thundering sixty feet into a flat graveled basin, Morrell Falls makes a fine destination for children and inexperienced hikers. Its easy grade and compelling destination mean Morrell Falls is not a place of solitude, but it's a peaceful hike nonetheless, through low-elevation forested bottomland and the grassy swales of several moose- and mosquito-friendly lakes.*

A woodpecker forages in the forest surrounding Morrell Falls.

GETTING THERE

At the north end of the town of Seeley Lake, turn east off Montana Highway 83 onto Morrell Creek Road (Forest Road 477). Drive 1.1 miles, then bear left onto FR 4353. Continue 5.9 miles, then turn right onto FR 4381. Cross the bridge, then bear left onto FR 4364, and continue 0.6 mile to the road's end and large trailhead (elev. 4750 feet). Privy available.

ON THE TRAIL

On the wide, nearly level tread of Morrell Falls Trail 30, enter an open lodgepole and fir forest. Low-growing plants—kinnikinnick, pipsissewa, beargrass, and grouseberry—form the understory. After a mile of level hiking, commence a quarter-mile climb; here, the forest character changes, old lightning-scarred larch replacing orderly rows of lodgepole. The canopy opens up, revealing scattered views of the sheer sedimentary face of Crescent Mountain to the right.

At 2 miles (elev. 4850 feet) pass an unnamed lake, its shallow, sandy shores a magnet for moose and mallards. Just past its outlet, bear right at a junction (to the left is Morrell Creek Trail), and, less than a quarter mile later, reach Morrell Lake (elev. 4850 feet). Grass shores encircle Morrell Lake,

which has several campsites (complete with fire grates) around its main body and subsidiary pools. Continue left past the lake into a lush creek drainage of thimbleberry and alder, and cross a large bridge at 2.4 miles (elev. 4840 feet). The trail curves to the east, passing a steep side trail to the upper falls and Grizzly Basin to the left, before running out in a broad gravel bar at the base of Morrell Falls at 2.7 miles (elev. 4920 feet).

Plunging some sixty feet down a sheer rock face, Morrell Falls roars at the height of snowmelt, filling its graveled catch-basin with spray. Late in the summer, Morrell mellows, its graceful cascades revealing the sculpted form of the rock underneath.

69 Pyramid Lake

RATING/ DIFFICULTY	ROUNDTRIP	ELEV GAIN/ HIGH POINT	SEASON
****/4	10.6 miles	2770 feet/ 7000 feet	Mid-June– Oct

Maps: USGS Morell Lake, MT; USGS Crimson Peak, MT; **Contact:** Lolo National Forest,

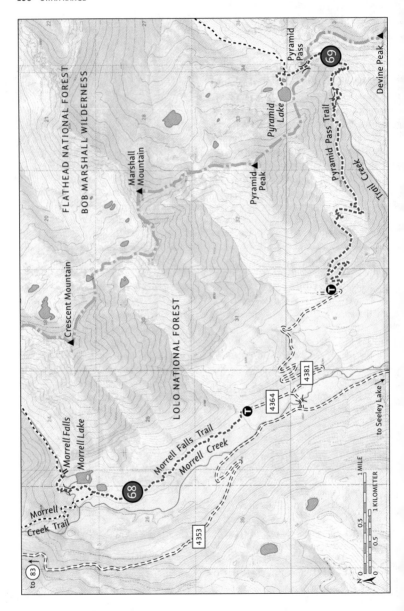

FLATHEAD NATIONAL FOREST

BOB MARSHALL WILDERNESS

LOLO NATIONAL FOREST

Crescent Mountain

Marshall Mountain

Pyramid Peak

Pyramid Pass

Pyramid Lake

Devine Peak

Pyramid Pass Trail

Trail Creek

69

4381

4364

to Seeley Lake

Morrell Falls

Morrell Lake

Morrell Falls Trail

Morrell Creek

Morrell Creek Trail

68

4353

to 83

N

0   0.5   1 MILE

0   0.5   1 KILOMETER

A bedrock bench above Pyramid Lake

Seeley Lake Ranger District; **Notes:** Wilderness rules apply. Open to horses; **GPS:** 47.2602°, -113.4254°

![icons] *A popular portal for pack trains headed into the southern interior of the Bob Marshall Wilderness Complex, Pyramid Lake also offers easily accessible high-country fare for hikers. Using a system of old roadbeds, the trail never exceeds a moderate grade as it climbs through second-growth timber and tumbling subalpine meadows with views of the Seeley Lake drainage and the snow-girded Missions beyond.*

GETTING THERE

At the north end of the town of Seeley Lake, turn east off Montana Highway 83 onto Morrell Creek Road (Forest Road 477). Drive 1.1 miles, then bear left onto FR 4353. Continue 5.9 miles, then turn right onto FR 4381. Continue 3 miles to the large trailhead loop (elev. 5240 feet). Privy available.

ON THE TRAIL

From the large Pyramid Pass Trail parking area, follow a disused roadbed through second growth Douglas-fir and larch, the latter particularly striking during October—when your hunting-season attire should be as bright as the larch needles. The route heads south before bending back into a drainage thickly timbered with second growth, kinnikinnick draped over old saw-cut stumps. Despite getting a pounding from a parade of hooves, especially during hunting season, the dry, well-drained slopes never get particularly muddy.

Numerous outfitters' trails join the main route as it steadily works its way uphill. The trail receives a particularly well-used outfitters' trail from the north on a switchback before ascending more steeply.

At 1.5 miles (elev. 5710 feet), round a bend and enter the base of a large meadow, above which sit the rounded summits and meadowy avalanche slopes of Pyramid Peak and its neighbors. Ascend to the first

BOB MARSHALL, WILDERNESS WARRIOR

The Big Sky country of Montana tends to breed big characters. And in the early 1900s, an entire era of characters, when Teddy Roosevelt clashed with the titans of industry, Bob Marshall made big strides—his own, and for the preservation of wilderness.

A scientist with a PhD in plant physiology, Marshall became independently wealthy after the death of his father in 1929. Rather than embrace the socialite scene, he self-funded trips to Alaska and other primeval areas. He developed a reputation as a mileage-chewing hiker: 50-mile days were typical for Marshall, and sojourns of 70 miles were not unheard of—in rugged country where trails were scarce and miles were hard-earned.

It was during these walks that Marshall began to conceive of a way to protect "primitive" or "wilderness" areas, places where a person "could spend at least a week or two of travel in them without crossing his own tracks." In 1935, Marshall founded the Wilderness Society, and, as head of recreation management of the Forest Service under Franklin D. Roosevelt, directed the setting aside of some five million acres for "primitive areas."

Marshall died young, of heart failure, in 1939. But two years later, Congress rewarded his efforts with the designation of the Bob Marshall Wilderness area. And twenty-five years later, in large part stemming from Marshall's efforts with the Wilderness Society, Congress passed the Wilderness Act.

Today, hikers need not hike the same number of miles to follow in Bob Marshall's footsteps; enjoying our public lands responsibly and spreading the word of their intrinsic worth continues his legacy.

of several overlooks, framed by old-growth Douglas-fir, of the Trail Creek drainage and Seeley Lake valley below.

The trail follows a steep old skid road for a short time before assuming the guise of true singletrack as it bears east across the flower-filled south-facing slope of the Trail Creek Valley. Enter the high hanging basin of Trail Creek as the trail crosses the first of several shallow fords of the creek at 3.5 miles (elev. 6420 feet).

Switchbacking out of the hanging valley through snow-worn subalpine firs, gain a bedrock ledge at 4.5 miles (elev. 6910 feet) in which sits a nameless, trout-stocked tarn at the base of a broad talus apron. Numerous outfitters' camps occupy the timbered

shore. Leaving the tarn, cross Pyramid Pass—a wooded cleft in the bedrock of the Swan Crest and the high point of this hike—and enter the Bob Marshall Wilderness at 4.8 miles (elev. 7000 feet).

As the main trail descends into dense forest, a braid of unsigned spurs take off left; take one, passing a reedy mosquito incubator of a pond before reaching Pyramid Lake at 5.3 miles (elev. 6930 feet). Pyramidal subalpine trees surround much of the shoreline, but the lake doesn't feel closed in, possibly because Pyramid Peak's exfoliated slopes sit so close. Well-used campsites perch on low rocks on the southwest shore of the lake, which recedes quite dramatically late in the season.

Opposite: *Still Hemlock Lake mirrors clouds and fall colors.*

mission mountains

East-Side Mission Mountains

The Mission Mountains are a familiar sight to travelers between Missoula and Flathead Lake: the serrated, snow-draped peaks, crowned by 9280-foot McDonald Peak and its dozen or so neighbors in the 9000-foot club, look impassable. But the Missions boast some of the most easily rewarding high-country day hiking in the Northwest. Short, shallow-grade trails access hundreds of high-elevation tarns—one of the highest densities of alpine lakes in the Northern Rockies. The centerpiece of the Mission Mountains is the nearly 75,000-acre Mission Mountains Wilderness on the east side of the range, overlooking the Seeley-Swan Valley. So, set up camp down low and make a long-weekend goal for a handful—or more—of high-mountain lakes. Missions accepted?

70 Cold Lakes

RATING/ DIFFICULTY	ROUNDTRIP	ELEV GAIN/ HIGH POINT	SEASON
****/3	5 miles	1500 feet/ 5890 feet	Mid-June– Oct

The Mission Crest caps Lower Cold Lake.

Maps: USGS Piper-Crow Pass, MT; USGS Peck Lake, MT; **Contact:** Flathead National Forest, Swan Lake Ranger District; **Notes:** Wilderness rules apply. Camping prohibited within a quarter mile of either lake; **GPS:** 47.5601°, -113.8560°

The Cold Lakes are among the hottest destinations in the Missions, but hikers averse to hordes should still make the trek. Cold Lakes initially gained their popularity from the harvest of cutthroat trout when they spawned in the stream between the two lakes. It's still a social trek: toddler-toting picnickers share the trail with anglers for a hike through shade-raked old-growth forest.

GETTING THERE

From Montana Highway 83, 4 miles north of Condon (between mileposts 46 and 47), turn left (west) onto Cold Creek Road (Forest Road 903). Continue for 2.9 miles, then bear right on FR 9568. Drive 3 miles, then turn left on FR 9599. Continue on this sometimes rocky road 1.6 miles to its end and the trailhead (elev. 5120 feet). Privy available.

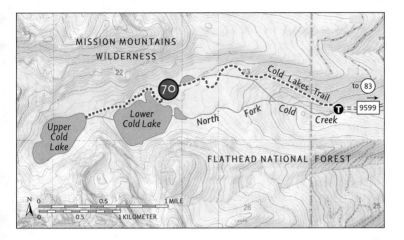

ON THE TRAIL

Cold Lakes Trail 121 parallels North Fork Cold Creek much of its length, widely spaced spruce casting dappled shadows on its shallow depths. Quickly entering the Mission Mountains Wilderness, continue upstream on the north side of the creek before making a sole-wetting crossing at 1.1 miles (elev. 5730 feet). On the south side of the creek, the trail levels out as it passes a shallow pool in the marshy environs of Lower Cold Lake's outlet.

At 1.7 miles (elev. 5750 feet), reach the lowermost lake. Heavy undergrowth limits shoreline access except at the lower lake's outlet. Of the two Cold Lakes, the upper is much prettier for sitting closer to the heavily glaciated cirques of the Missions peaks. No official trail connects Lower and Upper Cold Lakes, but hikers keen on clambering over logs on a rough-hewn user path can easily reach the upper lake; plan on taking as long to go the half mile from the lower to upper lake as it takes to travel from the trailhead to the lower lake.

Upper Cold Lake sits in a steep-walled cirque. Wave-deposited logs welter in the

chilly water; swimming options are few. Owing to a history of heavy use, the Forest Service has prohibited camping within a quarter mile of either lake; even day users should be mindful of the decades-long restoration efforts in the heavily denuded user sites. With few overnight options in the dense, deadfall-clogged understory, the Cold Lakes are better suited to a family picnic than a backpacking trip.

71 Glacier Lake and Heart and Crescent Lakes

Glacier Lake

RATING/ DIFFICULTY	ROUNDTRIP	ELEV GAIN/ HIGH POINT	SEASON
*****/3	3.2 miles	580 feet/ 5280 feet	Mid-June– Oct

Heart and Crescent Lakes

RATING/ DIFFICULTY	ROUNDTRIP	ELEV GAIN/ HIGH POINT	SEASON
*****/4	7.9 miles	1820 feet/ 6190 feet	Mid-June– Oct

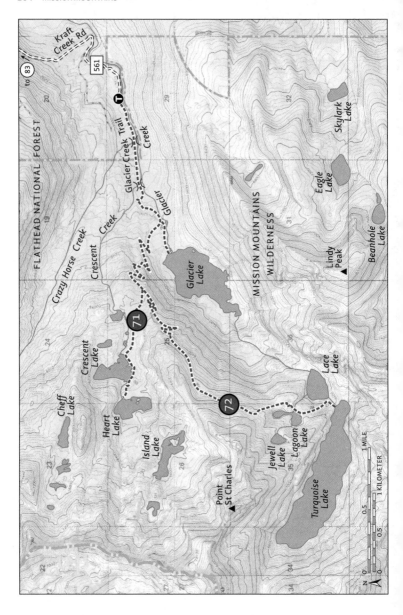

Maps: USGS Hemlock Lake, MT; USGS Lake Marshall, MT; **Contact:** Flathead National Forest, Swan Lake Ranger District; **Notes:** Wilderness rules apply. Camping prohibited within 0.25 mile of Glacier Lake. Open to horses; **GPS:** 47.3815°, -113.7933°

The Glacier Creek portal epitomizes the appeal of hiking in the Mission Mountains Wilderness: pleasant old-growth forest, well-maintained never-too-steep trails, and spectacular shoreline destinations that belie their ease of access. Few regions of the Northwest offer so many options for rewarding done-in-a-day outings. And few Missions hikes get as many done-in-a-day visitors as Glacier Lake. But most choose the shorter hike to Glacier Lake, meaning hikers en route to Heart and Crescent Lakes have little competition.

GETTING THERE

From Montana Highway 83, 13 miles south of Condon (between mileposts 37 and 38), turn right (west) onto Kraft Creek Road (Forest Road 561). Continue 11.6 miles on good, although washboarded, gravel to the road's end and trailhead (elev. 4850 feet). The large parking area can accommodate more than a dozen vehicles. Privy available.

ON THE TRAIL

Maintaining a shallow grade its entire length, Glacier Creek Trail 690 ambles streamside through an open old-growth forest of Engelmann spruce and Douglas-fir; the airy canopy allows plenty of fruit-sweetening light to reach the huckleberry shrubs below. At 0.4 mile (elev. 4910 feet) cross Crazy Horse Creek on a sturdy footbridge. Enter the wilderness, then make a quick series of creek crossings at 0.8 mile (elev. 5020 feet)

on split-log spans. At 1.3 miles, reach a junction: left goes to Glacier Lake; right goes to Heart and Crescent Lakes, and Turquoise Lake (see Hike 72).

Glacier Lake

For Glacier Lake, bear left, dipping into a boggy draw (trees screen a small pond to the left). Make a brief climb over a rocky moraine to reach the shore of Glacier Lake at 1.6 miles (elev. 5260 feet).

Glacier Lake occupies a vast cirque, the smooth granite shelves at the far end sheltering a handful of high tarns. To the left, Lindy Peak and Daughter-of-the-Sun Mountain loom. Logs jamming the shore make swimming in Glacier's cold, snow-stoked waters difficult.

As with Cold Lakes (Hike 70), the Forest Service prohibits camping here within a quarter mile of the shore, owing to a history of heavy use. No matter: the hike to Glacier Lake is better suited to a day of picnicking than to a backpacking trip.

Crescent and Heart Lakes

From the junction just before Glacier Lake, bear right; switchbacks soon leave level ground—and crowds—behind as they make their way up the spruce-adorned south face of Glacier Lake's cirque. Huckleberries grow in abundance in this airy forest.

At 1.5 miles from the junction to Glacier Lake, reach a second junction (elev. 5933 feet), this one splitting off the trail to Turquoise Lake. Keep right, contouring around the north side of the finger ridge separating the Glacier and Crescent Creek drainages. Above the shaded, boggy bottomlands of Crescent Creek's shallow outlet ponds, keep an eye out for moose. No need to look for mosquitoes here; they'll find you.

At 2.1 miles from the junction to Glacier Lake, reach the shore of Crescent Lake (elev. 6080 feet). Subalpine fir trace the rocky axe-head silhouette of the lake, and several high rock perches encourage cannonballing. A spacious tent site just across the outlet fills up quickly; latecomers can find cramped campsites on the peninsula poking into Crescent's middle.

Heart Lake lies another half mile beyond Crescent, its island-dotted waters dutifully reflecting the paired cirques of Point St. Charles above. One of the area's better backcountry tent sites lies across the raucous outlet stream under a rocky shelf.

72 Turquoise Lake

RATING/ DIFFICULTY	ROUNDTRIP	ELEV GAIN/ HIGH POINT	SEASON
*****/5	11.6 miles	2880 feet/ 6880 feet	Late June–Oct

Maps: USGS Hemlock Lake, MT; USGS Lake Marshall, MT; **Contact:** Flathead National Forest, Swan Lake Ranger District; **Notes:** Wilderness rules apply. Open to horses; **GPS:** 47.3815°, -113.7933°

Well above the masses at Glacier Lake's granite shores, the milelong Turquoise Lake hides in a high sedimentary shelf under the swooping shoulder of the Mission Divide. It's the longest, and best, hike out of the immensely popular Glacier Creek portal.

GETTING THERE
From Montana Highway 83, 13 miles south of Condon (between mileposts 37 and 38), turn right (west) onto to Kraft Creek Road (Forest Road 561). Continue 11.6 miles on good, although washboarded, gravel to the road's end and trailhead (elev. 4850 feet). The large parking area can accommodate over a dozen vehicles. Privy available.

ON THE TRAIL
Maintaining a shallow grade its entire length, Glacier Creek Trail 690 ambles streamside through an open old-growth forest of Engelmann spruce and Douglas-fir; the airy canopy allows plenty of fruit-sweetening light to reach the huckleberry shrubs below. At 0.4 mile (elev. 4910 feet) cross Crazy Horse Creek on a sturdy footbridge. Enter the wilderness, then make a quick series of creek crossings at 0.8 mile (elev. 5020 feet) on split-log spans. At 1.3 miles, reach a junction. The way left continues to Glacier Lake; bear right for Turquoise Lake.

Switchbacks soon leave level ground—and the crowds—behind as they make their way up the spruce-adorned south face of Glacier Lake's cirque. Huckleberries grow in abundance in this airy forest.

At 1.5 miles from the junction to Glacier Lake, reach a second junction (elev. 5933 feet) and bear left to Turquoise Lake. Settle in for a frustrating sidehill ascent on long, nearly level switchbacks, the Mission Divide, mirage-like, appearing to approach no closer as the trail repeatedly doubles back on itself.

After a mile or so, the trail assumes a more direct course, leaving tree cover behind for alpine tundra and scrubbed sedimentary rock. Daughter-of-the-Sun Mountain dominates the skyline before you, its diamond-tipped spires snow-covered well into summer.

Soon the tread fades as spongy snowmelt areas cede to bedrock. The route descends these bare crowns of bedrock; if in doubt here, plot a direct course toward Lagoon Lake, which pools into a bare bedrock shelf, then skirt between it and Lace Lake.

Soon, Turquoise Lake, until now hidden, comes into view, and at 5.8 miles from the trailhead (elev. 6420 feet), you reach its shore.

A picket line of Missions peaks stand guard over the expansive, wind-lapped waters of Turquoise Lake, its milelong shoreline difficult to take in from its narrow outlet. For the best views, scramble the smooth rocks above its north shore, which mirrors a swooping sedimentary ridgeline some

Fallen leaves and snow squalls mark autumn at Glacier Lake.

three thousand feet overhead: Daughter-of-the-Sun-Mountain, Panoramic Peak, Glacier Peaks, and Sunrise Glacier.

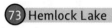

73 Hemlock Lake

RATING/ DIFFICULTY	ROUNDTRIP	ELEV GAIN/ HIGH POINT	SEASON
****/4	6.8 miles	1650 feet/ 6030 feet	June–Oct

Map: USGS Hemlock Lake, MT; **Contact:** Flathead National Forest, Swan Lake Ranger District; **Notes:** Wilderness rules apply. Open to horses; **GPS:** 47.4272°, -113.7281°

Hikers will be hard-pressed to find any hemlock on this 6.8-mile hike, which provides a unique opportunity in the typically wet Missions to travel through a recovering burn area. Overlooked by hikers in favor of Glacier Lake and its neighbors, Hemlock Lake has much to recommend it: spruce- and stone-buttressed shores, and, in season, a show of glowing larch.

GETTING THERE
From Montana Highway 83, 13 miles south of Condon (between mileposts 37 and 38), turn right (west) onto Kraft Creek Road (Forest Road 561). Continue 6.6 miles on good, although washboarded, gravel to FR 9576. Bear right and drive a bumpy 0.7 mile to the trailhead.

ON THE TRAIL
From the trailhead, Hemlock Lake Trail 407 immediately sets to work on a shadeless slope of shoulder-high larch and pioneering post-fire blooms. The 2003 burn revealed unobstructed views across the Seeley-Swan Valley to the snowcapped panorama of the Swans. Once you enter the wilderness at 1.4 miles (elev. 5700 feet), pockets of uniform lodgepole and low huckleberry provide some respite and refreshment, respectively.

The trail crosses a stream at 2 miles (elev. 5860 feet), then bends around the toe of a long timbered ridge and begins a gentle downward course paralleling Hemlock Creek. Now in a boulder-studded forest of survivor spruce, cross a bridge over Hemlock Creek followed by two smaller bridge-free crossings to reach a junction at 3.2 miles (elev. 5880 feet). Turn left; the way right traverses a long burn area to connect with the trail to North Hemlock Lake. Just shy of a quarter mile of climbing through fireweed and snags deposits hikers on the shores of Hemlock Lake.

Thick timber shelters the lake, which occupies a spot just below a slump in the crest of the Missions. A few small but

A hiker pauses above Glacier Lake en route to Turquoise Lake.

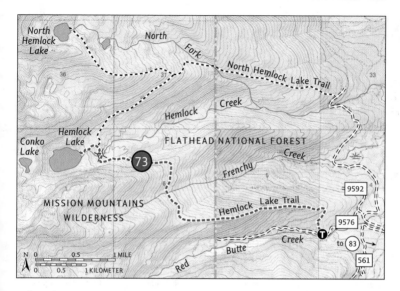

well-used tent sites occupy the lake's outlet; large bedrock boulders provide good picnic perches. Tiny Conko Lake sits on a high bedrock bench above Hemlock Lake's inlet; reaching it is more a matter of resolve than any technical climbing ability.

EXTENDING YOUR TRIP

From just below the junction to Hemlock Lake, hikers can follow the trail right for 1.3 shadeless miles to the North Hemlock Lake Trail. From here, it's another 1.5 miles of climbing through increasingly subalpine forest to tiny North Hemlock Lake, from which hikers might mount a scramble of Hemlock Point.

74 Crystal Lake

RATING/ DIFFICULTY	ROUNDTRIP	ELEV GAIN/ HIGH POINT	SEASON
****/3	4.6 miles	1680 feet/ 5830 feet	June–Oct

Map: USGS Gray Wolf Lake, MT; **Contact:** Flathead National Forest, Swan Lake Ranger District; **Notes:** Wilderness rules apply. Open to horses; **GPS:** 47.3538°, -113.7610°

Crystal Lake occupies the head of a large glacial valley upstream of the private shoreline lodges of Lindbergh Lake. While numerous routes—including a canoe portage from Lindbergh—access Crystal, the best day hike is the 2.3-mile dessert-first descent from the upper Bunyan Lake trailhead. Soak your feet on Crystal's shallow shore and save your sweat for the end.

GETTING THERE

From Montana Highway 83, 20 miles north of Seeley Lake (between mileposts 34 and 35), turn left (west) onto Lindbergh Lake Road (Forest Road 79). Continue on this well-maintained gravel road, bearing right

Fall colors reflected in the calm waters of Crystal Lake

to stay on FR 79 at 3 and 3.6 miles. From this second junction, continue 7.6 miles to the road's end and trailhead (elev. 5740 feet). The parking area accommodates a half dozen vehicles.

ON THE TRAIL

Immediately begin a gentle, quick ascent past a small clear-cut on Crystal Lake Trail 351, the young larch and fir allowing glimpses of Meadow Lake to the north. At 0.3 mile (elev. 5830 feet), crest the ridge above the Swan River and begin descending; from here, it's all downhill to the lake.

The trail showcases perhaps every tree species that grows in western Montana: gargantuan larch and ponderosa grow shoulder to shoulder with cedar and yew.

Enter the Mission Mountains Wilderness as the downhill grade begins to increase—remember you have to go back up this trail at the end. A lush understory of yew and thimbleberry encroaches on the tread as it nears the moist bottomlands below Crystal Lake. Negotiate the first in a series of split-log crossings, then reach a junction

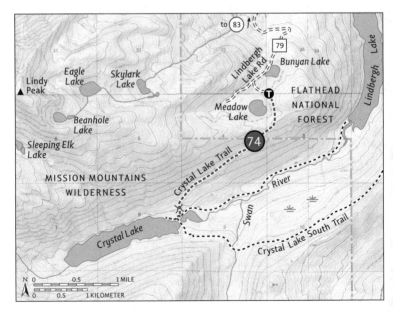

Grass and reeds ring Lake Elsina.

at 2.1 miles (elev. 4790 feet). Turn right (left traces the shaded Swan River downstream to Lindbergh Lake), and, 0.2 mile of level walking later, reach Crystal Lake at 2.3 miles (elev. 4790 feet).

Huckleberries, beargrass, and larch frame the relatively low-elevation lake. To the southwest stand the steeply tilted sedimentary summits of Sunset and Sugarloaf Peaks, a waterfall from High Park Lake above sheeting down much of the cirque's headwall. Befitting a lake that occupies a milder clime than most of its Missions neighbors, Crystal boasts a grass-lined beach with a gradual drop-off; it's ideal for foot-soaking or a post-snack float. Be sure to save energy for the post-lake haul back to up to the trailhead.

75 Lake Elsina to Lake Dinah

RATING/ DIFFICULTY	ROUNDTRIP	ELEV GAIN/ HIGH POINT	SEASON
****/3	4.4 miles	960 feet/ 6740 feet	Early July–Oct

Maps: USGS Upper Jocko Lake, MT; USGS Lake Marshall, MT; **Contact:** Lolo National Forest, Seeley Lake Ranger District; **Note:** Open to horses and bicycles; **GPS:** 47.2433°, -113.7024°

Lakes Elsina and Dinah lie just outside the Mission Mountains Wilderness, and although they lack the dramatic rock-and-ice aesthetic of the high-alpine tarns in the wilderness proper, they offer superb wildlife watching with a fraction of the crowds of their more chiseled kin.

GETTING THERE

From Montana Highway 83, 5 miles north of Seeley Lake (between mileposts 19 and 20), turn left (west) onto Boy Scout Road (Forest Road 77). Drive 0.8 mile, then turn right on Fawn Creek Road (FR 4349). Continue on this well-maintained road, bearing left at 1.2 and 1.7 miles, for 5.7 miles to Elsina Lake Road (FR 465). Turn right. Drive 5 miles, then bear left at a T-junction to stay on FR 465. Continue another 2.3 miles to the road's end and trailhead.

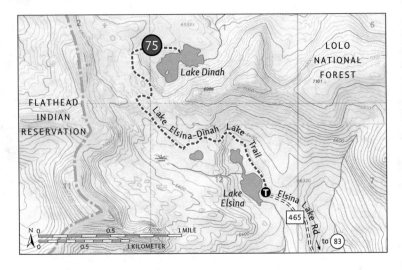

ON THE TRAIL

Beginning at the shallow, grass-fringed shores of Lake Elsina, contour around on Lake Elsina–Dinah Lake Trail 12, then make a slight climb, passing a small pond that used to connect to Elsina. Old-growth hemlock and glacial erratics make up the dense forest. Cross a couple of muddy spots, and climb a bit to crest the rocky sheaves of the Clearwater-Jocko Divide at 0.8 mile (elev. 6560 feet). Old ponds on the glacially carved shelf, some dried up, others on the way, show the life cycle of these shallow bodies of water. Low-growing rock-garden plants eke out a life amid late-lingering snow and frost-heaved stone; summer is but a brief visitor on the lee side of the Missions.

Continue northward. Old maps show a dizzying array of trails; they don't exist. Stay on the obvious path as it descends several bedrock benches past dried-up ponds, the first glimpse of Lake Dinah to the right.

At 1.4 miles, bear right, descending, sometimes steeply, down snag-covered shelves to reach the north shore of Lake Dinah at 2.2 miles (6490 feet). Surrounded by willow and sheltered by the ridge of Mount Henry and the Jocko Divide, Lake Dinah makes a reliable spot to watch moose paddle improbably fast across the frigid water.

Mission Mountains Tribal Wilderness

In 1979, the Confederated Kootenai and Salish Tribes of western Montana designated 89,500 acres along the western front of the Mission Mountains as wilderness—the only tribal-designated wilderness in the Wilderness Preservation System. The tribes manage the wilderness with the primary goal of wildlife habitat, with a large portion of the wilderness area around McDonald Peak closed to the public during the summer so that grizzlies can gorge themselves on glacier lilies and pawfuls of cutworm moth larvae. That also means that trails and roads are infrequently signed and maintained; hikers should plan on a higher level of self-reliance here than elsewhere.

In addition, portions of the wilderness are accessible only by tribal members; the public may access the remainder of the wilderness by purchasing two-day or annual recreation passes. The rewards here are immense, with glacier-crazed peaks, dense evergreen forest, and dramatic cascades comprising America's Alps. Consider it an awesome privilege to be granted access to such a special place.

76 Terrace Lake

RATING/ DIFFICULTY	ROUNDTRIP	ELEV GAIN/ HIGH POINT	SEASON
*****/4	8.6 miles	3910 feet/ 6620 feet	Mid-June– Oct

Maps: USGS Ronan, MT; USGS Piper-Crow Pass, MT; **Contact:** Confederated Salish and Kootenai Tribes (CSKT), Division of Fish, Wildlife, Recreation, and Conservation; **Notes:** Tribal Wilderness rules apply. CSKT recreation permit required for nontribal members. Open to horses; **GPS:** 47.5200°, -114.0015°

Occupying a hanging valley high on the bare sedimentary shoulders of the Mission Divide, Terrace

Playing fetch in Terrace Lake

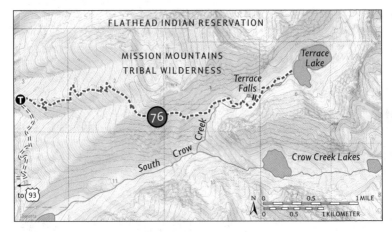

Lake reflects the steep scalloped skyline of its Missions kin. Riotous meadows and rushing streams accompany the rough-cut trail, which requires strong legs—and the drive to the trailhead may require a trip to the mechanic after you return to town.

GETTING THERE

From US Highway 93, 3 miles south of Ronan, turn east onto Mollman Pass Trail. Drive 3 miles, then turn left (north) on Hammer Dam Road, continuing north for half a mile before bearing east, off the pavement. Drive 1.6 miles northeast, following signs for Swartz Lake, to a junction. Bear left (the way right heads to Swartz Lake) and drive 2.5 miles to the trailhead (elev. 4470 feet). The increasingly steep, narrow, and rough road will test your driving ability and your relationships. Bring a spare tire—and perhaps a car you don't care for.

ON THE TRAIL

From the no-frills trailhead, climb steadily through a mixed forest of ponderosa pine, Douglas-fir, and larch. Thimbleberry and huckleberry inspire breaks on the trail, which, while steep, is a relief after the drive to the trailhead. The forest cover thins as lodgepole pine overtakes lower-elevation trees, permitting views of the steep canyon of South Crow Creek to the south and, in the distance, the steep summit block of 9820-foot McDonald Peak, the highest peak in the Mission Range.

After more than 2100 feet of elevation gained in 2.1 miles of climbing, the trail levels in open parkland meadows of lupine, pine grass, and fireweed. From here it retreats east, paralleling South Crow Creek upstream as the jagged, glacier-crazed peaks of the Mission Crest come into view. Rough tread threads through rock piles as the trail descends into a brushy valley just above the boulder-strewn confluence of several hanging valleys that pour into South Crow Creek. Indian paintbrush daubs the dry slope with color. If the trail grows faint under encroaching brush, head northeast toward the bedrock bench to the left side of the drainage upstream, which the trail vaults. From here, the path takes a hard right off the rocky bench, ducking into the trees briefly before entering a small valley at 3.5 miles (elev. 6250 feet).

Step across a shallow brook, and plunge into the brush tumbling down the steep north-facing meadow to your right. The braided trail climbs to a stream-cut above the 20-foot Terrace Falls before leveling out in thick timber. Windfall and wet seepage areas frequently threaten to swallow the trail here; maintain an upstream bearing to the lake, which is a half mile past Terrace Falls.

Terrace Lake occupies a wide glacial amphitheater, where contour lines constrict to form the high shoulders of the Missions. Nameless 8000-foot high points on the Mission Divide, bare rock shelves, reflect in the kidney-shaped contours. Trout trawl the timbered outlet of the lake, which several tent sites service. All told, Terrace Lake is one of the most striking subalpine lakes in western Montana. It's certainly worth a flat tire.

77 Mission Falls

RATING/ DIFFICULTY	ROUNDTRIP	ELEV GAIN/ HIGH POINT	SEASON
****/3	4.6 miles	1900 feet/ 4860 feet	May–Nov

Map: USGS St. Marys Lake, MT; **Contact:** Confederated Salish and Kootenai Tribes (CSKT), Division of Fish, Wildlife, Recreation, and Conservation; **Notes:** Tribal Wilderness rules apply. CSKT recreation permit required for nontribal members. Open to horses; **GPS:** 47.3241°, -113.9747°

The most popular hike in the Mission Mountains Tribal Wilderness, Mission Falls drops dramatically into a sea of evergreens above Mission Reser- *voir. From its sedimentary ledge, watch mountain goats scramble the escarpments of the Missions, and, should you dare, ascend to the lost paradise of Lucifer Lake.*

GETTING THERE

From US Highway 93 in St. Ignatius, head southeast on Mountain View Drive for 0.3 mile to Main Avenue. Turn right, and drive 0.2 mile to St. Mary's Drive, then turn left and drive 0.4 mile to St. Mary's Road. Turn left, and continue 2.9 miles, then bear left, crossing a bridge to Mission Reservoir and its campground. From the lower campground, continue 2.5 increasingly rough miles around the north side of the lake on Mission Dam Road to the road's end and trailhead (elev. 3560 feet).

ON THE TRAIL

From the trailhead, proceed upstream along Mission Creek, which sluices through a narrow bedrock shelf en route to the Mission Reservoir below. Cedar and hemlock shade the trail as it climbs away from the creek. Mossy rock gardens colored with purple camas flowers begin to mingle with the mid-elevation forest, the trail soon reaching a steep, rocky corridor, at the crest of which is a must-see side path to a viewpoint of Elizabeth Falls. Continue upstream, crossing a dry creek cobble under towering cedars and scattered larch before mounting a brief, stiff climb that opens up to views down valley of the National Bison Range and Camas Prairie to the west.

Soon, Mission Creek, absent for the last mile, comes back into view and earshot as the trail commences a steep, at times stressful, sidehill climb on decomposing tread high above the watercourse. Mountain goats, frequently seen scrambling among

A mountain goat makes easy work of the rocks above Mission Falls.

the waterfalls that streak the steep south face of the valley, make it look easy.

Finally, at 2.3 miles (elev. 4680 feet), the narrow tread reaches Mission Falls. Here, Mission Creek squeezes through a steep-sided canyon before plunging some hundred feet off a sheer sedimentary bench. Mission Falls is not the dramatic horsetail cascade visible from the Flathead Valley; that's Elizabeth Falls, which plunges into a pool immediately upstream. Nonetheless, Mission Falls demands respect;

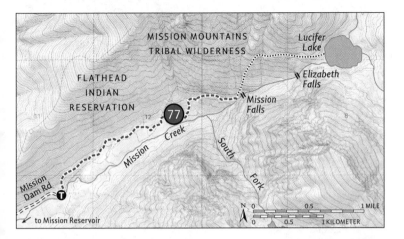

hikers have died here from wading out into the shallow pools and slipping on the algae-slimed rocks. The surrounding wilderness demands respect, too; the Confederated Salish and Kootenai Tribes have graciously allowed the general public to recreate here, and only through courteous use will that privilege continue.

EXTENDING YOUR TRIP
From the falls, a steep, brush-obscured climbers' path tacks on some 1800 feet in 1.5 miles to reach the subalpine shores of Lucifer Lake, which mirror the imposing slab of Mountaineer Peak to the east. The descent into hell is easy—so said Virgil—but the ascent to Lucifer is not; in many places, you will be hauling yourself up by roots and branches.

78 Lost Sheep Lake

RATING/ DIFFICULTY	ROUNDTRIP	ELEV GAIN/ HIGH POINT	SEASON
****/5	7.8 miles	2220 feet/ 6440 feet	June–Oct

Maps: USGS Gray Wolf Lake, MT; USGS Belmore Sloughs, MT; **Contact:** Confederated Salish and Kootenai Tribes (CSKT), Division of Fish, Wildlife, Recreation, and Conservation; **Notes:** Tribal Wilderness rules apply. CSKT recreation permit required for nontribal members. Open to horses; **GPS:** 47.2326°, -113.8015°

Hike to a high, hidden lake above the straight, shaded banks of the North Fork Jocko River on the southern edge of the Mission Mountains Tribal Wilderness. Despite its proximity to Missoula, Lost Sheep Lake sees far fewer visitors than equivalent lakes in the area.

GETTING THERE
From US Highway 93 on the south end of Arlee, turn east onto Jocko River Road (Montana Highway 559). Continue 3.1 paved miles, then, leaving pavement, bear left to continue on Jocko Canyon Road. Drive 5.6 miles, then, at a Y-junction, bear left to stay on Jocko Canyon Road. Continue 5 miles, then, at a Y-intersection, bear left onto North

The full spring flow of North Fork Jocko River

Fork Jocko Road. Continue for 1.3 increasingly rough miles—a passenger vehicle can slowly navigate this road—to the road's end and trailhead (elev. 4450 feet).

ON THE TRAIL

Immediately cross a sturdy footbridge over the North Fork Jocko River just upstream of a series of rock-rimmed cascades. Continue

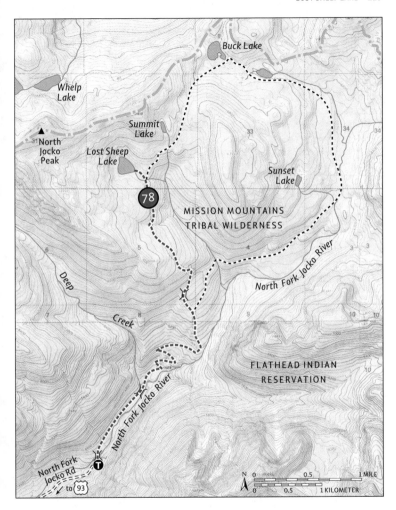

on an old roadbed as it parallels this larch-lined watercourse, crossing a footbridge over a tributary creek before reaching, at 1 mile (elev. 4700 feet), the first in a series of switchbacks that climb away from the creek. Open lodgepole forest—good huckleberry picking—borders the increasingly narrow and rough roadbed, revealing glimpses of the steep couloirs and castle-like abutments of Blacktail Peak's south face. A backward glance shows the finely mortised mudstone walls of the cliff faces to the south.

After a mile of gradual ascent, the trail—now true tread—takes a more northerly bearing as it dips into a shallow creek bed and then launches a steep ascent, gaining more than a thousand feet in the next mile on a path that could only nominally be called a switchback.

Easing into a shallower grade among old-growth spruce, cross a small rivulet at 3.4 miles (elev. 6320 feet), then cross several small pocket meadows before reaching Lost Sheep Lake's outlet. Leaving the main trail, cross and then parallel the shallow outlet stream to reach the lake at 3.8 miles (elev. 6420 feet).

Tree cover shields the view south, limiting the vistas to the slumped sedimentary benches of North Jocko Peak immediately on the other side of the lake. Nonetheless, the wide, open shoreline at the outlet invites lingering; there are far worse places to be lost.

EXTENDING YOUR TRIP

From Lost Sheep Lake, the main trail continues in a loop past the high cirque of Summit Lake and the marshy environs of Buck Lake before returning to the North Fork Jocko drainage for a 10-mile lollipop.

Opposite: *The sun sets on the gray granite of Ch-paa-qn (Hike 80).*

reservation divide

High, rolling meadows characterize the Reservation Divide, the east-to-west ridge that forms the border between the Lolo National Forest and the Flathead Reservation to the north. In contrast to the ranges surrounding it, the Reservation Divide lacks dramatic vertical relief and boasts few lakes of any size, none of which are accessible by trail—in fact, water of any kind is in short supply on this dry, wind-swept terrain. But hikers should have little reservation about this region, for, at their feet, they'll find a wealth of wildflowers and some of the finest ridgetop walking around, capped by near-constant views of the Mission Mountains, the Flathead and Missoula valleys, and, on a clear day, the jagged peaks of the Selway-Bitterroot Wilderness.

79 Three Lakes Peak

RATING/ DIFFICULTY	ROUNDTRIP	ELEV GAIN/ HIGH POINT	SEASON
****/5	12.4 miles	3890 feet/ 7792 feet	July–early Oct

Maps: USGS Horsehead Peak, MT; USGS Stark North, MT; USGS Perma, MT; **Contact:** Lolo National Forest, Ninemile Ranger District; **Note:** Open to horses and bicycles; **GPS:** 47.2345°, -114.6271°

Ascend a rocky buttress and peer down to three small lakes tucked in a scooped-out cirque. Along the way, amble among vast tracts of burnt-but-blooming meadows.

GETTING THERE

From Interstate 90, take exit 82 (Ninemile). From the north side of the freeway, drive north on Ninemile Road 1.7 miles. Turn right on West Ninemile Road, and drive 4.6 miles to a bridge crossing and T-intersection. Turn left onto Ninemile Road (Forest Road 412), and drive 11.2 miles to Foothills Road (FR 5498). Turn right, and continue 4.9 miles to the trailhead (elev. 4380 feet). A pullout on the left shoulder accommodates a few vehicles.

ON THE TRAIL

The first 1.5 miles of Burnt Fork Trail 418 traverses an old burn area on the aptly named Burnt Fork drainage. Scattered Douglas-fir, ponderosa, and larch compete with vigorous shrubs, the waxy leaves of snowbrush, willow, falsebox, and kinnikinnick made to withstand the desiccating winds and sunlight of the shadeless ridge. At 1.5 miles (elev. 5480 feet), the trail enters timber on the edge of the burn, then traverses open, grassy slopes; yellow balsamroot blooms gird old-growth larch and Douglas-fir as the switchbacks get shorter and steeper.

Now in subalpine forest, the trail climbs onto Burnt Fork Pinnacle, a small notch filled with boulder-sized talus. From the boulder field, an off-trail bushwhack of a hundred yards will reach the old Burnt Fork lookout cabin site. Nothing is left of the old fourteen-foot-square lookout cabin that stood here; the Forest Service razed it in 1950. Imagine living in its cozy confines for a season, then imagine how cozy it was when, during an early-summer snowstorm some eighty years ago, the two newlyweds who'd just arrived at the cabin for their summer posting had to share the tight space with the pack mule who'd hauled in their supplies and was rightfully reluctant to return to its post at the Ninemile Remount Depot down the valley.

At 3.1 miles (elev. 6790 feet), turn right onto the Reservation Divide Trail. This

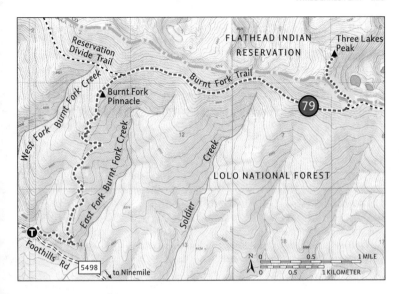

22-mile-long ridge-running trail, the center-piece of the nearly 20,000-acre Reservation Divide Roadless Area, never strays too far from the 6800-foot elevation contour as it traverses beargrass-clad balds and steep talus slopes. A 2002 wildfire left lupine and low huckleberry growing amid scattered snags and a few stands of arrow-like subalpine firs—there's little for shelter in case a thunderstorm threatens.

Cross the flank of Three Lakes Peak and ascend into a wooded saddle on its eastern shoulder, and at 5.7 miles (elev. 7220 feet), at a signed junction, bear left into the timber. From here the trail grows rather faint—sometimes nonexistent—as it ascends to the summit of Three Lakes Peak. If in doubt, bear right and up. At 6.2 miles climb the final few rocks to the small summit of Three Lakes Peak. Small, ice-stunted trees crowd the west side; the east side drops precipitously toward the trio of unnamed tarns below. Maps show

a trail approaching the summit from the north and then intersecting the Reservation Divide to the west of where you left, which would provide a shorter, more direct return option, but I found no such tread on the ground. It's a safer bet to simply return the way you came.

Grouse are by turns credulous and easily startled.

80 Ch-paa-qn

RATING/ DIFFICULTY	ROUNDTRIP	ELEV GAIN/ HIGH POINT	SEASON
*****/4	7 miles	2090 feet/ 7996 feet	July–early Oct

Map: USGS Hewolf Mountain, MT; **Contact:** Lolo National Forest, Ninemile Ranger District; **Note:** Open to horses and bicycles; **GPS:** 47.1357°, -114.3103°

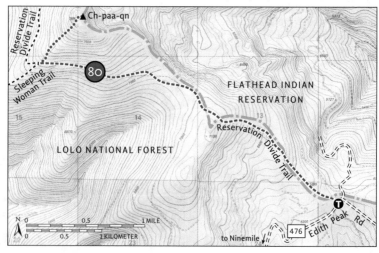

The Salish meaning of Ch-paa-qn, the 7996-foot pyramidal peak west of Missoula, is "shining peak," or, more accurately, "gray, treeless peak"—but it's the views that truly shine from the prominent summit of this local landmark.

GETTING THERE
From Interstate 90, take exit 82 (Ninemile). From the north side of the freeway, drive north on Ninemile Road 1.4 miles. Turn right on Remount Road, and drive 2.7 miles, bearing right at the historic Ninemile Ranger Station onto Edith Peak Road (Forest Road 476). Stay on this road, bearing right at well-signed junctions at 1.5 and 2.8 miles, for 11.4 miles to the trailhead (elev. 6240 feet). A parking area on the left side of the road accommodates a half dozen vehicles.

ON THE TRAIL
The striking symmetrical pyramid of 7996-foot Ch-paa-qn hovers above Missoula's western skyline, its form as unmistakable as the story of its name is convoluted. The United States Geographic Board originally labeled it Skiotah Peak, a name given to it by Captain John Mullan. It quickly dropped the moniker in favor of "Squaw," an appellation that stuck for eighty years until 1999 legislation tasked a subcommittee with soliciting new names for seventy-six sites around the state that contained the offensive term. After lengthy public input, the peak has been known as Ch-paa-qn (pronounced "Cha-paw-quin") since 2004, a name that

Surveying the long shadow cast by Ch-paa-qn

means "shining peak" in the Salish language of the area's Confederated Salish, Pend Oreille, and Kootenai Tribes. A more accurate translation is "gray, treeless peak," but either description is fitting, especially in the late evening light of summer.

Three routes approach the shoulder of Ch-paa-qn. The steep 16-mile roundtrip hike from Kennedy Creek is more than most day hikers want to handle; the 5-mile hike on the Sleeping Woman Trail has more views early on, but it is reached by an incredibly rough access road. The Reservation Divide route hits the sweet spot in terms of ease of access—it's a forty-five-minute drive from Missoula to the trailhead—and length of hike. Consequently, it's a popular hike.

From the eastern terminus of the 22-mile Reservation Divide Trail, ascend on wide tread flanked by head-high fool's huckleberry. The first 0.9 mile is a steady ascent, but then a short, steep stretch gains 400 feet in about a quarter of a mile. Now on level tread, stroll through a thick subalpine forest, crossing a couple of boggy areas on footbridges at 1.8 miles (elev. 6970 feet).

At 2.2 miles, ascend out of the trees and traverse a steep ridge of talus and beargrass. The views get progressively better; spread out below lie the sparsely populated farmlands of the Ninemile Valley, which in 1989 became home to the first pair of denning wolves in Montana outside Glacier National Park in more than a half century. You're unlikely to see any evidence of these elusive creatures, but keep an eye out for owls and other cavity-nesting critters in the standing snags of the Reservation Divide.

At 3 miles (elev. 7250 feet), reach a junction. To the left descends the Sleeping Woman Trail ("Sleeping Woman" was an alternate name proposed for the peak). Turn right, and ascend rocky, root-crossed tread. In a quarter of a mile, a large cairn marks the end of the trail. Aside from a few tenacious whitebark pines, it's pure rock from here to the summit—about 500 feet of climbing in a quarter mile. If the weather threatens thunderstorms or fog engulfs the peak, save the summit for another day. Otherwise, carefully negotiate the rocks. Ten minutes of scrambling, none of it steep or exposed, will gain the summit at 3.5 miles (elev. 7996 feet).

Scree and tiny, wind-cowed juniper carpet the barren summit; a small rock wall provides a windscreen. There's nothing to obstruct the awesome panorama: to the east, the steep, dry defiles of the west face of the Missions; to the north, the rolling foothills of the Camas Prairie; to the west, the timber-clad Coeur d'Alene and northern Bitterroot Ranges; and, to the south, the crenellated peaks of the Selway-Bitterroot Wilderness.

EXTENDING YOUR TRIP

Continue on the Reservation Divide for almost twenty more miles of fine ridgeline walking.

Opposite: A lone arrowleaf balsamroot dots the top of Mount Sentinel (Hike 81).

missoula area

Home to the University of Montana in the whole-foods-and-hiking-boots heart of the state, Missoula is a community of fit free spirits. In recent years, the city's running and river surfing communities have put it on the adventure-sports map, but hiking remains king here. Full parking lots belie quiet footpaths, with nearly a hundred miles of trails around the city to absorb trail runners and toddler-toting strollers. Its location in a miniature banana belt means that Missoula's hiking season gets into full swing in spring, when the region's high-country hiking opportunities are still encased in snow.

81 Crazy Canyon to Mount Sentinel

RATING/ DIFFICULTY	ROUNDTRIP	ELEV GAIN/ HIGH POINT	SEASON
***/3	6.6 miles	1430 feet/ 5158 feet	May–Nov

Map: USGS Southeast Missoula, MT; **Contacts:** Lolo National Forest, Missoula Ranger District; City of Missoula Parks and Recreation; **Note:** Open to horses, bicycles, and paragliders; **GPS:** 46.8257°, -113.9386°

Mount Jumbo (Hike 82) as viewed from the summit of Mount Sentinel

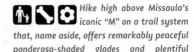

Hike high above Missoula's iconic "M" on a trail system that, name aside, offers remarkably peaceful ponderosa-shaded glades and plentiful wildflowers.

GETTING THERE
From downtown Missoula, drive south on South Higgins Avenue for 2.1 miles, then turn left on Pattee Canyon Road. Drive 3.5 miles to the Crazy Canyon parking lot on the left side of the road (elev. 3960 feet). Privy available.

ON THE TRAIL
The large white "M" on Mount Sentinel above the University of Montana campus is the most immediately visible of the city's landmarks, the short trail leading up to it a favorite destination for students showing visiting relatives around. But it's merely the public face of a sprawling trail system that connects forested Pattee Canyon on the east side of town with the letter-stamped Mount Sentinel. Named after an early Bitterroot Valley settler, the Pattee Canyon trail system crisscrosses gently sloping meadows and old-growth ponderosa and larch groves. From the Crazy Canyon trailhead—one of the primary portals into Pattee Canyon—the 3.3-mile hike to Sentinel's summit stitches together a crazy-quilt collection of spur trails and skid roads through old-growth ponderosa forest.

From the trailhead, follow the old skid road through sun-streaked evergreen forest of ponderosa pine, Douglas-fir, and larch. Arnica, serviceberry, balsamroot, shooting star, and trillium color the understory.

At 1.3 miles, bear right at a junction, continuing to climb through excellent white-tailed deer habitat. The trail dips into

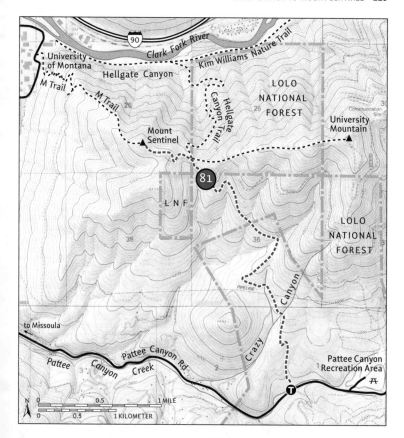

and out of a lupine-lush draw before reaching a junction at 2.5 miles. Bear left at this four-way junction, then head uphill as the path nears Sentinel's summit, where the thinning understory reveals views north to the S-shaped folds of the Rattlesnake Creek drainage.

A grove of large old-growth ponderosa quickly gives way to Sentinel's rocky crown. Snags surround a wind-swept summit; bluebirds can often be spotted flitting among these gray perches, as can the occasional paraglider departing from the summit's launch platform. Views abound, of the forested lower reaches of Rattlesnake National Recreation Area to the north and the broad granite defiles of the Bitterroot Valley to the south. To the west lies the immediately recognizable pyramid of Ch-paa-qn; to the southwest, the shaded and snow-covered north aspect of Lolo Peak demarcates the north end of the Bitterroots.

EXTENDING YOUR TRIP

From the junction just below the summit, hikers can tackle a series of steep climbs to reach University Mountain.

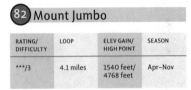

82 Mount Jumbo

RATING/ DIFFICULTY	LOOP	ELEV GAIN/ HIGH POINT	SEASON
***/3	4.1 miles	1540 feet/ 4768 feet	Apr–Nov

Maps: USGS Northeast Missoula, MT; USGS Southeast Missoula, MT; **Contact:** City of Missoula Parks and Recreation; **Note:** Open to paragliders; **GPS:** 46.8683°, -113.9755°

A jumble of user-created paths wind toward the Loyola High School "L" on broad, grassy Mount Jumbo, which, with the "M" on Mount Sentinel, bookends Hellgate Canyon. Balsam-root and bunchgrass blanket the broad, south-facing slope that overlooks the confluence of Rattlesnake Creek and the Clark Fork River. Beyond the "L," continue up to copses of firs surrounding Jumbo's flat summit, from which the views down the Bitterroot Valley are unmatched.

GETTING THERE

From Interstate 90 in Missoula, take exit 105 (Van Buren Street). Turn north on Van Buren Street, and continue for two blocks to Poplar Street. Turn right, and drive 0.3 mile to the trailhead (elev. 3250 feet), located on the 90-degree bend in the street. Street parking only.

ON THE TRAIL

From the trailhead, follow the obvious path uphill on the shade-scarce, south-facing slope. This is a social trail system, with myriad user-created paths crisscrossing the

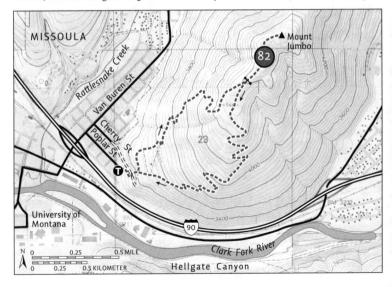

mountain. Fortunately, the destination—the giant white "L," painted every year by Loyola High School students—is quite obvious; pick the path that suits you, but generally head right to the mountain's southern side.

In three-quarters of a mile, reach the "L." It's a logical place to stop and enjoy the view of Missoula. The University of Montana sits just below Mount Sentinel to the south; on the far side of the city, Blue Mountain beckons.

For Jumbo's summit and even better views, continue on the trail to the left. Balsamroot blankets the slope as the trail steadily switchbacks north up the canyon. In a half mile, the grade eases, and at 1.4 miles the trail reaches a junction. Turn left for Jumbo; the righthand path is your return route.

Pass through an open fence, small copses of fir paralleling Jumbo's grass-clad humps, to the summit. From here, admire the tight cleft where the Clark Fork River passes through Hellgate Canyon. To the north lies the timbered "urban" wilderness of Stuart Peak and the Rattlesnake Creek drainage.

Speaking of rattlesnakes: although they don't dwell in the eponymous recreation area farther up the creek, the snakes do inhabit Mount Jumbo; it's not uncommon to encounter a rattler sunning itself in the middle of the trail come late spring. Fortunately, you're more likely to encounter a passel of paragliders toting their massive packs to the Jumbo summit.

From the summit, return the way you came, this time going straight at the junction just beyond the gate. The trail curves around the south face of Mount Jumbo, gradually descending to the trailhead over the din of the interstate.

Arrowleaf balsamroot blankets the slopes of Mount Jumbo.

83 South O'Brien Creek Loop

RATING/ DIFFICULTY	LOOP	ELEV GAIN/ HIGH POINT	SEASON
***/3	7.1 miles	1110 feet/ 4340 feet	May–Nov

Map: USGS Blue Mountain, MT; **Contact:** Lolo National Forest, Missoula Ranger District; **Notes:** Horses, bicycles, and dogs permitted. Seasonal closure December to May 1; **GPS:** 46.8523°, -114.1686°

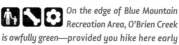 *On the edge of Blue Mountain Recreation Area, O'Brien Creek is awfully green—provided you hike here early in the season, before the shadeless slopes have*

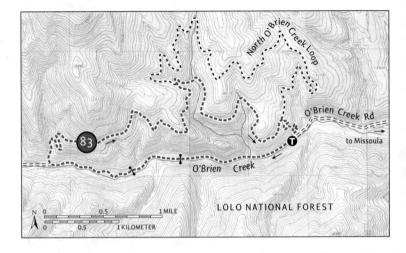

LOLO NATIONAL FOREST

you looking pink. Whereas many of Blue Mountain's trails are open to motorized vehicles, O'Brien Creek is motor-free, and often it is free of other recreationists of any kind.

GETTING THERE

From the intersection of South Avenue and Reserve Street in Missoula, drive 2.5 miles west on South Avenue to Humble Road. Turn right, and go 0.2 mile to North Avenue. Turn left and continue 1 mile, crossing the Maclay Bridge over the Bitterroot River, to the Blue Mountain Road–Big Flat Road junction. Proceed through the intersection onto O'Brien Creek Road, and continue 3.1 miles to the trailhead at road's end (elev. 3550 feet). A large parking area will accommodate a half dozen vehicles.

ON THE TRAIL

Ask an avid Missoula hiker about the O'Brien Creek trail system, and—assuming they don't respond with a blank stare—their reply will likely be "Is that the one with all the ceramic angels?" Yes, it is—courtesy of a homeowner with a whimsical sense of style along the gated gravel right-of-way that constitutes the first part of this 7-mile hike. But there's no shortage of earthly delights in this drainage that abuts Blue Mountain Recreation Area on the southwest edge of Missoula. With only modest elevation gain, the South O'Brien Creek Loop makes for a pleasant early-season conditioner.

From the usually empty trailhead, the South O'Brien Creek Loop passes private property (please respect their property by staying on the road) on the lush O'Brien Creek drainage before reaching a gate at 1 mile (elev. 3680 feet). Continue through an open riparian area—scan for elk bedding areas in the brush—then pass a second gate. Butterflies and early-summer flowering shrubs are plentiful here.

At 2.2 miles (elev. 3800 feet), bear right at a signed junction and begin ascending a dry south-facing draw; the trail is faint but easy to follow. Leaving the draw, the trail switchbacks steeply up sunbaked south-facing slopes of ponderosa and wildflowers before intersecting an old roadbed at 3 miles (elev. 4300 feet). Bear right and enjoy nearly level walking amid expansive dry-land wildflowers. The grassy ridges afford unobstructed views of Blue Mountain and its lookout tower to the south and Missoula and Mount Sentinel to the east. The road bends north and parallels a rocky, lush canyon; at 4.7 miles (elev. 4270 feet), leave the road and bear right into this canyon (the way straight continues the North O'Brien Creek Loop). Dip down into a brushy draw, cross two boggy areas, and then ascend a short, steep sidehill out of the drainage.

At 5.2 miles (elev. 4220 feet), bear right onto roadbed again as it curves around the octopus-like contours of the dry slope. And then bear right once more onto forested, lupine-lined singletrack at 6.6 miles (elev. 3920 feet) for a pleasantly shaded final half mile to the trailhead.

A hiker traverses the open slopes of Sawmill Gulch.

EXTENDING YOUR TRIP

Hikers have the option of tacking on nearly three miles in figure-eight fashion on the adjoining North O'Brien Creek Loop for more ponderosa wandering.

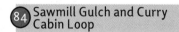 *Travel the paths of ax-men and cattle ranchers on this history-rich introduction to the Rattlesnake National Recreation Area. Lively wildflowers carpet derelict cabins and ancient ponderosas on a trail system more lightly visited than the main Rattlesnake portal (Hike 85).*

84 Sawmill Gulch and Curry Cabin Loop

RATING/ DIFFICULTY	LOOP	ELEV GAIN/ HIGH POINT	SEASON
***/3	5 miles	1280 feet/ 4920 feet	May–Nov

Map: USGS Northeast Missoula, MT; **Contact:** Lolo National Forest, Missoula Ranger District; **Notes:** Dogs prohibited. Open to bicycles; **GPS:** 46.9352°, -113.9812°

GETTING THERE

From Interstate 90 in Missoula, take exit 105 (Van Buren Street). Proceed north on Van Buren Street, which becomes Rattlesnake Drive. At 2.3 miles, bear right to stay on Rattlesnake Drive. At 4 miles from I-90, turn left on Sawmill Gulch Road. Cross the bridge over Rattlesnake Creek, and proceed 1.5

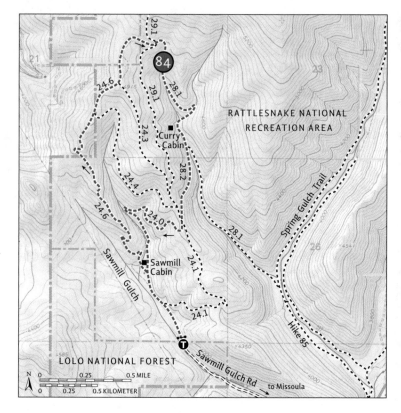

miles to the road's end and trailhead (elev. 3900 feet).

ON THE TRAIL

Before the Forest Service acquired the land that now comprises the Sawmill-Curry portion of the Rattlesnake National Recreation Area in a land exchange with a private landowner in 1986, a century of ranchers and axe-swingers made their homes and livelihoods here. Connecting old timber skid roads and livestock driveways, this 5-mile loop visits moldering homesteads

and ancient orchard trees, which mingle with old-growth ponderosa pines spared the saw. It's a hike rife with history, but there's lots of life here, thanks to a profusion of open-forest blooms—lupine, balsamroot, buckwheat, and more.

Be sure to pick up a brochure at the trailhead; the seventy or so miles of trail in Rattlesnake can bewilder newcomers, nowhere more so than this portion of the recreation area.

From beyond the gate, follow the old dirt road north as it traces the broad, bowl-shaped meadow of Sawmill Gulch. Yellow arnica garlands the fluted trunks of fir and pine on the steep slopes to the right. Continue straight at a junction, soon arriving at a homestead known as the Sawmill Cabin. Vestigial orchard trees shade only foundations and moldering rock walls.

Just past the homesite, bear right at a junction (trail 24.7 descends left back into Sawmill Gulch). Hordes of burrowing critters call this hill home. Switchbacking, leave Sawmill Gulch behind and climb through flower-filled Douglas-fir forest. As the trail ascends, thinning tree cover reveals views of Mount Sentinel to the east and the Grant Creek drainage to the west. Having reached the crest of the ridge above Grant Creek, the grade eases, and the path tracks north through pleasant larch forest. Continue straight at a junction with Trail 24.4 at 1.8 miles and at a second junction at 1.9 miles before reaching a third junction at 2.2 miles (elev. 4900 feet). Stay straight and continue downhill through a wooded gully to Curry Cabin at 3.1 miles (elev. 4390 feet).

Built in the 1800s by Jacob Curry, the two-room cabin included an earthen root cellar and old shed. Aspen has colonized the cabin, where scattered tin cans and sections of stovepipe are all that remain.

From Curry Cabin, take Trail 28.2, an old roadbed that cuts across Curry Gulch to connect with the forested ridge above Sawmill Gulch at 3.6 miles (elev. 4410 feet). At this confusing three-way junction, angle downhill onto Trail 24.1, then immediately bear right onto an old road that descends into the wooded gulch above Sawmill Cabin to close the cherry-stem loop.

EXTENDING YOUR TRIP

Hikers can string together myriad connectors for loops of varying lengths. Be sure to

pick up a trail map from the trailhead kiosk; the numbered trails can stymie first-time visitors.

85 Stuart Peak

RATING/ DIFFICULTY	ROUNDTRIP	ELEV GAIN/ HIGH POINT	SEASON
*****/5	18.4 miles	4500 feet/ 7960 feet	July–Oct

Maps: USGS Northeast Missoula, MT; USGS Stuart Peak, MT; **Contact:** Lolo National Forest, Missoula Ranger District; **Notes:** "South Zone" restrictions in place first 3 miles from main Rattlesnake trailhead. Camping and firearms are prohibited. Wilderness rules apply, although hikers should expect to encounter cyclists up to the wilderness boundary; **GPS:** 46.9249°, -113.9596°

The nearly 8000-foot gray and granite dome of Stuart Peak crowns the Rattlesnake Wilderness. Don't be put off by the mileage: only Glacier rivals Stuart Peak's penchant for smooth, pleasantly graded tread; the trip is well within the realm of seasoned day hikers. Worthy based solely on its scenic merits, Stuart has added appeal as an exemplar of urban wilderness: where else can you find a nearly twenty-mile subalpine summit hike with a trailhead accessible by city bus?

GETTING THERE

From Interstate 90 in Missoula, take exit 105 (Van Buren Street). Proceed north on Van Buren Street, which becomes Rattlesnake Drive. At 2.3 miles, bear right to stay on Rattlesnake Drive. At 4 miles from I-90, turn left on Sawmill Gulch Road. Cross the bridge over Rattlesnake Creek and proceed

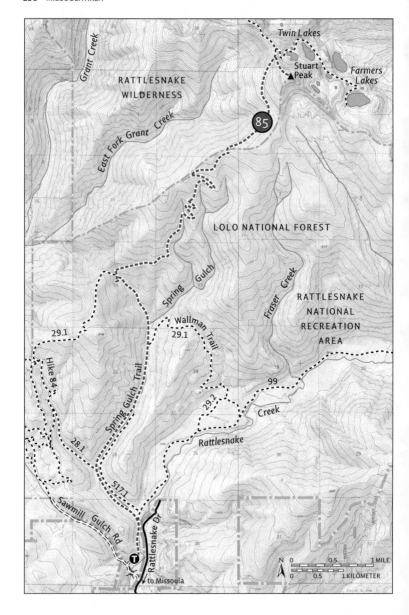

Grant Creek

Twin Lakes

RATTLESNAKE
WILDERNESS

Stuart
Peak

Farmers
Lakes

East Fork Grant Creek

85

LOLO NATIONAL FOREST

Spring Gulch

Fraser Creek

RATTLESNAKE
NATIONAL
RECREATION
AREA

Wallman Trail
29.1

29.1

Hike 84

Spring Gulch Trail

29.2

99

Creek

28.1

Rattlesnake

517.1

Sawmill Gulch Rd

Rattlesnake Dr

T

to Missoula

N   0   0.5   1 MILE

0   0.5   1 KILOMETER

Twin Lakes and their neighbors sit below Stuart Peak.

a quarter mile to the large parking area on the right (elev. 3590 feet). Privy available.

ON THE TRAIL

A century ago, travelers up the Rattlesnake Creek drainage north of Missoula would have found a bustling community, complete with a school, post office, and hundreds of homesteaders. Today Rattlesnake bustles with the sound of running shoes slapping gravel and mountain bikes clattering down high-speed trails.

Protected because it was the watershed for the municipal water supply, the Rattlesnake drainage remained in private hands until the early 1980s, when Congress set aside 61,000 acres in the drainage to foster watershed health, recreation, wildlife, and education: 28,000 acres were designated a national recreation area; the remaining 33,000 acres were designated wilderness. Today the Rattlesnake is one of the closest wilderness areas to a major metropolitan area in the United States.

The origin of the Rattlesnake appellation is unclear: some historical sources claim it is in honor of a homesteader who succumbed to a rattlesnake bite in the drainage; other sources state it is an echo of the Salish word for "rattlesnake." Either way, hikers need not worry about snakes, which don't live this far up the creek valley. But black bears and cougars should be top of mind; sightings of both are common.

The granddaddy of Rattlesnake hikes is the more than 18-mile roundtrip trek to Stuart Peak. Don't be put off by the mileage: outside of Glacier National Park, few trails in Montana match Rattlesnake's penchant for pleasantly graded and buffed tread. Determined hikers and trail runners can do Stuart Peak as a day hike. A procession of shallow-grade switchbacks gain elevation in lazy loops like a fledgling bird; in late spring, lupine garland larch in the open, fire-prone forest.

From the large parking area, pass through the road barrier on Forest Road 99, the original access road that parallels Rattle-snake Creek and is still occasionally used by city workers accessing the watershed. In 0.4 mile, bear left on Trail 517, the Spring Gulch Trail, which assumes a straight course toward the head of the gulch, passing the twisted forms of old orchard trees and the broad clearings of old homesteads.

Begin climbing steeply out of the gulch and, now in thick timber, bear right at a junction at 4.1 miles (elev. 5010 feet); the way left provides an alternate approach from the Grant Creek drainage (see Extending Your Trip). A series of seemingly endless switchbacks ensue, casually making their way through brushy Douglas-fir forest like a rudderless ship. As fir gradually gives way to stock-straight lodgepole pine, the trail gains the ridge and, at 6.8 miles (elev. 6820 feet), makes one final switchback to enter the Rattlesnake Wilderness.

The hall of lodgepole pine along the ridgeline occasionally grants views of the Montana Snowbowl ski area and Point Six as it proceeds northeast. Nearing the northern end of the ridge of which Stuart Peak marks the high point, lodgepole gives way to broad and snow-bent whitebark pine.

Boulder Lake sprawls beneath Boulder Point.

At 8.9 miles (elev. 7600 feet) reach the pass at the top of Twin Lakes cirque. From here, abandon the official trail, which descends to the lakes basin. Rather, follow a well-worn climbers' path as it hugs the ridgeline in a workmanlike ascent toward the summit, gaining nearly 400 feet in a quarter mile.

Wind-stunted whitebark pines surround the summit, a gray and granite dome that overlooks no fewer than a half dozen lakes on broad sedimentary benches in the interior of the Rattlesnake Wilderness. To the south sprawls Missoula; to the north runs the ragged picket line of the Missions.

EXTENDING YOUR TRIP

The Rattlesnake trailhead off Grant Creek allows for an open loop of sorts that can ameliorate the tedium of the lower several miles of trail. Backpackers will find numerous campsites near the shallow lakes just below Stuart Peak.

86 Boulder Point and Boulder Lake

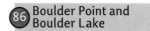

RATING/ DIFFICULTY	ROUNDTRIP	ELEV GAIN/ HIGH POINT	SEASON
****/4	12.4 miles	2980 feet/ 7280 feet	July–Oct

Map: USGS Wapiti Lake, MT; **Contact:** Lolo National Forest, Missoula Ranger District; **Notes:** Wilderness rules apply. Dogs and horses permitted; **GPS:** 47.0280°, -113.7993°

Access the lightly used east side of the Rattlesnake Wilderness, where deer and elk outnumber hikers. From the broad prow of Boulder Point, a former lookout site, peer down upon Boulder Lake, where snow often lies thick until mid-

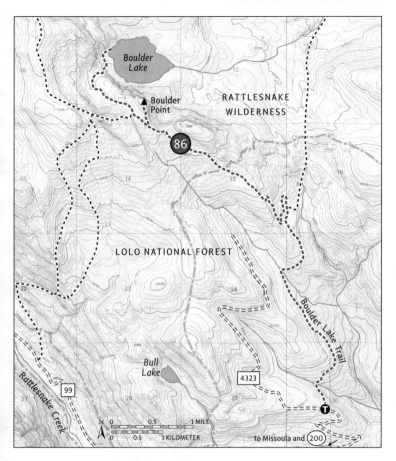

summer, and the expansive wet, moose-friendly meadows and forests of golden larch of the Gold Creek drainage.

GETTING THERE

From Montana Highway 200 northeast of Missoula, just past milepost 9, turn north on Gold Creek Road (Forest Road 126). Drive 6 miles, then turn left on West Fork Gold Creek Road (FR 2103). Continue 5.1 miles before turning left on FR 4323. From here, drive 5.6 rough, rocky miles—a passenger car can do it, but at a snail's pace—to the large trailhead parking area (elev. 5700 feet).

ON THE TRAIL

From the no-frills Boulder Lake Trail 333 trailhead hike north through an open landscape burned in a 2003 fire. The few remaining snags offer little in the way of sun or rain protection, but they do permit views of the Gold Creek drainage—larch and snags in a sea of clear-cuts. Crossing a small brook, the trail bends northwesterly as it parallels a road-scarred drainage. The trail, despite its relative lack of use, is in good shape, the crushed rock surface easy to follow through beargrass, willow, snowbrush, and fireweed—post-fire colonizing flora all.

Cairns begin to mark the sometimes faint tread as it passes through burnt-over bottomland, creek water occasionally making use of the trail. At 1.6 miles (elev. 5890 feet), cross a small creek and swing north. Look behind for a glimpse of Mineral Peak Lookout. Cross an old roadbed; cairns mark the trail's continuation on the far side. Immediately cross the old road again and, at 2 miles (elev. 6000 feet), find the signed singletrack. Continue northeasterly through the open, shallow-sloped foothills. Briefly enter a copse of unburnt fir and lodgepole before returning to a boulder-studded forest of snags. In contrast to the heavily forested main portion of the Rattlesnake Wilderness, this side is much more open, a product of regular fires through the dry ponderosa stands.

At 2.5 miles (elev. 6110 feet), turn left at a signed junction. Now climbing in earnest, the trail doubles back the way you just came before ascending a sparsely vegetated ridge and reaching the wilderness boundary at 3.6 miles (elev. 6570 feet). Continue through austere, talus-strewn beauty as the trail climbs to a saddle south of Boulder Point; Boulder Lake eventually comes into view.

At 4.5 miles (elev. 7050 feet), turn right at a signed junction for Boulder Point. The path quickly fades, but it's an easy walk through

fallen lodgepole to the site of the old lookout, which once surveyed snowcapped Stuart Peak to the north and the wet meadows and expansive larch forests of the northern Rattlesnake Wilderness to the northeast.

Having descended back to the main trail, continue northwest, and in a few minutes bear right at a signed junction. Descend through a cool forest of lodgepole and subalpine heath, past the broad, wet meadow benches above Boulder Lake. The trail, now rougher and steeper, stays above the lake as it crosses muddy ground alongside the inlet creek before reaching the shore at 6.2 miles (elev. 6530 feet). Boulder Point's sheer prow looms over the southwest shore; large campsites at the north end of the lake invite an overnight fishing trip.

87 Sheep Mountain

RATING/ DIFFICULTY	ROUNDTRIP	ELEV GAIN/ HIGH POINT	SEASON
****/4	7.4 miles	2020 feet/ 7646 feet	Mid-June–Oct

Map: USGS Blue Point, MT; **Contact:** Lolo National Forest, Missoula Ranger District; **Note:** Dogs, bicycles, and horses permitted; **GPS:** 46.9531°, -113.7704°

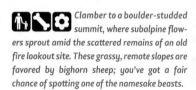 *Clamber to a boulder-studded summit, where subalpine flowers sprout amid the scattered remains of an old fire lookout site. These grassy, remote slopes are favored by bighorn sheep; you've got a fair chance of spotting one of the namesake beasts.*

GETTING THERE

From Montana Highway 200 northeast of Missoula, just past milepost 9, turn north on Gold Creek Road (Forest Road 126). Drive

Looking out over the Blackfoot River country from Sheep Mountain

0.5 mile, then bear left on FR 2117. Negotiate this at times slow, bumpy road for 5 miles, then continue right on FR 2119. Drive 2.9 miles to the trailhead on the left (elev. 5740 feet). Pullouts on the shoulder will accommodate a half dozen vehicles.

ON THE TRAIL

From the trailhead, follow the old roadbed, rapidly deteriorating in places, as it travels in a southwesterly fashion through an open forest of evergreens and birch. Round a switchback at 0.6 mile, and then proceed to walk a lodgepole gauntlet before intersecting the Sheep Mountain Trail a quarter mile beyond. At the junction, proceed straight then immediately bear left. The next 0.5 mile is a steady grind through shady lodgepole

and high fool's huckleberry. Breaks in the trees reveal glimpses of the Gold Creek drainage and the foothills of the Blackfoot River Valley beyond; below, tiny Sheep Mountain Bog is barely visible.

At 2.8 miles (elev. 6800 feet), begin switchbacking up the east face of Sheep Mountain, lodgepole yielding to thick mats of heather topped by subalpine fir. Trees give way to grass and talus just before the summit at 3.7 miles (elev. 7646 feet). An old rock shelter and tangled telegraph wire mark the only remains of an old lookout, although 50 yards distant red-painted bricks mark an extant helipad site. Whitebark pine skeletons do little to obscure views of, in clockwise fashion, the Bob Marshall country to the far northeast, the Garnet Range, the Bitterroots, and, to the immediate northwest, Stuart Peak. Pine beetle die-off is evident on burnt-bare Wisherd Ridge to the south. If you're lucky, you'll hear the clatter of rams from this grass-clad summit.

EXTENDING YOUR TRIP
The Sheep Mountain Trail continues some 11 miles southwest to the Rattlesnake drainage; this trail is more often used by mountain bikers owing to its length.

Opposite: The shoulder of Boulder Peak as viewed from Boulder Point Lookout (Hike 121)

bitterroot range

Northern Bitterroot Range

The Bitterroot Range unfolds some several hundred miles along the Idaho-Montana border from Lake Pend Oreille well into the Salmon River country of central Idaho. Although Bitterroot Valley residents might quibble with the particulars, broadly speaking the term "Bitterroot Range" spans this entire stretch, whereas the Bitterroot Mountains include only the granite-carved masses west of the Bitterroot Valley. And while the Bitterroot Mountains tend to grab all the glory with their chasm-like canyons and cloud-catching crags, the northern reaches of the greater Bitterroot Range—the area bounded roughly by Lolo and Lookout Passes—offer their own quietly rugged charm. Dozens of lakes dot the landscape, many of them accessed via anyone-can-do-it trails. Although for the most part below tree line, the ridges boast expansive vistas, thanks to the catastrophic wildfires of the 1910 Great Burn, which left a patchwork of forested and flower-clad ridges that include several wilderness-worthy roadless areas, most notably the 250,000-acre Great Burn Proposed Wilderness Area that stretches into the upper Clearwater River country of Idaho.

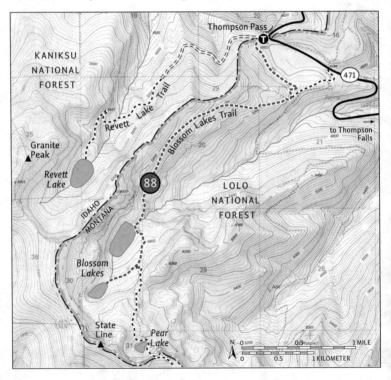

The boulder-strewn shore of Lower Blossom Lake

88 Blossom Lakes

RATING/ DIFFICULTY	ROUNDTRIP	ELEV GAIN/ HIGH POINT	SEASON
****/4	7.1 miles	2030 feet/ 5930 feet	Late June–Oct

Map: USGS Thompson Pass, MT; **Contact:** Lolo National Forest, Plains/Thompson Falls Ranger District; **Note:** Open to horses and bicycles; **GPS:** 47.5675°, -115.7168°

A pair of blossoms—and the possibility for a pear—make for a pretty, and popular, hike high in the Coeur d'Alene Range of the Bitterroots on the Idaho-Montana border.

GETTING THERE

From Montana Highway 200 about 2 miles northwest of Thompson Falls, head west on MT 471 (Prospect Creek Road, also named Forest Road 7) for 22 miles to Thompson Pass,

245

on the Idaho-Montana border. The trail begins on the south side of the large parking area (elev. 4850 feet). Privy available a half mile up the gravel road to Revett Lake trailhead.

ON THE TRAIL

Blossom Lakes Trail begins atop an old dike. In the 1800s, Chinese laborers dug a drainage ditch to sluice water from Blossom Lakes to the mining camp of Murray across the border in Idaho. However, a competitor dynamited the dam at the lakes' outlet, and Blossom Lakes' mining history ended there.

In half a mile, the trail leaves the dike, bending to the southwest as it parallels the lakes' outlet stream under old-growth hemlock and fir cocooned in lichen. The trail begins to gain elevation in stairstep fashion for the next mile, hemlock giving way to larch and lodgepole as the trail reaches higher and drier aspects. At 2 miles, the grade reverses; descend through doghair fir, their uniformly bent basal trunks evidence of heavy snows. Briefly leave thick timber, a sedimentary perch revealing the steep scree slopes of Glidden Ridge to the south, before tracing Lower Blossom Lake's outlet stream to its source at 2.8 miles (elev. 5720 feet).

Diving into the perennially frigid waters of Lower St. Regis Lake

Surrounded by timber on three sides and a steep sedimentary slope on the west side, Lower Blossom Lake offers fair fishing from its log-jammed east shore. Tenters will find several large sites on the north side of the lake's outlet.

To reach Upper Blossom Lake, cross the outlet and continue a quarter mile through thick fool's huckleberry to a junction with the spur trail to Upper Blossom Lake. Long abandoned, this spur has in recent years been restored, and a half mile of easy hiking deposits hikers at Upper Blossom's northeast shore. Smaller and more lightly visited than its lower kin, Upper Blossom is arguably the prettier of the two, with an open forest at its outlet feeling less hemmed-in.

EXTENDING YOUR TRIP

Tiny Pear Lake, just over a mile beyond Lower Blossom Lake, is a must-see side trip. Tucked into a deep depression just below Glidden Ridge, Pear offers a few camps at its grassy "stem." From here, a quarter mile of steep switchbacks gain Glidden Ridge; from its talus-strewn slopes, the views of the Bitterroots and Idaho's Silver Valley are superb.

89 St. Regis Lakes

RATING/ DIFFICULTY	ROUNDTRIP	ELEV GAIN/ HIGH POINT	SEASON
****/3	5.4 miles	1350 feet/ 5610 feet	Late June–Oct

Maps: USGS Mullan, ID; USGS Lookout Pass, ID; **Contact:** Lolo National Forest, Superior Ranger District; **Note:** Open to horses and bicycles; **GPS:** 47.4450°, -115.7063°

 *The headwaters of the St. Regis River, the*

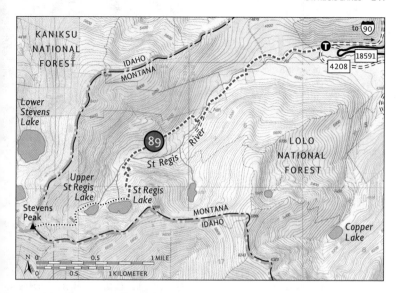

snow-fed St. Regis Lakes provide icy refreshment all summer long. All this and slopes that cascade with color—from the many-hued mountain flowers of early summer to the crimson and purple of huckleberries at its end.

GETTING THERE

From Interstate 90, take exit 0 (Lookout Pass) south. At the stop sign, turn left onto Forest Road 7896. Continue 1 mile to a steep, rocky spur road on the right (FR 18591). If you don't have a high-clearance vehicle, park here; otherwise, proceed uphill 0.1 mile to the trailhead on FR 4208 (elev. 4510 feet).

ON THE TRAIL

On a closed-to-motors old mine road—now maintained as a cross-country ski trail—climb past the bottom of Lookout Pass Ski Area's Chair 4. The roadbed leaves the ski slope and levels out in a forest harboring some impressive and increasingly rare old white pine. Cross a small creek, and at 0.5 mile, bear left at the junction of two old roads. At 0.8 mile (elev. 4650 feet), the roadbed makes an ankle-deep crossing of the St. Regis River, which provides some relief in the heat of summer. After a brief climb, the forest flanking the trail opens up to provide views of the St. Regis River drainage. Keep an eye out, too, for old mining cabins, now in an advanced state of decay, alongside the water.

At 1.3 miles (elev. 4780 feet), pass the official trailhead; now on singletrack, travel a short ways, then bear right on a hikers-only trail. Cross the St. Regis River again—here, a mere rock hop—and then sidehill across a hot, shadeless slope. The trail enters a mountain meadow surrounded by cirques and punctuated by elephant head and the pungent scent of horsemint. Cross the St. Regis River again and commence climbing the last half mile to the lake. It's a steep, switchbacking ascent with little shade; aster, agastache, and mountain ash threaten to overtake the dusty tread. Snakes seem to enjoy it, though.

At 2.7 miles (elev. 5610 feet), crest the hill at lake's edge. Subalpine firs and steep meadows surround St. Regis Lake, limiting shoreline access; follow the trail to the right for the best spots, as well as good dispersed campsites. The lake harbors a population of vigorous fish. Numerous tiny waterfalls from late-melting snowfields feed the lake and keep it bracingly cold; although the shoreline boulders and immediate drop-off in lake depth invite a dive, most hikers will be scrambling for shore after only a few seconds.

EXTENDING YOUR TRIP

From the lower lake, follow a faint boot path west a half mile to Upper St. Regis Lake. No fish inhabit its shallow waters. From here, peak baggers can scramble out of the brush and up steep avalanche chutes to Stevens Peak, which peers down onto Upper Stevens Lake.

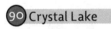

90 Crystal Lake

RATING/ DIFFICULTY	ROUNDTRIP	ELEV GAIN/ HIGH POINT	SEASON
***/3	3.2 miles	1370 feet/ 5480 feet	June–Oct

Map: USGS McGee Peak, MT; **Contact:** Lolo National Forest, Superior Ranger District; **Note:** Open to horses and bicycles; **GPS:** 47.3141°, -115.4052°

  Fishing poles and huckleberry buckets have replaced pickaxes in the hands of visitors to this quiet little lake. A bustling mining community once crowded the forested shores of Crystal Lake; today hikers will find scant evi-

Boulders line swift-running Deer Creek.

dence of its existence, save the steep mining road under their feet.

GETTING THERE

From Interstate 90, take exit 18 (De Borgia) and head south to Dry Creek Road (Forest Road 236). Turn right and drive east, bearing left at 0.5 mile to stay on FR 236. Continue for 6.7 miles to the trailhead on the left side of the road (elev. 4150 feet). A parking pullout on the right shoulder accommodates two vehicles.

ON THE TRAIL

The trail to Crystal Lake uses an old roadbed that accessed the gold-lode town of Deer Creek Mining Company Town, and it mines the 1.5-mile-long path for every foot of elevation. Climb through a shady forest of hemlock, fir, and western redcedar. Huckleberries border the wide path, which has occasional views of Up Up Mountain and Eagle Peak on the far side of the Deer Creek drainage. Cross a trio of small creeks, and enter a brushy slide area thick with thimbleberry and, in midsummer, the white, sweetly scented blossoms of syringa and honeysuckle.

After 1 mile (elev. 4770 feet), commence a calf-cramping half-mile ascent through

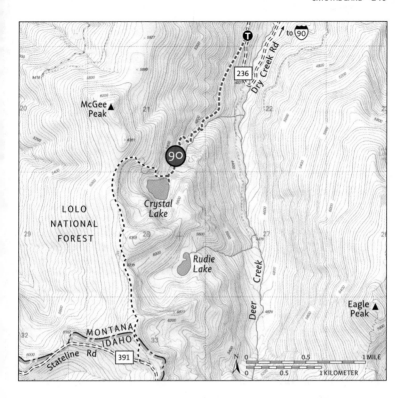

dense timber. At 1.5 miles (elev. 5430 feet), the trail, now true singletrack, levels before reaching the outlet of Crystal Lake. Here you'll reach the remains of the Deer Creek Mining Company Town, which once bustled with nearly one hundred miners. The gold dried up, and the town after it, by 1913. Thick timber has reclaimed most of the townsite's cabins. But vestiges of three flumes, once used to harness the lake's water for power, remain near the lake's outlet, in addition to some old pilings.

A well-used camp overlooks the rocky shore (a privy hides in the trees about fifty feet back). The deep waters invite a swim, and anglers will find biting brook trout. In the open lodgepole forest above the north shore, berry pickers will find a mother lode of huckleberries, the purple prize of Montana summers.

EXTENDING YOUR TRIP

From the dike works at the outlet of the lake, follow a crude but well-marked path up through prime huckleberry picking to the ridgeline above the lake and finally to Stateline Road (FR 391) 2.3 miles from the lake. The first 0.5 mile gains a steep 700 feet, but the grade mellows out after that. In contrast to much of the Bitterroot Divide, thick hemlock casts the ridge here in deep shade. At 1.2 miles, a faint boot path bears left across an open slope to tiny Rudie Lake a steep half mile distant.

For an easier view of Rudie Lake, continue on the main trail another quarter mile to an arrow carved in a tree trunk, which points the way through thick deadfall to a rock knob with an aerial view of the drainage below.

91 Hazel and Hub Lakes

RATING/ DIFFICULTY	ROUNDTRIP	ELEV GAIN/ HIGH POINT	SEASON
*****/3	6.4 miles	2440 feet/ 5740 feet	Late June–Oct

Map: USGS De Borgia S, MT; **Contact:** Lolo National Forest, Superior Ranger District; **Note:** Open to horses and bicycles; **GPS:** 47.2863°, -115.3391°

Tiny Hazel and Hub Lakes occupy a steep, flower-choked slope high on the Bitterroot Divide. But they are only part of the scenic appeal of this 6-mile roundtrip hike. The trail passes gargantuan cedars that escaped the 1910 Great Burn and a scenic view of the dramatic 60-foot Dipper Falls. Only occasionally steep, this hike is ideal for kids and canine companions.

GETTING THERE

From St. Regis, travel west on Interstate 90 to exit 25 (Drexel). Get back on I-90 and head east to exit 26 (Ward Creek). The Ward Creek exit is only accessible to eastbound travelers. Travelers heading west after the hike will have to drive east to exit 28 and turn around. From exit 26, travel south on Ward

Creek Road (Forest Road 889) for 6.25 miles to its crossing of Ward Creek and the trailhead (elev. 4060 feet). The road shoulder accommodates parking for several vehicles.

ON THE TRAIL

From the trailhead, wander upstream along Ward Creek, the mossy cobbles of its bed shaded by some truly gargantuan cedars—some upwards of six feet in diameter. This grotto-like grove survived the big blowup of the 1910 fires, one of the only such stands in the Great Burn to do so.

At 1 mile, leaving cedars behind, climb past a charming waterfall on Ward Creek, and stay right at a junction with a trail that ascends off to the left. From here, spruce replace cedar and huckleberries begin to grow in earnest as the trail climbs away from Ward Creek. At 2.4 miles (elev. 5480 feet), cross a shallow brook and, a few hundred yards later, a steep side trail to Hazel Lake. Waterfalls streak the beargrass slopes above Hazel Lake's south face, but because steep lodgepole forest prevents easy shoreline access from the main trail, most hikers walk right past this lake in favor of Hub Lake.

Enjoying the view from the shoulder of Ward Peak

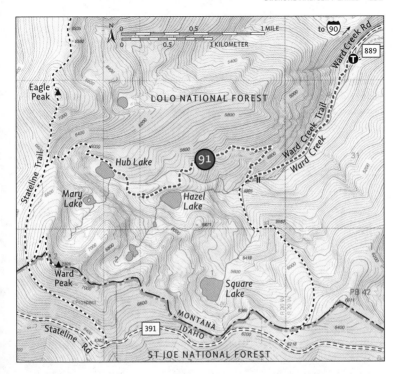

From Hazel, continue uphill, ascending a huckleberry-flush slope before dipping down into Hub Lake's outlet creek at 3 miles (elev. 5660 feet). Cross the creek, aided by logs, and walk another two hundred yards to Hub's shore. Hub is the smaller but more scenic of the two lakes, its shores, bounded by beargrass and huckleberries, perfect for a quick overnight stay. Late in the summer, otherwise waterlogged tent sites near the inlet dry out and make a good base for exploration. Whether you're staying for the day or weekend, climb the beargrass slope above the lake's inlet to investigate an old mine shaft that runs some 300 feet back into the slopes, a remnant of the Silver Valley's get-rich roots.

EXTENDING YOUR TRIP

Ambitious hikers can climb 1 mile and another thousand feet to the Stateline Trail on the divide, and from there follow a faint footpath to either Ward or Eagle Peaks for even better views of the endless pickets of the Bitterroots.

92 Diamond and Cliff Lakes

RATING/ DIFFICULTY	ROUNDTRIP	ELEV GAIN/ HIGH POINT	SEASON
****/2	2 miles	600 feet/ 5940 feet	Mid-June– Oct

Map: USGS Torino Peak, MT; **Contact:** Lolo National Forest, Superior Ranger District;

Note: Open to horses and bicycles; **GPS:** 47.1482°, -115.1735°

Cliff Lake provides a miniature dose of Bitterroots wilderness, with crashing waterfalls and cliff-rimmed waters. Car campers at Diamond Lake Campground can enjoy Cliff Lake for a post-picnic stroll; backpackers can take kids and *tenderfoots there. For the effort, there may be no better lake in the northern Bitterroots.*

GETTING THERE

From Interstate 90, take exit 47 (Superior) south to Southside Frontage Road. Turn right (west) and drive 4.9 miles to Dry Creek Road (Forest Road 342). Turn left and drive 9.9 miles, then bear left on FR 7843. At 3.5 miles,

Casting about in Cliff Lake

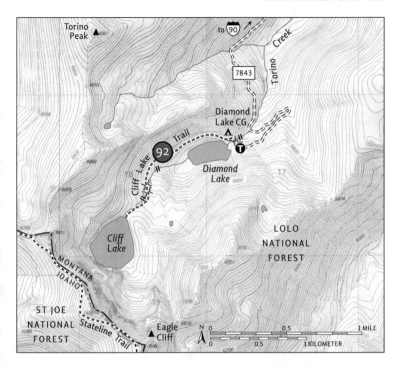

stay right, and at 4 miles reach the road's end at Diamond Lake Campground and trailhead (elev. 5410 feet). Privy available.

ON THE TRAIL

On Cliff Lake Trail 100, cross the closed-to-motors bridge and pass campsites, joining an old roadbed as it ascends gradually through thick forest for 0.5 mile. Scan shallow Diamond Lake and its marshy margins for moose.

Now maintained as singletrack, the trail briefly levels before ascending across an avalanche slope swollen with blooms—agastache, western coneflower, and cow parsnip prominent. To the left, a waterfall tumbles toward Diamond Lake. Cross a couple soggy sections of tread, and enter cool forest. At 0.7 mile cross the first of two sturdy footbridges that span Torino Creek, the latter at the base of a small cascades.

Pass another two-tiered waterfall, and reach the outlet of Cliff Lake. Tall fool's huckleberry surrounds several well-beaten tent sites, but for better picnic spots contour around the east side of the lake. Anywhere on the easily accessible shoreline will work for anglers—and for those angling for a view of icy-hued Eagle Cliff and its permanent snowfield. Consider this a miniature dose of western Montana wilderness, with the corresponding lack of crowds to match.

93 Lost Lake

RATING/ DIFFICULTY	ROUNDTRIP	ELEV GAIN/ HIGH POINT	SEASON
***/3	7.6 miles	1950 feet/ 6170 feet	June–Oct

Maps: USGS Sherlock Peak, MT; USGS Illinois Peak, MT; USGS Wilson Gulch, MT; **Contact:** Lolo National Forest, Superior Ranger District; **Note:** Open to horses and bicycles; **GPS:** 47.1275°, -115.1014°

Traverse broad meadows and flower-choked slopes past a series of hidden waterfalls to a small lake shrouded in willows and subalpine firs. Lost Lake lacks the high-mountain mystique of other Bitterroots lakes, but it's the least of the charms on this rarely used trail. And even if its namesake lake doesn't stack up to some, there's plenty to recommend it— especially in early summer when the wildflowers are blooming and Lost Falls is at its peak.

GETTING THERE

From Interstate 90, take exit 47 (Superior). On the south side of the freeway, turn left (east) on Diamond Match Road. Drive 1 mile, then turn right on Cedar Creek Road (Forest Road 320). Continue 5.8 miles (paved for the first 2.8 miles, good gravel thereafter) to Oregon Gulch Road (FR 7865). Turn right, and continue 8.3 miles to the trailhead at

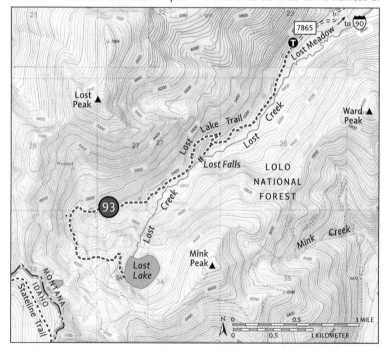

a hairpin turn just before road's end (elev. 4830 feet).

ON THE TRAIL
Lost Lake Trail 804 begins by skirting Lost Meadow, a flat, mid-elevation meadow of a type rarely seen on Bitterroots hikes. It's a great spot to scan for wildlife, particularly in the morning. A spur trail immediately leads to a dispersed camp on the creek; stay right.

Enter a thick forest of fir and western redcedar, cross a couple small hop-over brooks, then hike cool forest within earshot of Lost Creek. Western coneflowers crowd the trail anywhere the sun can breach the thick branches above.

At 1.1 miles (elev. 4960 feet), reach a marked junction. To the right is the route to Lost Lake, but first take the 200-yard spur to the base of Lost Falls. Set back from the end of the path and well-hidden behind a screen of streamside vegetation, the narrow sixty-foot drop of Lost Falls certainly lives up to its name.

Back on the main trail, ascend a handful of switchbacks over an exposed rock knob with views into the Lost Creek drainage. Following the course of Lost Creek, the trail alternates between open meadows of waist-high wildflowers—aster, agastache, pearly everlasting—and dense timber, including a few old Engelmann spruce and western red-cedar, survivors of the 1910 Great Burn. Pass a series of small shaded cascades—at 2.4 miles look for a small trailside sign marking "Canteen Falls." Matted vegetation marks deer and elk bedding spots, and the occasional wolf tracks chart the return of this elusive predator. The trail begins ascending more steeply, taking on an increasingly subalpine character, and at 2.7 miles (elev. 5800 feet) enters an open, expansive meadow at the base of Lost Peak.

Late summer at Lost Lake

Shouldering through unruly blooms, the yellow flowers of shrubby cinquefoil underfoot, round the contour of the meadow as it climbs into subalpine basins. At 3.3 miles (elev. 6110 feet), bear left at a junction with an old roadbed (see Extending Your Trip) and descend through fool's huckleberry; shortly after, bear right at another junction and drop down to the lake basin at 3.8 miles (elev. 6030 feet).

Surrounded by willows on its west and south shores and subalpine firs elsewhere, Lost Lake's shallow, silty waters are difficult to access—or even see—except from one small campsite at trail's end. No peaks or cirques crown the shoreline. But anglers willing to wade should find eager fish rising.

EXTENDING YOUR TRIP

From the old roadbed above Lost Lake, ascend to the Stateline Trail. Following the faint tread south, hikers can bag Bonanza Lakes (Hike 95) too.

94 Oregon Lakes

RATING/ DIFFICULTY	ROUNDTRIP	ELEV GAIN/ HIGH POINT	SEASON
***/2	1.2 miles	580 feet/ 5900 feet	June–Oct

Map: USGS Illinois Peak, MT; **Contact:** Lolo National Forest, Superior Ranger District; **Note:** Open to horses and bicycles; **GPS:** 47.0620°, -155.0850°

The 1.2-mile roundtrip hike to the Oregon Lakes is one of the shortest lake hikes in the Bitterroot Mountains, but that doesn't make the destination any less spectacular.

GETTING THERE

From Interstate 90, take exit 47 (Superior). On the south side of the freeway, turn left (east) on Diamond Match Road. Drive 1 mile, then turn right on Cedar Creek Road (Forest Road 320). Drive 20.9 miles (paved for the first 2.8 miles, good gravel thereafter) to FR 18688. Turn left, and drive 0.4 mile to a sharp turn in the road and the trailhead (elev. 5340 feet).

ON THE TRAIL

Oregon Lakes Trail is almost too easy: hikers can reach the lower lake in a short but steep fifteen minutes, then the middle lake with another five minutes of effort. But the trail puts its short length to good use, gaining 400 feet in a quarter mile. Beginning in a lush creek drainage, the trail steeply ascends on narrow, brushy tread, thimbleberries and columbine lining the path. Several small cascades course down the narrow gulch.

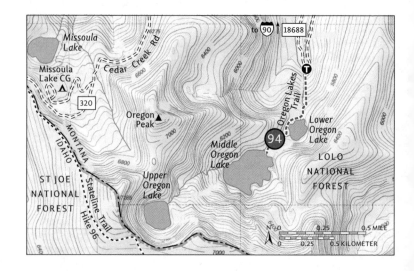

Middle Oregon Lake mirrors dusk-colored clouds.

The grade relents and then dips down to the outlet of Lower Oregon Lake at 0.3 mile (elev. 5730 feet). With the exception of a wide avalanche path on the steep east shore, timber surrounds much of the tiny tarn. A raft of logs crowds much of the shoreline, but hikers will find good access to the water on a tiny forested finger that juts into the lake about fifty yards from the outlet. Twisted spruce shelter several well-worn campsites.

To reach Lower Oregon Lake's prettier kin, cross the inlet and continue climbing steeply up the creek course to Middle Oregon Lake at 0.6 mile (elev. 5900 feet). Sitting in a lush cirque with stringers of subalpine fir, Middle Oregon Lake offers many granite rocks on which to watch the waterfall crashing down its west shore. As might be expected of lakes with such easy access, Middle and Lower Oregon Lakes are popular spots, and it shows: be sure to practice a zero-impact visit.

EXTENDING YOUR TRIP

Middle Oregon Lake will satisfy all but those desperate to crawl off-trail through a labyrinth of alder limbs to reach Upper Oregon Lake. A cross-country descent to the upper lake from the Stateline Trail (see Hike 96) would be a steep, but safer, bet.

95 Stateline Trail to Bonanza Lakes

RATING/ DIFFICULTY	ROUNDTRIP	ELEV GAIN/ HIGH POINT	SEASON
*****/3	5.4 miles	1040 feet/ 6630 feet	Late June–Oct

Maps: USGS Sherlock Peak, MT; USGS Illinois Peak, MT; **Contact:** Lolo National Forest, Superior Ranger District; **Note:** Open to motorcycles, horses, and bicycles; **GPS:** 47.0610°, -115.1205°

Strike it rich with two subalpine lakes, each with its own character, in a region of the Bitterroots that hasn't been mined heavily for recreation. Save for one short steep stretch, the only difficult part of this hike is deciding which lake to linger at.

GETTING THERE

From Interstate 90, take exit 47 (Superior). On the south side of the freeway, turn left (east) on Diamond Match Road. Drive 1 mile, then turn right on Cedar Creek Road (Forest Road 320). Drive 24.9 miles (paved for the first 2.8 miles, good gravel thereafter) to the trailhead at Cascade Pass on the Idaho-Montana border (elev. 6470 feet).

ON THE TRAIL

From the Cascade Pass trailhead for Stateline Trail 738, trace the crest of the Bitterroot Divide north through dry lodgepole forest, stunted subalpine groves, and grassy meadows. It's a wildflower bonanza: beargrass, harebell, and western coneflower carpet the open subalpine forest. The walking is as easy as it comes, so admire the blooms and, beyond, the bare, burnt-over ridges to

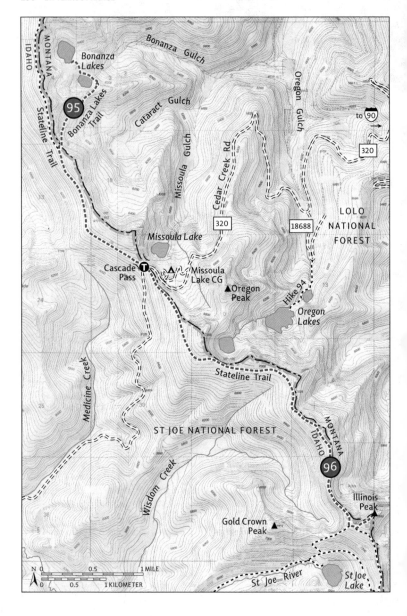

Traversing the open slopes of the Stateline Trail on the way to Bonanza Lakes

the west. This section of the Stateline Trail is open to motorcycles, but the narrow tread belies light use of any kind.

On the pleasant, level tread, small chunks of quartz catch the eye, the sparkling stones an indicator of potential mineral wealth. In fact, in 1869 Cedar Creek experienced a miniature midwinter gold rush, as nearly three thousand miners flooded into the drainage, staking the entire gulch in one day; little paid out, but the miners left their mark, both on the ground and on maps, the name Bonanza Lakes commemorating a strike either real or hoped-for. The high mineral content—and high, tree-free ridge the trail traverses—should also be a clue that the area gets its share of lightning. Stay off the ridge if thunderstorms are in the forecast and avoid an unlucky strike of your own.

Cross several small talus fields, and in open, subalpine forest, turn right at a junction at 1.5 miles (elev. 6630 feet). Descend the steep, rocky tread as it traverses above a vast, two-tiered meadow. Drop into a saddle, then climb a low, lodgepole-forested ridge, the bowl of lower Bonanza Lake visible below. Descend long, loping switchbacks to the lower lake's east shore at 2.5 miles (elev. 6280 feet). The sandy-bottomed lake is well-suited to swimming, and the shaded, huckleberry-laden shore is ideal for whiling away an hour or two. But first, continue another quarter mile to the upper lake (elev. 6320 feet). Compare the two bodies of water, which exemplify the spectrum of Bitterroots lakes: the lower ringed by forest and the upper set into granite shores at the base of a vast, nearly vertical meadow. Take your pick; it's an embarrassment of riches.

EXTENDING YOUR TRIP

Continue north on the Stateline Trail to Eagle Cliff Peak some six miles distant. Past the junction with the Bonanza Lakes Trail, the tread grows increasingly faint.

259

96 Stateline Trail to Illinois Peak

RATING/ DIFFICULTY	ROUNDTRIP	ELEV GAIN/ HIGH POINT	SEASON
*****/3	8 miles	1840 feet/ 7690 feet	Late June–Oct

Map: USGS Illinois Peak, MT; **Contact:** Lolo National Forest, Superior Ranger District; **Note:** Open to horses and bicycles; **GPS:** 47.0610°, -115.1205°

Ramble high on the Bitterroot Divide to the flat, flower-topped summit of 7690-foot Illinois Peak. From the footings of its old lookout, gaze upon the seemingly endless sea of rounded Bitterroot ridges, and imagine the vigilance of those tasked with protecting this landscape from a repeat of the catastrophic Great Burn of 1910.

GETTING THERE

From Interstate 90, take exit 47 (Superior). On the south side of the freeway, turn left (east) on Diamond Match Road. Drive 1 mile, then turn right on Cedar Creek Road (Forest Road 320). Drive 24.9 miles (paved for the first 2.8 miles, good gravel thereafter) to the trailhead at Cascade Pass on the Idaho-Montana border (elev. 6470 feet).

ON THE TRAIL

From the Cascade Pass trailhead for Stateline Trail 738 on the Idaho-Montana border, ascend wide, rocky tread for nearly a mile, the only significant climbing until the shoulder of Illinois Peak. At 0.9 mile, the tread, now true singletrack, begins to level out among diminutive subalpine firs.

The views, and wildflowers, get progressively more impressive—some of the best in

Pausing among purple vetch on the way to Illinois Peak

the northern Bitterroots. At 1.3 miles (elev. 7000 feet), a twenty-five-foot spur trail accesses an incredible aerial vista of Upper Oregon Lake from the top of a steep meadow on the shoulder of Oregon Peak. A rich palette of color—creamy-colored collomia and bear-grass, purple-hued penstemon and vetch, yellow arnica, hawkweed, and blue aster—carpets the ground beneath Christmas-tree firs. Turn around, too, for views of Gold Crown Peak just across the border in Idaho.

Continue through a tundra-like landscape laid bare by the Great Burn as the trail undulates under a few wizened whitebark pine and across broad wet meadows, which, in early summer, burst with shooting star. The trail stays to the west of the ridge, intersecting at 2.9 miles (elev. 7210 feet) a defunct path that stayed higher on the crest.

Now on the exposed spine of the ridge, cross a narrow notch in the rocks. To the left, well below the ridgeline, lies a small tarn. Straight ahead loom the steep-sided east-facing couloirs of Illinois Peak. Climb a narrow path blasted into the rock, and at 3.7 miles (elev. 7450 feet), bear left (the trail right descends steeply to the St. Joe River just downstream of St. Joe Lake). In a hundred yards, bear left again, and on steep, rutted tread, climb the last quarter mile to the summit (elev. 7690 feet).

In contrast to the couloir-cut east face of the peak seen from farther north on the trail, the summit is broad and flat, filled with diminutive alpine flowers. A lookout tower once sat on this summit, from which a fire lookout scanned nearby peaks for signs of wildfire, part of the Forest Service's zeal, in the wake of the 1910 Great Burn, to prevent future fires. Ironically, the Forest Service razed this and thousands of similar structures in its midcentury mission to modernize wildfire detection. Fortunately, the views remain, of the "Shadowy St. Joe" River drainage to the west and the sea of Bitterroots summits all around.

Dalton Lake sits amid diminutive heather.

EXTENDING YOUR TRIP

The Stateline Trail continues south for another two dozen miles. Parties with two vehicles could arrange a point-to-point hike between Cascade Pass and Hoodoo Pass to the south, but it would entail a long shuttle. A short, though steep, alternative is the trail to St. Joe River just downstream of St. Joe Lake. A spring just above the lake is the source of the famed fly-fishing waters.

97 Heart Lake

RATING/ DIFFICULTY	ROUNDTRIP	ELEV GAIN/ HIGH POINT	SEASON
*****/3	5.4 miles	1330 feet/ 5760 feet	Late June–Oct

Map: USGS Straight Peak, MT-ID; **Contact:** Lolo National Forest, Superior Ranger District; **Note:** Open to horses and bicycles; **GPS:** 46.9831°, -114.9779°

The largest subalpine lake in this part of the Bitterroot Range, Heart Lake is the centerpiece of the 250,000-acre Great Burn Proposed Wilderness Area. One of the most well-known of the northern Bitterroots hikes—but by no means crowded—it's one of the few places in the area where hikers can expect to see out-of-state plates in the summer.

GETTING THERE

From Interstate 90, take exit 47 (Superior). On the south side of the freeway, turn left (east) on Diamond Match Road (County Road 257, which becomes Forest Road 250). Travel 20 miles (paved for the first 6 miles), past Trout Creek Campground, to the trailhead on the left side of the road (elev. 4690 feet). Overflow parking on the opposite side

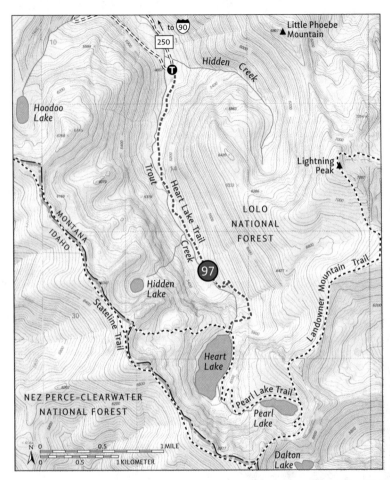

of the road accommodates several vehicles and offers a privy.

ON THE TRAIL

On Heart Lake Trail 171, immediately enter cool Engelmann spruce forest, crossing a creek on a split-log span. The forest stands in stark contrast to the brushy, tundra-like slopes of much of its surroundings. The intensity of the 1910 Great Burn scorched the soil such that, combined with the short growing season at elevation, little but ground-hugging tundra plants have managed to survive on the Bitterroot Divide.

Cross a long, shadeless avalanche slope, keeping an eye on the brush-obscured rocks

THE GREAT BURN

On August 20, 1910, strong "Palousers"—powerful northeasterly winds out of the Palouse farming country of eastern Washington—kicked up a hot, dry gale across the pine forests of northern Idaho and western Montana. It had already been a long fire season; crews had been battling fires since April following a nearly nonexistent winter. The Palouse winds woke nearly eighteen hundred small blazes and stoked them into a historic hellstorm known as the Great Burn.

When the catastrophic wildfires of the summer of 1910 finally subsided, they left behind more than three million acres of ravaged forest. At least eighty-five people died. Overnight, the firestorm reduced several mining towns to ash and removed them from the map; half of Wallace burned down. They left behind a legacy of US Forest Service wildfire management, the repercussions of which are still being felt today.

In response to the wildfires, the fledgling Forest Service committed to systematic wildfire suppression across the lands in its jurisdiction, culminating in the "10 AM" rule, which stated that all wildfires had to be extinguished by 10 AM the day after they were spotted.

Over the course of the 20th century, the Forest Service did its job exceedingly well, such that fire was excluded from many of our nation's forests. However, the last two decades have produced much research that demonstrates wildfires are a natural, and integral, part of healthy forest ecosystems.

In western Montana, the wildfires played a particularly large role in shaping the ecosystem. The intensity of the 1910 Great Burn scorched the soil such that, combined with the short growing season at elevation, little but ground-hugging tundra plants have managed to survive on the Bitterroot Divide. Elsewhere, drainages that escaped the conflagration harbor ancient cedars. The combination of landscapes—high and barren and low and lush—in such close proximity is one reason conservationists and the Forest Service have for decades supported the protection of 250,000 acres of the Bitterroot Range as wilderness.

at your feet. The trail enters unburnt forest again as it meanders southward, crossing several waterlogged areas as it maintains a stream-level gradient.

At 2 miles (elev. 5310 feet) mount several steep switchbacks as the trail climbs out of the creek drainage. Cross a small side channel before making a shallow ford of Trout Creek at 2.5 miles (elev. 5680 feet). Immediately after, come to a junction. The way straight is a continuation of the Heart Lake Trail but doesn't approach the lake; instead, it climbs a steep mile to the Bitterroot Divide.

Rather, bear left and follow Trout Creek upstream to Heart Lake's log-jammed outlet at 2.7 miles (elev. 5760 feet).

The largest lake in the Great Burn Proposed Wilderness Area, Heart Lake occupies the base of a steep cirque on which mountain goats frequently scramble (when they're not making sweat-seeking circuits of the campsites). Several tent sites dot the north shore of the lake; a backcountry pit toilet sits just uphill. Even better lunching spots, complete with shallow ramps of rock perfect for sunning or swimming, lie on the other side of the lake's outlet, on the trail to Pearl Lake.

EXTENDING YOUR TRIP

From Heart Lake, another mile of walking deposits hikers at Pearl Lake, set in a granite bench high on the Bitterroot Divide. From there, continue climbing for a mile through heathered tundra to a short, steep side trail to tiny Dalton Lake. Either lake makes for a worthwhile spot to stretch legs, splash in the lake, or set up a tent for a weekend of Great Burn exploration. From above Dalton Lake, it's a short climb to the Bitterroot Crest, from which you can make a loop north to return to Heart Lake for an 11-mile roundtrip.

98 Straight Creek

RATING/ DIFFICULTY	ROUNDTRIP	ELEV GAIN/ HIGH POINT	SEASON
****/3	10.4 miles	2160 feet/ 4840 feet	Late June– early Nov

Map: USGS Saint Patrick Peak, MT; **Contact:** Lolo National Forest, Ninemile Ranger District; **Note:** Dogs, horses, and bicycles permitted; **GPS:** 46.9088°, -114.8047°

 *Sluicing through the Great Burn of the Bitterroots, Straight Creek offers a look at the 1910 fire's effects as well as those of more recent conflagrations.*

GETTING THERE

From Interstate 90 about 35 miles west of Missoula, take exit 66 (Fish Creek). Head south on Fish Creek Road, which becomes Forest Road 343, passing Montana's champion ponderosa pine tree, for 9.3 miles to West Fork Fish Creek Road (FR 7750). Bear right and continue 6.6 miles, past the old Hole-in-the-Wall Lodge, to the road's end at Clearwater Crossing Campground (elev. 3490 feet). Privy available.

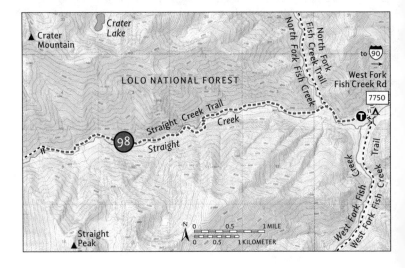

Straight Creek Falls surges with early summer snowmelt.

ON THE TRAIL

From the Clearwater Crossing Campground, North Fork Fish Creek Trail 103 follows the remains of an old administrative road past closed-to-the-public Forest Service outbuildings. A 2015 wildfire razed much of the Fish Creek drainage; at peak intensity, its flames cauterized the deep root systems of old-growth cedar and spruce spared by the Great Burn and reduced lodgepole and ponderosa to acres of stark, blackened snags. However, some of the stateliest old-growth ponderosa pines survived thanks to their thick plated bark, and new life abounds.

After a few minutes of hiking, the trail—now on true singletrack—joins the course of North Fork Fish Creek. Unburdened by bends of any significance, the watercourse sluices through cottonwoods and willows. In three-quarters of a mile, continue straight at a junction with the North Fork Fish Creek Trail. Now on the Straight Creek Trail, immediately come to the confluence of Straight Creek and North Fork Fish Creek. Early in the season, when they're thundering with snowmelt, crossing both creeks can be downright treacherous; if in doubt, turn around—the North Fork Fish Creek Trail provides pleasant walking through alternating stands of snags and intact cedars safely above creek level.

Once across, head west at stream gradient along Straight Creek and immediately cross Straight Creek again. Now on the north side of the creek, the trail repeatedly climbs away from and rejoins the creek, clover and creeping dogbane encroaching upon the narrow tread.

At 2.6 miles (elev. 3950 feet), reach a wide, slippery crossing of Straight Creek. On the other side, the trail climbs away from and then returns to creek level, crossing

Calm Kid Lake reflects fall colors.

the waterway yet again at 3.2 miles; a wider, calmer creek greets hikers at this ford.

Again on the north side of the creek, hop across a trio of trail-crossing trickles over the next mile before the trail departs brushy forest for the last time, reaching a broad avalanche-cut opening at 5.2 miles (elev. 4840 feet). Here, Straight Creek stepladders down a series of cockeyed bedrock cascades as it negotiates one of the watercourse's few curves. Meanwhile, wildflowers—purple fireweed, creamy death camas, silvery tufts of prairie smoke—cascade down the south-facing slope. Here, the heat of the 1910 Great Burn effectively created a tundra ecosystem at a much lower elevation than it would otherwise be found; in this rocky, frequently snowbound environment, only a few stunted trees have managed to take hold in the century hence.

Beat poet Gary Snyder, considered the poet laureate of deep ecology, memorialized this creek in his eponymous poem, writing of its sluicing stream that it "spills out / rock lip pool, bends over, / braided, white, foaming." After you have witnessed Straight Creek's cascades up close, especially in the fervor of early summer, Snyder's propulsive, poetic language should come as no surprise.

EXTENDING YOUR TRIP

Beyond the first set of cascades, the Straight Creek Trail continues upstream with several foot-soaking crossings toward the Siamese Lakes high on the Bitterroot Divide.

99 Kid and Mud Lakes

RATING/ DIFFICULTY	ROUNDTRIP	ELEV GAIN/ HIGH POINT	SEASON
****/3	9 miles	2210 feet/ 6920 feet	July–Oct

Map: USGS Schley Mountain, MT; **Contact:** Lolo National Forest, Ninemile Ranger District; **Note:** Horses, bicycles, and dogs permitted; **GPS:** 46.7918°, -114.7878°

Let your vehicle do most of the climbing to these charming tarns in the southern portion of the Great Burn. It's a landscape of dramatic cliff faces and alpine tundra, spare, low-growing subalpine firs, and fields of bear-grass. Families with little ones will find the effort to their liking, but all will enjoy the berry picking and flower viewing.

GETTING THERE

From Interstate 90 about 35 miles west of Missoula, take exit 66 (Fish Creek). Head south on Fish Creek Road (becomes Forest Road 343), passing Montana's champion ponderosa pine tree, for 16 miles to Surveyor Creek Road (FR 7734). Turn right and proceed 12 miles to the lower trailhead at Schley Saddle. If the road past Schley Saddle is not gated, continue 3 miles to the main trailhead; otherwise, park here, adding 3 miles to the hike in each direction. Privy available at Schley Saddle.

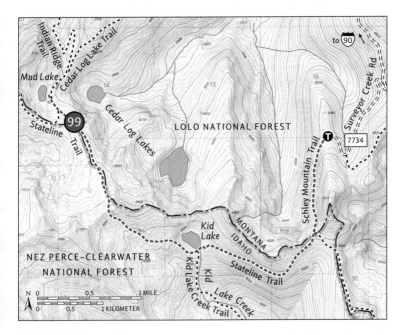

ON THE TRAIL

Making use of a relic roadbed, climb above the blasted rock of an old mine at a gentle pace on Schley Mountain Trail 110. After a mile, having gained only 150 feet, pass over a low, sparsely wooded saddle into Idaho, then begin a gradual descent as the rough roadbed traverses a broad, talus-strewn slope high above the Kelly Creek drainage, a blue-ribbon Bitterroots trout stream. As the trail bends to the west, trees replace talus, and at 2.3 miles (elev. 6250 feet) the trail crosses the shallow outlet of Kid Lake. Beargrass and boulders hug the south shore of this infinity-pool pond, beyond which the landscape drops dramatically toward Kelly Creek. Horse-trampled camps can be found among the miniature subalpine firs, as can huckleberries.

Pass the signed junction at the outlet (the way left follows Kid Lake Creek Trail downstream toward Kelly Creek) and continue westward as the trail climbs, finally with some vigor, up increasingly sparsely vegetated slopes. The rounded, rocky balds bloom profusely in the summer. Having climbed 700 feet in the previous mile, the trail passes back into Montana and proceeds to lose an equal amount of elevation as it parallels the crest of the Bitterroot Divide, now under the cover of thick subalpine timber.

At 4.4 miles, bear right at a junction (the way left proceeds to Admiral Peak; see Extending Your Trip), and in another tenth of a mile reach the outlet of miniscule Mud Lake. Despite its unflattering appellation, Mud Lake is a serene spot, occupying a sheltered north-facing shoulder of Admiral Peak. Surprisingly, given its meadow surroundings and shallow bottom, Mud Lake seems to attract fewer biting bugs than similarly appointed neighbors. Below lie several tributaries of Fish Creek, which survived the Great Burn of 1910 and the same fate in 2015.

EXTENDING YOUR TRIP

From just before Mud Lake, hikers can climb 1000 feet to the rocky cap of Admiral Peak.

100 Burdette Creek

RATING/ DIFFICULTY	ROUNDTRIP	ELEV GAIN/ HIGH POINT	SEASON
***/3	9.8 miles	1660 feet/ 4270 feet	May–Nov

Map: USGS Lupine Creek, MT; **Contact:** Lolo National Forest, Ninemile Ranger District; **Note:** Open to horses and bicycles; **GPS:** 46.8069°, -114.6089°

Burdette Creek boasts—albeit quietly—an increasingly rare low-elevation old-growth ponderosa and larch

The author walks among larch above Burdette Creek.

parkland. It's perfect for a shoulder-season stroll, its low elevation meaning snow-free spring access and its larch lighting up with autumn glow. No destination here, just one statuesque tree after another.

GETTING THERE

From the junction of US Highways 12 and 93 in Lolo, drive 26.5 miles west on US 12, 0.4 mile past Lolo Hot Springs, to Fish Creek Road (Forest Road 343). Turn right (north) and drive 9.4 miles to the trailhead on the right side of the road (elev. 3890 feet). A pullout on the left-side shoulder accommodates two vehicles.

ON THE TRAIL

Burdette Creek Trail 2 forms the centerpiece of the 16,000-acre Burdette Creek Roadless Area, its low-elevation parkland possessing a quieter character than the glittering lakes and towering battlements of the high-elevation Bitterroots. From the trailhead the route, an old roadbed, skirts private property in a steep climb before cresting the toe of a ridge at 0.5 mile (elev. 4180 feet). From here the trail descends through gradually thinning timber to cross Burdette Creek at 1.2 miles (elev. 3790 feet). A few side-by-side skinned logs might provide a dry crossing; otherwise it's a shin-deep ford across four feet of sluggish creek.

Now on dry ground, the trail wanders among a fabulous open parkland of old-growth larch and ponderosa—some of the finest such habitat in western Montana, and increasingly rare. (Some 15 miles to the north, just off FR 343, Montana's champion ponderosa pine makes for a fine post-hike side trip.) The two species' thickly furrowed, fire-resistant bark looks similar, particularly on old trees; a peek into the trees' high, sun-loving

canopy will identify them. Of course, at the peak of autumn there's no question—larch is the star. Western larch is the only species of larch whose distribution is largely confined to the Inland Northwest. Like other larch, the western larch is a deciduous conifer, meaning that it loses its needles every fall and produces a completely new set in the spring. In the fall, the needles go out in a blaze of glory, lighting up mid-elevation slopes with yellow and gold. Speaking of bright colors, Burdette Creek has been set aside as wintering range for a large herd of elk; wear orange during

hunting season, when this otherwise-silent trail gets its only traffic.

As it travels upstream, the trail closes in on Burdette Creek and its willow-filled bottomlands. Black bear scat and beaver dams provide good visual evidence of the wildlife-viewing opportunities here. Brush begins to encroach, serviceberry and ferns occasionally obscuring the narrow tread although the route is never hard to follow. The trail crosses small feeder creeks at 3.2 and 4.2 miles before beginning a half-mile traverse of a long talus toe of the steep ridgeline. Just shy of 5 miles (elev. 4260 feet) the trail fades out in a broad clearing of prickly hawthorn and other upland valley shrubs. From here, retrace your steps back to the trailhead.

Bitterroot Mountains

South of Lolo Pass, the 200-mile-long mass of granite known as the Idaho Batholith lies exposed on the Bitterroot Divide, like a half-extracted fossil. The advance of alpine glaciers during the most recent ice age sculpted the Bitterroot Mountains into a series of rugged peaks and steep, incredibly straight canyons cut by swift-running streams, some of the Northern Rockies most

The first snow of the season slickens the descent off Lolo Peak

rugged terrain. The largest wilderness area in the continental United States to be designated in the original 1964 Wilderness Act, the Selway-Bitterroot Wilderness protects 1.3 million acres—2000 square miles—of the heart of this landscape, and with it some of western Montana's most iconic hikes. Alpine larch towers over granite-flanked lakes, and serrated, heavily glaciated peaks tower even higher still: this is the quintessential Bitterroot Mountains.

101 Lolo Peak

RATING/ DIFFICULTY	ROUNDTRIP	ELEV GAIN/ HIGH POINT	SEASON
*****/5	11.4 miles	4170 feet/ 9096 feet	July–Sept

Map: USGS Carlton Lake, MT; **Contacts:** Bitterroot National Forest, Stevensville Ranger District; Lolo National Forest, Missoula Ranger District; **Notes:** Wilderness rules apply. Open to horses; **GPS:** 46.7168°, -114.1922°

The northernmost of the Bitterroot Range's 9000-foot peaks, Lolo Peak stands guard over the vast granite wilderness of the Selway-Bitterroot. This popular nontechnical summit, a mere 15 miles from Missoula, offers day hikers one of the easiest—and best—peak-bagging opportunities in the Bitterroots.

GETTING THERE

From Lolo, drive west on US Highway 12 for 3.8 miles to Mormon Peak Road (Forest Road 612). Turn left (south), cross the bridge over Lolo Creek, and proceed 8.5 miles on good gravel to the trailhead (elev. 5850 feet). The wide pullout accommodates a half dozen vehicles.

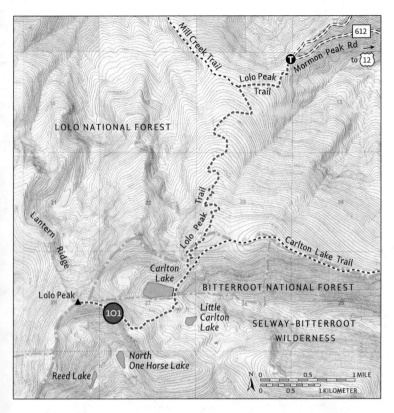

ON THE TRAIL

Wide, well-tended Lolo Peak Trail 1311 ambles aimlessly uphill through a thick forest of fir, passing a junction with Mill Creek Trail at 0.8 mile. The low-incline tread and loping switchbacks are clearly a reconstruction of a switchback-eschewing old route. An open parkland of alpine larch underlain by grouseberry gradually replaces lodgepole as openings in the trees reveal glimpses of Missoula and the Bitterroot foothills. Pass a small rock ledge at 1.7 miles (elev. 7040 feet) and Vista Point at 3.5 miles (elev. 8250

feet), both offering a preview of the granite gendarmes of Lolo's north ridge.

From here the trail switchbacks down to a rocky road-trail; bear right as it heads toward the rather unsightly outlet dam of Carlton Lake (elev. 7800 feet). Like many of its dammed Bitterroot kin, Carlton loses much of its charm late in the summer. But a raucous waterfall at the outlet hints at Little Carlton Lake not far below. For the summit, cross the outlet dam, and, just past the wilderness boundary, leave the trail—now true singletrack—and pick up

TRAIL ANGELS: SELWAY-BITTERROOT FRANK CHURCH FOUNDATION

On summer weekends, as many as several hundred hikers will make the pilgrimage to the 9351-foot summit of Saint Mary Peak and its restored lookout west of Stevensville in the Selway-Bitterroot Wilderness. Once every summer, staff and volunteers from the Selway-Bitterroot Frank Church Foundation (SBFC) make the same trip. But it's not just a walk. It's work. Wearing hard hats and leather gloves in the dry mountain heat, they cut back trail-swallowing brush and clean out drainage ditches with Pulaskis, the half-axe, half-adze tool that's the hallmark of trail hand tools. Teams with two-man crosscut saws—those six-foot-long blades now more commonly seen on the wall of a rustic saloon than in the hands of a lumberjack—make short work of the lanky lodgepole and sun-bleached and snow-sculpted whitebark pine snags crisscrossing the trail. A shower of sawdust, a four-person hiking boot heave-ho shove, and the trail is clear. One down, dozens to go.

Together with the adjacent 2.4-million-acre Frank Church–River of No Return Wilderness in central Idaho, the 1.3-million-acre Selway-Bitterroot Wilderness in north-central Idaho and western Montana spans an area nearly the size of Delaware—the largest block of roadless lands in the Lower 48. Laid out end to end, their trails would stretch from Washington to Florida and halfway back again. And the Forest Service and its volunteers maintain nearly all of them, using primitive hand tools, because the Wilderness Act prohibits, except in special circumstances, mechanized tools.

Chances are, if you've hiked in Montana, you've hiked on a trail maintained, at least in part, by volunteer labor. It's the reality in a political climate in which the Forest Service has seen ongoing significant budget reductions over the last several decades for recreational management. Wilderness trails are a concession to the human desire for exploration, but, in the end, the wilderness has the final say.

Land managers and their volunteer partners, then, must reconcile the Wilderness Act's stated aims of "future use and enjoyment as wilderness" with access to "primitive and un-confined . . . recreation" and the act's description that wilderness "generally appears to have been affected primarily by the forces of nature"—admonishments that seem to limit the guiding hand of government, well-intentioned as it may be.

Below St. Mary Peak's summit, the orderly parcels of farmland in the Bitterroot Valley, carved at right angles by roads, contrast with the serrated mass of Bitterroot spires to the west. The same type of labor, paid for in sweat, that settled the valley now keeps the mountains open for hikers, anglers, outfitters, and guides.

hints of an intermittent user trail that takes a southwesterly bearing toward the summit. The path angles around larch and over loose talus and ground-hugging heather as it gains the northernmost toe of the summit ridge; if in doubt, steer right. As it gains the ridge, the path runs a general course just below the rocky ridgeline; there's no exposure unless you go out of your way to find it.

Leave the last of the snow-cowed larch behind, and, at 5.7 miles (elev. 9096 feet), reach the summit. To the north are the gray granite pyramid of Ch-paa-qn and the blue-hued forested peaks of the "northern" Bitterroots, a contrast to the craggy cirques and spires of the Selway-Bitterroots. To the south curves the slightly higher South Lolo Peak, which shades the steep talus drainage of One Horse Creek below, and, beyond, the visible bones of the 200-mile Bitterroot Crest.

EXTENDING YOUR TRIP

Most day hikers consider this the true summit, owing to a quirk in the US Geological Survey nomenclature. But the south summit is actually higher by a little more than forty feet. It's easily reachable by descending off the north summit, passing a three-sided stone windbreak and the erroneously placed summit register, and crossing talus-flecked tundra to the south peak a half mile hence.

102 Sweeney Creek Lakes

RATING/ DIFFICULTY	ROUNDTRIP	ELEV GAIN/ HIGH POINT	SEASON
****/5	12.6 miles	3990 feet/ 7450 feet	Late June–Oct

Maps: USGS Carlton Lake, MT; USGS Dick Creek, MT; USGS Saint Joseph Peak, MT; USGS MT; Saint Mary Peak, **Contact:** Bitterroot National Forest, Stevensville Ranger District; **Notes:** Wilderness rules apply. Open to horses; **GPS:** 46.6222°, -114.1487°

In contrast to many of its canyon kin, the hike above Sweeney Creek starts high and stays high, treating hikers to open old-growth parkland en route to a series of subalpine lakes, each more austerely grand than the last.

GETTING THERE

From Florence, drive south on US Highway 93 for 1.5 miles to Sweeney Creek Loop (near milepost 73). Turn right (west), and proceed 1 mile; at the end of the pavement, continue straight (west) onto Sweeney Trail Road (Forest Road 1315). Bear right at the junction with Koepplin Lane and Upper Sweeney Creek Loop in 0.5 mile, and continue 5.5 miles to the road's end and trailhead (elev. 6000 feet). The last 0.5 mile is increasingly steep and deeply rutted; drivers of low-clearance vehicles may wish to park at one of the penultimate switchbacks and walk the last stretch of road.

ON THE TRAIL

From its high-elevation trailhead, Sweeney Ridge Trail 393 immediately retreats steeply upward through a series of switchbacks. Deeply furrowed Douglas-fir, some centuries old, crown a widely spaced parkland. Climb, with little relief, for 1.6 miles, whereupon the trail reaches a spire of split granite (elev. 7450 feet) from which Little Saint Joe Peak can be seen towering above the steep, dry Sweeney

Early summer ice encases Duffy Lake.

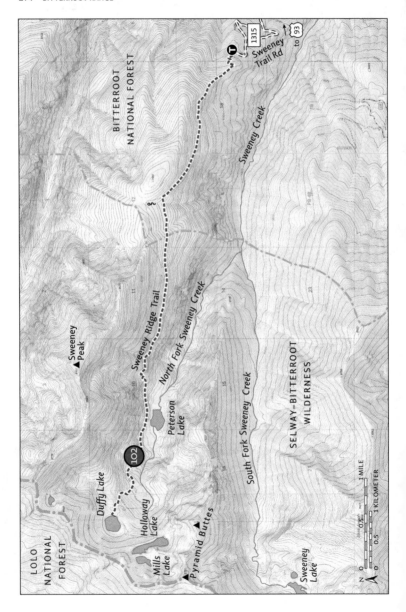

Creek drainage. Distant Bitterroot peaks shimmer, still a half dozen miles out of reach.

Pass a spring and, shortly after, enter wilderness at 2.5 miles (elev. 7420 feet). From here the trail follows a generally descending course through uniform lodgepole forest, Sweeney Creek's cascades unseen but audible far below. Peterson Lake, ringed in timber, can be glimpsed nearly a mile distant. Two swift but shallow stream crossings precede a couple of steep, rocky switchbacks, which deposit hikers on grassy and wildflower-dotted meadows—beargrass, lomatium, alpine forget-me-not—for the final half mile to Peterson Lake at 4.9 miles (elev. 6520 feet).

Steep, thick timber surrounds the reed-choked outlet of Peterson Lake, this unassuming body of water lacking the hard-edged granite grandeur of its neighbors. A well-used, shaded campsite at the inlet is the only real access, but good swimming and fishing can be found from rock perches nearby.

Back on the main trail, continue as it begins ascending across open rock and through patchy forest, the trail occasionally faint but easy to follow. Cross the swift waters of an unnamed tributary of North Fork Sweeney Creek and switchback past its granite cascades; a backward glance reveals the seldom-summited Pyramid Buttes to the south.

Pass several small marshy areas, and, in a broad, sparsely timbered bench, reach Duffy Lake at 6.3 miles (elev. 7350 feet). Clumps of spruce and subalpine fir dot the shallow cirque of the lake; a swift creek pours forth from below a rotting dam at the outlet. Several small campsites on the south side of the outlet make a fine base for scrambling Sweeney Peak to the north or to Holloway

and Mills Lakes, hidden in a hanging valley to the south.

EXTENDING YOUR TRIP

Occupying a narrow hanging valley to the immediate southwest of Duffy Lake, Holloway Lake is perhaps the most attractive of the three Sweeney Creek Lakes. To get there, head uphill around the crest of the toe ridge just to the southwest of Duffy Lake.

103 Bass Lake

RATING/ DIFFICULTY	ROUNDTRIP	ELEV GAIN/ HIGH POINT	SEASON
*****/5	15.4 miles	3550 feet/ 6830 feet	Late June–Sept

Maps: USFS Selway-Bitterroot Wilderness; USGS Saint Joseph Peak, MT; USGS Saint Mary Peak, MT; **Contact:** Bitterroot National Forest, Stevensville Ranger District; **Notes:** Wilderness rules apply. Open to horses; **GPS:** 46.5739°, -114.1450°

Bass Lake sits high on the Bitterroot Divide, its mile-long talus shores tucked at the head of an impressive U-shaped glacial valley. The lake itself, dammed for irrigation, is secondary to the beauty of Bass Creek Valley: high craggy colonnades, rushing cascades, and sprawling streamside meadows.

GETTING THERE

From Florence, drive south on US Highway 93 for 4 miles (between milepost 70 and 71) to Bass Creek Road. Turn right (west), and drive 2.6 miles to the large trailhead parking area just west of Charles Waters Memorial Campground (elev. 3760 feet). Privy available.

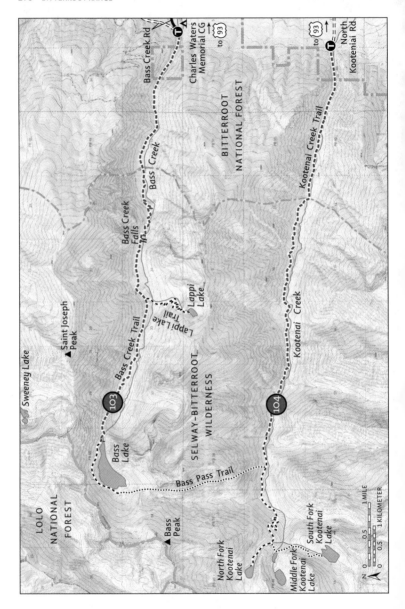

Snow-coated "Stormy Joe" overlooks Bass Lake.

ON THE TRAIL

Beginning on an old roadbed, Bass Creek Trail 4 never strays far from the rushing, cottonwood- and maple-shaded stream. At 0.25 mile, enter a half-mile stretch of private inholding; make sure to stay on the trail. The road-trail, never steep, passes a small, muddy pond at 1.8 miles (elev. 4540 feet) and enters dense larch forest and the Selway-Bitterroot Wilderness at 2.5 miles (elev. 4590 feet).

At 2.8 miles, look out for a cairn-marked but easy-to-miss junction to the right. If you reach the creek, you've gone a couple hundred yards too far. (The old trail, now rerouted, used to make a tricky crossing of the creek, unaided by a bridge, to continue on the west side of Bass Creek.) Switchback through talus and larch as the terrain opens up from the lush creek drainage now below you. The open forest reveals the battlements of the Bass Creek crags on the south side of the canyon, an appealing objective for rock climbers.

At 3.7 miles pass Bass Creek Falls, a popular destination for shorter hikes. Cross a couple small creeks, and at 4.4 miles (elev. 5690 feet) intersect the old trail. The trail enters

a pretty grove of young aspen in the broad, cliff-flanked canyon, then dives back into dense subalpine forest, passing the unsigned junction for Lappi Lake Trail at 5.5 miles.

Now on true singletrack, enter a broad, streamside subalpine meadow at 6.5 miles (elev. 6250 feet)—a relatively uncommon, and uncommonly scenic, sight in the normally tightly packed creek canyons of the Bitterroots. This is definitely bear country, and although grizzlies disappeared from the Bitterroots in the 1940s, hikers may encounter black bears here.

The final half mile to the lake—a strenuous climb on a steep, talus-packed path across the flank of Saint Joseph Peak—will tax the calves. But the view—a waterfall splashing out of the outlet of the lake into a broad, glacier-cut U-shaped valley with rugged pinnacles framing it on both sides—will provide plenty of excuses to pause. It's one of the best canyon views in the Bitterroots.

After that spectacle, Bass Lake's manmade outlet dam at 7.7 miles might underwhelm, especially when the late-summer drawdown for irrigation leaves it with the "bathtub-ring" look. But the bare, worn-down battlements of the Bitterroot Divide frame the lake nicely, and Saint Joseph Peak hovers to the north. The trail continues another mile along the lake's steep talus shoreline, providing plenty of room to stretch out. Backpackers will find the best tent sites in a flat copse of subalpine fir at the lake's southwest end.

EXTENDING YOUR TRIP

Hikers with two vehicles can arrange a nearly twenty-mile point-to-point hike connecting Bass Creek with the Kootenai Creek Trail (Hike 104) one drainage south. The shuttle is easy; the hike over the Bass Pass Trail, no longer maintained, is not. From the southwest end of Bass Lake, climb up to the steep forested saddle south of the lake. Dotted with dwarven subalpine firs, Bass Pass provides a seldom-viewed vantage over both Bass and Kootenai Creek Valleys. From here hikers must negotiate a pick-up sticks tangle of downed trees to intersect with the Kootenai Creek Trail about 0.7 mile south of Kootenai Lakes. Plan on two hours to hike this trail-less 1-mile stretch of the point-to-point route.

104 Kootenai Creek

RATING/ DIFFICULTY	ROUNDTRIP	ELEV GAIN/ HIGH POINT	SEASON
*****/5	14.6 miles	2700 feet/ 5290 feet	May–Nov

Maps: USGS Saint Joseph Peak, ID-MT; USGS Saint Mary Peak, MT; **Contact:** Bitterroot National Forest, Stevensville Ranger District; **Notes:** Wilderness rules apply. Open to horses; **GPS:** 46.5377°, -114.1510°

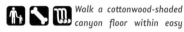

Walk a cottonwood-shaded canyon floor within easy reach of Kootenai Creek, its myriad clear pools, cascades, and riffles echoing off the moss-covered walls. One of the most popular portals to the Bitterroots, Kootenai Creek's lower reaches teem with hikers, joggers, dog-walkers, and equestrians most weekends. But solitude is easy to find in the rough-hewn upper miles of the canyon, as are a trio of sparkling pools in one of the Bitterroot's prettiest subalpine settings.

GETTING THERE

From Florence, drive south on US Highway 93 for 6 miles to North Kootenai Road (between mileposts 67 and 68). Turn right (west) and drive this good gravel road 2 miles past private property to the road's end and trailhead (elev. 3570 feet). Privy available.

ON THE TRAIL

From the large and busy trailhead for Kootenai Creek Trail 53, the wide, well-tended tread immediately retreats upstream underneath the walls of Kootenai Creek canyon. Expect lots of company on this first portion; it's a local favorite for those looking for easy access to Kootenai Creek's numerous clear pools, riffles, and rocky shores. Craggy, precipitous walls of gneiss and schist shade ponderosa and cottonwood as the trail crosses a private inholding its first half mile.

Eventually the canyon broadens somewhat on the terminal moraine of the glacier that originally carved the U-shaped profile of this valley. Here the stream bullies through a great mass of boulders. Scattered snags from an old burn provide scant shade as the trail negotiates a boggy log crossing at 2.6 miles (elev. 4080 feet). A half mile later, the trail reaches the wilderness boundary, a logical turnaround point for short treks. Otherwise, continue onward upstream as the trail traverses an open burn area, the heat of which can be withering on cloudless days. With only occasional forays into unburnt forest, the trail gains elevation in gulps on increasingly rougher tread.

At nearly 6 miles, enter cool bottomland of larch and tall yew—a welcoming respite on a hot day after the shadeless burn. A mile later, cross a large perennial stream and, at 7.3 miles (elev. 5280 feet), reach multitiered cascades in the shade of old-growth spruce. For day hikers, this is the last logical turnaround spot before committing to a steep ascent to the Kootenai Lakes (see Extending Your Trip).

EXTENDING YOUR TRIP

To continue to the Kootenai Lakes, continue upstream through old-growth spruce bottomland, ferns obscuring a faint junction to Bass Pass at 7.9 miles. The trail then begins ascending an agonizing number of meandering, seemingly aimless switchbacks, leavened only by views of the serrated peaks above each drainage. Following tread that occasionally fades as it angles across the sideslope, cross the North Fork Kootenai Creek at 9.3 miles and, immediately after, reach a junction. Proceed straight to the South Fork Kootenai Creek (right goes to the North Fork).

At 9.5 miles, cross the outlet of Middle Kootenai Lake. Beyond this crossing, the tread, heavily trenched and obscured by head-high vegetation, switchbacks up rocky ledges and sidehills across ballast blasted out of the talus for equestrian benefit. The trail hasn't seen loppers in years and is essentially gone; although the occasional cairn guides the way, plan on an hour of bushwhacking to reach South Kootenai

Lake. You'll have the bruised-up shins of a soccer player to show for it. But it's worth the effort: sheltered among three sides of steep, angular granite and exfoliated rock, with thick, moose-friendly meadows at the head and foot, South Kootenai Lake is among the Bitterroots' best. Deceptively well-used tent sites flank the outlet stream. Anglers will find active brook trout.

Kootenai Creek sluices through a granite canyon.

A hiker celebrates at the summit of Saint Mary Peak.

105 Saint Mary Peak

RATING/ DIFFICULTY	ROUNDTRIP	ELEV GAIN/ HIGH POINT	SEASON
*****/3	7 miles	2480 feet/ 9351 feet	July–late Sept

Maps: USFS Selway-Bitterroot Wilderness; USGS Saint Mary Peak, MT; **Contact:** Bitterroot National Forest, Stevensville Ranger District; **Notes:** Wilderness rules apply. Open to horses; **GPS:** 46.5004°, -114.2036°

Jesuit missionaries named the tallest peak on the Stevensville skyline after their Bitterroot Valley mission; on summer weekends, several hundred hikers will make the pilgrimage to the 9351-foot summit of Saint Mary Peak and its restored lookout. Graced with great views,

Saint Mary is at its most glorious under the golden vestments of late-September larch.

GETTING THERE

From Stevensville, drive south on US Highway 93 for 2 miles to Indian Prairie Loop (between mileposts 63 and 64). Drive west for 1.3 miles to Saint Mary's Road and turn right, continuing 0.5 mile to Saint Mary Peak Road (Forest Road 739). Follow this road, which gets progressively steeper, rougher, and narrower—make sure to bring a spare tire—for 12 miles to the road's end and large trailhead parking area (elev. 6870 feet). Privy available.

ON THE TRAIL

Don't be surprised to find, on a summer weekend, a dozen or so vehicles at the Saint Mary Peak Trail 116 trailhead; it's a popular

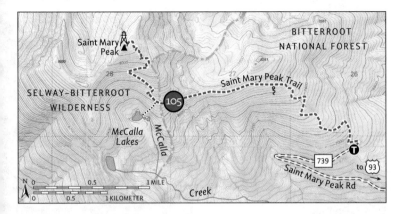

destination for Missoula-area residents. If it's solitude you seek, come midweek. Better yet, come in late September: the steep, east-facing prow of Saint Mary Peak has one of the Bitterroot Valley's best larch displays, an extensive intermixing of western larch and its alpine kin.

The wide, well-constructed Saint Mary Peak Trail makes numerous long switchbacks in its first mile, lodgepole, beargrass, and purple vetch flanking the path high and low. It's unremarkable hiking, although occasional gaps in the tree cover permit views of the Bitterroot Valley. The trail passes a spring and stock camp at 1 mile (elev. 7620 feet) and soon levels out among bleached whitebark pine snags, their forms sculpted by persistent snow and wind.

Traversing the south side of Saint Mary Peak among exposed bedrock and scattered subalpine cover, pass the wilderness boundary at 2.2 miles (elev. 8310 feet) and, immediately after, a cairn marking a rough spur trail to McCalla Lakes, visible below. Straight ahead is the first peek of Saint Mary Peak's active lookout.

Switchbacking up the south face of the peak, enter a krummholz corridor of stunted whitebark pine before leaving the tree line at 3 miles (elev. 8960 feet) and reaching a flat "false summit." With red mylonite rock and masses of mat-like alpine plants underfoot, enjoy the view before the final approach. The orderly parcels of farmland in the Bitterroot Valley below, carved at right angles by roads, contrast with the serrated mass of Bitterroot spires to the west.

The trail makes several shadeless switchbacks before reaching the lookout at 3.5 miles (elev. 9351 feet). The lookout, a fourteen-foot-square white cabin set atop a natural stone base, is the second to perch on the summit; a 1952 windstorm blew the first tower off the mountain. Today, the Selway-Bitterroot Frank Church Foundation provides volunteers to staff the lookout throughout the summer, performing maintenance and answering the questions of throngs of visitors.

Close by are the Castle Crags and the molar-like forms of the Heavenly Twins. On a clear day scan the horizon for mountains farther afield: the Rattlesnakes, Swans, Missions, and Lewis and Clark Range to the north; the Bitterroot and Beaverhead Ranges to the south; the Sapphires and, beyond, the

Flint Creek and Anaconda Ranges to the east; and to the west, the expansive interior of the Bitterroots.

EXTENDING YOUR TRIP

Just beyond the wilderness boundary, a cairn marks a faint boot path that descends 0.25 mile to the northernmost McCalla Lake, the first of two shallow fishless pools situated in the smooth granite and stunted whitebark pine of the McCalla Creek drainage. The path peters out before reaching the southernmost lake a half mile distant.

106 Glen Lake

RATING/ DIFFICULTY	ROUNDTRIP	ELEV GAIN/ HIGH POINT	SEASON
****/3	5.4 miles	1430 feet/ 7590 feet	Mid-June– early Oct

Maps: USFS Selway-Bitterroot Wilderness; USGS Gash Point, MT; **Contact:** Bitterroot National Forest, Stevensville Ranger District; **Notes:** Wilderness rules apply. Open to horses; **GPS:** 46.4355°, -114.2524°

No glacier-carved glens here: this is one of few lake destinations in the Bitterroot Valley that doesn't follow a major creek canyon. In fact, the drive to the high-elevation trailhead does most of the climbing, making Glen Lake ideal for families with children or first-time backpackers.

GETTING THERE

From Victor, drive north on US Highway 93 for 2 miles to Bell Crossing (between mileposts 61 and 62). Turn left (west) on Bell Crossing Road, and drive 0.5 mile to a T-junction. Turn right onto Meridian Road, and continue 0.25 mile to Curlew Orchard Road. Turn left, and

Snags and flowers surround Glen Lake.

drive 1.1 miles, then bear right onto Big Creek Road (Forest Road 738). Drive 1.7 miles, then turn left onto Smith Creek Road (FR 1321). Drive 7.9 miles, bearing left at 3 miles to stay on FR 1321, to the large trailhead parking area (elev. 6660 feet).

ON THE TRAIL

Glen Lake Trail 232 gradually ascends on wide tread through an area that was completely engulfed by the 2006 Gash Point Fire. The nearly 9000-acre conflagration eliminated shade and shelter but opened up unimpeded views of the Bitterroot Valley and the Sapphire Range beyond. Post-fire colonizing flowers—purple vetch, pearly everlasting, fireweed, and beargrass—bloom in profusion among the thousands of wraith-like snags creaking in the breeze.

At 1.3 miles, crest the ridge and enter the Selway-Bitterroot Wilderness. Lone ridgeline gendarmes frame views of Gash Point above the Sweathouse Creek drainage to the south. Descend on dusty sidehill tread, admiring the

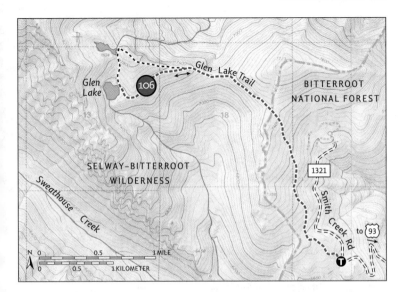

view of South Heavenly Twin, its steep-sided pyramidal form plainly visible to the north. Cross a small saddle and climb slightly to a junction at 2 miles (see Extending Your Trip); bear left, and follow a gradually descending contour to your destination at 2.7 miles.

Glen Lake sits high on the shoulder of a fire-bare ridge, surrounded by snags. Surprisingly, the lake remains relatively free of floating logs. On the south shore, a small patch of flat ground sheltered by widely spaced trees overlooks the lake to one side and the steep drainage of the outlet drain to the other. It's the best spot to set up a tent or dip a toe. Or a line: anglers will find plenty of room for a backcast here.

EXTENDING YOUR TRIP

Hikers who don't mind stepping over deadfall can follow unmaintained tread 0.25 mile from the north end of the lake to two tiny unnamed tarns above Glen Lake. Surrounded by a

parklike stand of alpine larch spared the Gash Point Fire, these lakes, small enough to skip a stone across, sit in an arguably prettier setting than the larger body of water below. From their outlet stream, it is a 1-mile hike back to the junction you passed at 2 miles, then up and over the same rock knob for a second look at those divine views of South Heavenly Twin and Saint Mary Peak.

107 Bear Creek Overlook

RATING/ DIFFICULTY	ROUNDTRIP	ELEV GAIN/ HIGH POINT	SEASON
*****/3	4 miles	1370 feet/ 7070 feet	Late June– early Oct

Maps: USFS Selway-Bitterroot Wilderness; USGS Gash Point, MT; **Contact:** Bitterroot National Forest, Stevensville Ranger District; **Notes:** Wilderness rules apply. Open to horses; **GPS:** 49.3955°, -114.2668°

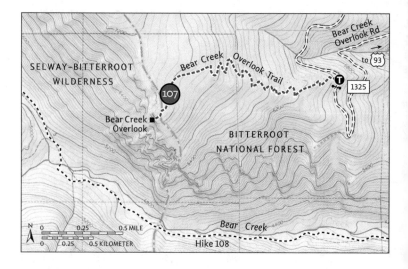

Hike 108

Peer into a grand, glacier-plowed Bitterroot canyon with a fraction of the effort of most trails in the Selway-Bitterroot Wilderness. Mile for mile—and switchback for endless switchback—there may be no better hike for viewing the craggy interior of the Selway-Bitterroot.

GETTING THERE

From US Highway 93 in Victor, drive west on Fifth Street for 1 mile to a T-intersection with Pleasant View Road. Turn left, and drive 2.3 miles to Red Crow Road; stay left as the road changes to Red Crow Road, then immediately turn right to continue on Pleasant View Road. After 1.5 miles the road changes to Gash Creek Road (Forest Road 737); continue another 2.5 miles to Bear Creek Overlook Road (FR 1325). Turn left, and follow this narrow, winding road 4 miles to the trailhead just before a gate across the road (elev. 5930 feet).

ON THE TRAIL

Bear Creek Overlook Trail departs at an unmarked spot through uniform lodgepole forest. Following a few minutes' brisk climbing, settle in for several dozen switchbacks, seeming to gain no elevation.

At 1.25 miles (elev. 6780 feet), the trail curves around and changes both aspect and character; now in subalpine whitebark pine forest, follow the wide tread west as it gains the ridgeline. Reaching rocky gendarmes, bear left as the trail descends slightly to its obvious end at Bear Creek Overlook at 2 miles (elev. 7070 feet).

Only lichen and a few ice-stunted whitebark pine have eked out a living on the smooth, wind-scoured slab of granite. From as close to the edge of the overlook as you dare, peer down into the deep canyon where the three forks of Bear Creek converge. Ruddy mylonite walls gird the near side of the canyon. Beyond, the scalloped canyon

Watching the last light leak from the sky at Bear Creek Overlook

walls drop into the wooded ravines of Bear Creek. The pyramid-shaped peak of Sky Pilot stands prominent on the northern skyline. From here the seemingly endless pickets of the Bitterroots seem humbling in scale but close enough to reach out and touch—just mind the 900-foot sheer drop.

108 Bear Creek to Bryan Lake

RATING/ DIFFICULTY	ROUNDTRIP	ELEV GAIN/ HIGH POINT	SEASON
*****/5	16.5 miles	3590 feet/ 6780 feet	June–early Oct

Maps: USFS Selway-Bitterroot Wilderness; USGS Gash Point, MT; USGS White Sand Lake, ID-MT; **Contact:** Bitterroot National Forest, Stevensville Ranger District; **Notes:** Wilderness rules apply. Open to horses; **GPS:** 46.3795°, -114.2531°

Bear Creek boasts some of the finest forested streamside hiking in the Bitterroots, thanks to its unburnt and diverse forest of old-growth larch and yew and brawling cascades. The forest and falls are their own reward, but because the trail gains elevation so gradually, on such a soft trail surface, a 16.5-mile roundtrip to Bryan Lake is well within the reach of day hikers.

GETTING THERE

From Tucker Crossing on US Highway 93, 3 miles south of Victor (milepost 56), head west on Bear Creek Road. Continue for 2.3 miles to the T-intersection with Red Crow Road. Turn right, and continue on Red Crow Road for 1 mile, then continue straight on graveled Bear Creek Road (Forest Road 1326) for 2.8 miles to the road's end and trailhead (elev. 4120 feet). Privy available.

ON THE TRAIL

On Bear Creek Trail 5, a narrow but well-maintained tread immediately heads westward through lush north-facing forest and stays that way for most of its length, the moss-covered rocks and soft forest floor doing little to muffle the sound of brash Bear Creek. The trail swings within view of the creek before entering a broad talus apron at 0.5 mile. It's not until reaching a second broad talus bench that the scale of the sheer canyon walls of Bear Creek become apparent, the lofty aerie of Bear Creek Overlook high overhead.

At 1.4 miles, enter an opening: broad bedrock benches flank the rushing cascades of Bear Creek; it's quite a show, particularly

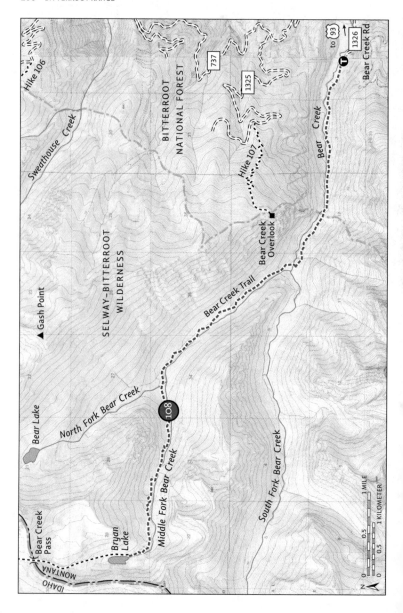

in the springtime, and a common destination for day hikers. With the precipitous granite walls of Bear Creek above and soft larch needles underfoot, enter the wilderness.

Shortly after entering the wilderness, the trail makes one crossing of Bear Creek, its insistent, knee-deep current potentially a barrier to early-season travel. Once on the other side, ascend several switchbacks and pass a rarely used junction with the South Fork Bear Creek Trail. Aside from one talus incursion and a marshy pool at 4 miles or so, enjoy pleasant forest walking through yew and old-growth larch. You might see—or at least smell—moose in these moist bottomland environs.

The trail bends west and makes an easy crossing of North Fork Bear Creek at 5.5 miles (elev. 5350 feet). For the next mile or so, the trail stays near the narrow ribbon of Middle Fork Bear Creek. Climb a handful of switchbacks as larch and yew yield to wide granite slabs. A series of small cascades announce the presence of the creek; backpackers will find several worthwhile campsites here. Drawing nearer to Bryan Lake, make two boggy crossings before bending north toward Bryan Lake's outlet.

Expanses of beargrass and bright granite talus form the broad amphitheater of Bryan Lake, which occupies a north-south basin directly below the Bitterroot Divide. The filed-granite finial of Sky Pilot flies overhead, a worthwhile destination for hikers staying over at the lake.

EXTENDING YOUR TRIP

Sky Pilot offers an attractive, nontechnical summit from Bryan Lake. Follow the lake's shore north, climbing 1 mile among beargrass to Bear Creek Pass on the Bitterroot Divide. From here, it's a short scramble to the summit.

Granite and subalpine fir frame Bryan Lake.

109 Sheafman Creek Lakes

RATING/ DIFFICULTY	ROUNDTRIP	ELEV GAIN/ HIGH POINT	SEASON
*****/5	13.8 miles	3390 feet/ 7980 feet	Late June– mid-Oct

Maps: USGS Hamilton North, MT; USGS Printz Ridge, MT; **Contact:** Bitterroot National Forest, Stevensville Ranger District; **Notes:** Wilderness rules apply. Open to horses. See road closure note below; **GPS:** 46.3309°, -114.2474°

Climb to parklands of alpine larch and the progressively more beautiful pools of a trio of lakes set in a broad hanging valley under the sky-grabbing granite spires of the Bitterroot Divide. The infinity-pool of Aichele Lake surely ranks as one of the best in Glacier Country.

287

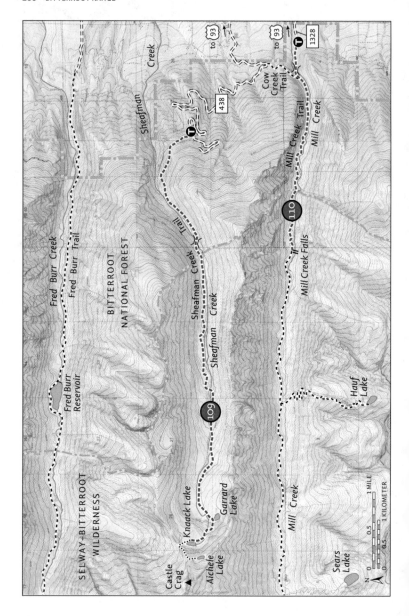

Looking into the Fred Burr Creek drainage from above Knaack Lake

GETTING THERE

From the Woodside Exchange on US Highway 93, 4 miles north of Hamilton (milepost 52), head left (west) on Dutch Hill Road (signed for Ferndale). Drive 2.5 miles, and at a T-intersection turn right (north) onto Bowman Road. Continue 1.2 miles, and turn left (west) onto West Cow Creek Road (Forest Road 438). Pass several residences and climb this narrow, frequently rutted high-elevation road to the trailhead pullout in 5 miles (elev. 5450 feet). A wide spot on the shoulder accommodates a half dozen vehicles. (Note: The upper 4 miles of FR 438 are closed October 15–June 15 to protect winter elk habitat.)

ON THE TRAIL

From the high-elevation trailhead for Sheafman Creek Trail 82, follow a skid road north across an old clear-cut blackened by the Blodgett Trailhead Fire of 2000. Turn after a half mile to head up the Sheafman Creek

drainage, which was spared the brunt of the burn thanks to fire suppression.

Now in shaded stream-bottom forest, there's little to mark the distance save the occasional creek crossing (and re-crossing). At 2.1 miles (elev. 6220 feet), cross Sheafman Creek on a split-log bridge and then enter the wilderness. The trail continues to gain elevation in shallow-stream-grade increments, and at 4 miles (elev. 6610 feet), following a knee-deep ford—early in the summer, the snowmelt-stoked torrent of Sheafman Creek can make this crossing tricky—it takes the form of a creek itself, making several more shallow crossings in the next mile as it negotiates dark bottomland.

At 5.7 miles, the shoe-sucking tread passes a tiny pond, its shallow waters reflecting Castle Crag above. A quarter mile later, reach the small outlet dam at Garrard Lake (elev. 7150 feet). Named for John T. Garrard, an early Bitterroot Valley resident, Garrard Lake guards the base of an expansive talus field on the southeast buttress of Castle Crag. A few large-diameter alpine larch tower over the lake, which harbors pan-sized trout.

To continue to Knaack Lake, cross the outlet dam and angle upward through rough, switchbacking tread, crossing Sheafman's boggy waters before reaching the larch-fronted lake a half mile later. Set beneath a sheer, scrubbed face of granite, Knaack's narrow shoreline offers spacious, if saturated, tent sites.

EXTENDING YOUR TRIP

Determined day hikers can—and should—continue to Aichele Lake. From Knaack, follow the obvious path to the low pass to the northeast. Here, peer down into the glacier-born Fred Burr Valley before angling upward to the left. The granite slabs will test your balance; an easier, if steeper, approach stays in the trees on the high side of the toe ridge. A half mile from Knaack Lake, reach the freshly scrubbed granite pool of Aichele Lake. The thick, twisted limbs of alpine larch frame a view of Sheafman Creek in its entirety and the granite gendarmes that separate it from Mill Creek to the south. From here only a steep talus slope defends Castle Crag; it's a nontechnical climb for those camping at one of the lakes.

110 Mill Creek Falls

RATING/ DIFFICULTY	ROUNDTRIP	ELEV GAIN/ HIGH POINT	SEASON
****/3	6.2 miles	1520 feet/ 4900 feet	May–Oct

Maps: USFS Selway-Bitterroot Wilderness; USGS Printz Ridge, MT; USGS Hamilton North, MT; **Contact:** Bitterroot National Forest, Stevensville Ranger District; **Notes:**

Wilderness rules apply. Open to horses; **GPS:** 46.3103°, -114.2223°

Rock climbers clamor to Mill Creek to work its steep canyon walls, but there is also much to recommend it for day hikers. Follow the fast-moving creek through a diverse post-fire landscape to the narrow flume of Mill Creek Falls and its inviting plunge pool.

GETTING THERE

From the Woodside Exchange on US Highway 93, 4 miles north of Hamilton (milepost 52), head left (west) on Dutch Hill Road (signed for Ferndale). Drive 2.5 miles, and at a T-intersection turn left onto Bowman Road. Continue 0.3 mile, then turn right onto Mill Creek Road (Forest Road 1328) and continue 0.8 mile to the large trailhead parking area (elev. 4060 feet). Privy available. Camping is prohibited at the popular trailhead.

ON THE TRAIL

Mill Creek Trail follows an old bulldozer grade as it parallels fast-moving Mill Creek, old flumes and other irrigation detritus twisting in its waters. Ignoring an old roadbed branching down to the creek on the right, follow the creek course as the canyon narrows. Look skyward at the "flatirons," the prominent features of mylonite along the eastern front of the Bitterroots that show where the Sapphires sheared off before sliding to their present location.

At 0.5 mile (elev. 4280 feet), a sturdy footbridge spans Mill Creek; cross it and continue upstream past the ingress of the Cow Creek Trail, an alternate access to the Mill Creek drainage. Leave the trees behind and enter a landscape razed by the 2000 Blodgett Trailhead Fire. Colonies of aspen

Mill Creek Falls plunges into a deep, granite-carved pool.

and head-high pines have replaced cool forest; fireweed and other sun-loving flowers provide summer color. With Mill Creek never far from sight, the trail continues to plot an upward course, never gaining or losing too much elevation on the way. Turn around for views of the Mill Creek canyon, its crags and mylonite columns standing starkly about the creek drainage. It's pretty clear why climbers have begun to migrate here from popular Blodgett Canyon, but the rough tread underfoot on the trail proper indicates its light use.

At 2.1 miles (elev. 4640 feet) enter the wilderness, passing a small marsh as the trail wanders through patches of birch, aspens, and ferns spared the fire. After another mile of easy hiking, leave the trail and cross exposed bedrock fifty feet to Mill Creek Falls (elev. 4900 feet). Here the granite flume of Mill Creek sluices forty feet into a small but deep plunge pool, a refreshing destination on shadeless summer days.

EXTENDING YOUR TRIP

Determined day hikers can continue upstream for a 15-mile roundtrip hike to Hauf Lake. From Mill Creek Falls, go another 2.5 miles upstream along the now-meandering Mill Creek. At an unmarked junction, turn left (south) for a calf-deep ford of the creek, then climb 2100 lung-scorching feet in 2 miles to Hauf Lake. The tiny lake occupies a basin high on the north side of Printz Ridge. The forest has begun to subsume a bunkhouse and a handful of outbuildings set back in the trees from the lake's shore.

111 Blodgett Canyon

RATING/ DIFFICULTY	ROUNDTRIP	ELEV GAIN/ HIGH POINT	SEASON
*****/3	9.8 miles	1750 feet/ 5400 feet	Apr–Nov

Maps: USGS Hamilton North, MT; USGS Printz Ridge, MT; **Contact:** Bitterroot National Forest, Stevensville Ranger District; **Note:** Open to horses and bicycles (until the wilderness boundary at 7 miles); **GPS:** 46.2685°, -114.2433°

Popular with hikers, equestrians, and rock climbers who revere its rocky spires, Blodgett Canyon sees more visitors on a given weekday than neighboring trails might see in a year—not surprising since it is the showpiece of the Bitterroot canyons. Blodgett Canyon's dramatic relief and wide, U-shaped profile inspire awe in first-time visitors. It's a hike to be done more than once, the dramatic canyon lighting changing minute by minute, season by season.

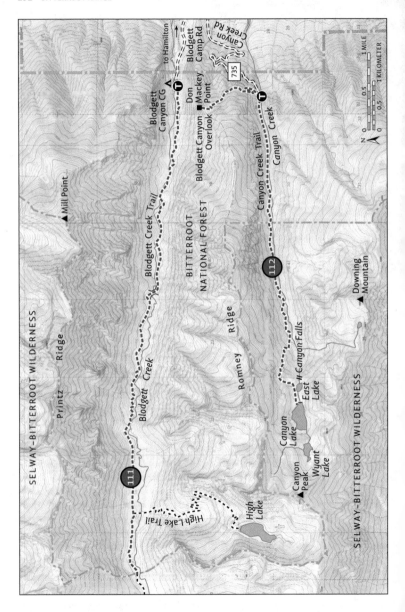

to Hamilton

Blodgett
Camp Rd

Canyon
Creek Rd

735

Blodgett Canyon CG

Don
Mackey
Point

Blodgett Canyon
Overlook

Canyon Creek

BITTERROOT
NATIONAL
FOREST

Blodgett Creek Trail

Canyon Creek Trail

Mill Point

SELWAY–BITTERROOT WILDERNESS

Printz   Ridge

112

Romney   Ridge

Downing
Mountain

Blodgett   Creek

Canyon Falls

East
Lake

Canyon
Lake

Wyant
Lake

111

High Lake Trail

Canyon
Peak

High
Lake

SELWAY–BITTERROOT WILDERNESS

N

0   0.5   1 KILOMETER

0   0.5   1 MILE

Making a log crossing of Blodgett Creek

GETTING THERE

From US Highway 93 in downtown Hamilton, drive west on Main Street 1.3 miles to Ricketts Road. Turn right (north), and drive 0.5 mile to Blodgett Camp Road. Turn left, and drive 4 miles to the trailhead just before the Blodgett Canyon Campground (elev. 4240 feet). Privy available.

ON THE TRAIL

For its first mile, Blodgett Creek Trail 19 stays mostly in the thick cover of towering ponderosa pines, little hint of the spectacle to come—although the sight of giddy rock climbers on the trail might give some indication. Occasional side paths access side channels and pools, while scattered openings in the tree cover—much of this area burned in the 2000 Blodgett Trailhead Fire, the largest in the Bitterroot Valley in recent memory—provide glimpses at the grandeur to come.

It's not until the trail breaks out onto the first in a series of talus aprons that the granite grandeur of Blodgett Canyon is revealed. Of particular note are a series of helms and spires on Printz Ridge on the north side of the canyon; even if the names Blackfoot Dome, Nez Perce and Shoshone Spires, and Flathead Buttress mean little to nonclimbers, all will marvel at the constantly shifting play of light and shadow on the canyon's walls—it's a spectacular sight early in the evening as the sun dips toward the Bitterroot Divide. To the south of the canyon are Horsehead Arch and Blodgett Canyon Overlook, the latter's canyon-bottom vantage giving a good preview of the scene afforded by that trail (Hike 112). It's a vista straight out of a John Ford western.

At 3 miles, cross a mechanical marvel of a pack bridge—each of the support beams weighs more than a thousand pounds and had to be lifted into place via an impressive cable pulley system—and enjoy the view upstream, the opening in the canyon floor courtesy of a large beaver dam and its accompanying ponds. Rocky talus tread underfoot, skirt the north side of the wetland. Vigorous pine striplings surround this and many of the open areas in the canyon. Curiously, the trail remains outside the Selway-Bitterroot Wilderness boundary for another 4 miles, the result of an excision that carved the canyon out of the original wilderness proposal in anticipation of an irrigation project that never materialized.

At 4.3 miles, venture upon a small cascade in a small carved channel just off-trail. Amble off-trail to the rock ledge to view the cascades, which can be heard but not seen from the trail. The trail gains elevation in a stairstep fashion before encountering a set of small cascades at 4.9 miles. Either is a good turnaround point, or a lunch spot in pursuit of a journey farther up the canyon. This is a classic "just around the next bend" hike, the level, well-tended tread and dynamic woodland scenery always spurring one on for just a little longer.

EXTENDING YOUR TRIP

Day hikers interested in some extra miles or backpackers planning a multiday trek have several options, all of them appealing. From the cascades, the trail ambles at an easy grade through heavy stream-bottom spruce forest. At 6.2 miles from the trailhead, just past a viewpoint of the granite horn of Canyon Peak, the trail meets a junction with the spur to High Lake. It's more than 2000 feet of elevation gain in less than 2 miles, much of

it on steep boulder slopes, to reach this eerie, seldom-visited lake and the moldering cabin on its fringes. Hikers can also continue on Blodgett Creek Trail, reaching the wilderness boundary at 7 miles and Seven Mile Meadows, a broad aspen-shaded expanse, shortly after.

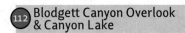

112 Blodgett Canyon Overlook & Canyon Lake

Blodgett Canyon Overlook

RATING/ DIFFICULTY	ROUNDTRIP	ELEV GAIN/ HIGH POINT	SEASON
*****/2	2.8 miles	900 feet/ 5540 feet	May–Nov

Canyon Lake

RATING/ DIFFICULTY	ROUNDTRIP	ELEV GAIN/ HIGH POINT	SEASON
****/5	9.8 miles	3030 feet/ 7420 feet	July–early Oct

Maps: USGS Hamilton North, MT; USGS Printz Ridge, MT; **Contact:** Bitterroot National Forest, Darby Ranger District; **Notes:** Dogs and horses permitted. Wilderness rules apply on Canyon Creek Trail; **GPS:** 46.2527°, -114.2473°

An easy jaunt to a breathtaking vista of a broad, glacier-cut chasm, Blodgett Canyon Overlook is where locals take their out-of-town guests and where photographers go for epic sunsets. There's no better—or easier—way to appreciate the effects of ice-age glaciers on the Bitterroots landscape. Meanwhile, hikers looking for a rugged lake escape will find it at Canyon Lake.

GETTING THERE

From US Highway 93 in downtown Hamilton, drive west on Main Street 1.3 miles to

The evening's final light shines on the towers of Blodgett Creek canyon.

Ricketts Road. Turn right (north) and drive 0.5 mile to Blodgett Camp Road. Turn left and drive 2.5 miles to Canyon Creek Road (Forest Road 735), then bear left and follow this good gravel road 2.8 miles to the road's end and large trailhead (elev. 5030 feet). Privy available.

ON THE TRAIL

Follow wide, well-traveled Blodgett Overlook Trail 101 a few steps to the junction with Canyon Creek Trail 525. The way right climbs to Blodgett Canyon Overlook; the way left continues to Canyon Lake.

Blodgett Canyon Overlook

From the junction, Blodgett Overlook Trail begins switchbacking a handful of times across a skiff of talus on steep bedrock. Wooden benches placed along the first three-quarters of a mile of trail provide viewpoints of Hamilton and the Sapphires beyond, but the going is so easy, and the rewards so great at the end, that there's little reason to linger.

Round Romney Ridge through Douglas-fir forest and scattered patches of the brushy aftermath of the 2000 Blodgett Trailhead Fire, then crest the ridge to reach the Blodgett Canyon Overlook at 1.4 miles (elev. 5440 feet).

Well-beaten paths weave through the rocky lip of the overlook to reach numerous viewpoints, all of them good. Across the canyon, 8467-foot Mill Point caps Printz Ridge and its steep talus-strewn slopes. Below lies broad, nearly straight Blodgett Canyon, the story of ice-age glacial movement laid bare on its steep, U-shaped profile. In the summer, time your arrival for late evening to watch the sun dip between the canyon walls.

Canyon Lake

From the junction with the Blodgett Overlook Trail, the Canyon Creek Trail retreats up the canyon under lofty pines. Boulder fields and the burn boles of lodgepole pine—remnants of the Blodgett Trailhead Fire—border the trail. Navigate patchy aspen groves and clumps of timber as it constantly gains and loses elevation, but generally takes an upward course. At 1.7 miles, the trail enters the wilderness and settles into thick timber. From here, it eschews switchbacks for stone step-ups as it charges straight up the canyon wall. Periodically, Canyon Falls comes into view as it sluices some four hundred feet down sheer granite. In early summer, water runnels down the trail, making it particularly slippery. Shoulder aside slide alder and climb, following cairns, as the route crosses a talus slope and regains level ground. Begin a gentle descent across smooth granite and into the long glacial moraine at the foot of Canyon Peak's cirque, first passing the moldering vegetation and bleached stumps surrounding the remnants of East Lake that, following a dam breach, now exists in name only.

At 4.9 miles, reach the uninspired concrete dam at the outlet of Canyon Lake. Surrounded on three sides by gray talus and granite benches, Canyon Lake, like many of its neighbors, bears the "bathtub-ring" look of irrigation drawdowns as the summer wears on. But the gradually smaller surface nonetheless does a fine job reflecting the imposing form of Canyon Peak at its head.

EXTENDING YOUR TRIP

Sitting some 600 feet higher than Canyon Lake, Wyant Lake provides an even more attractive destination than its dammed downstream neighbor. To reach it, follow the user-defined footpath along the east shore of the lake, passing several appealing tent sites. When the trail reaches the first of several talus fans, leave the trail and climb upslope toward the head of the canyon; although steep, the route is never exposed.

113 Camas Lake

RATING/ DIFFICULTY	ROUNDTRIP	ELEV GAIN/ HIGH POINT	SEASON
****/3	5.6 miles	1670 feet/ 6930 feet	Late June–Oct

Map: USGS Ward Mountain, MT; **Contact:** Bitterroot National Forest, Darby Ranger District; **Notes:** Dogs and horses permitted. Wilderness rules apply; **GPS:** 46.1322°, -114.2552°

A small, reed-ringed tarn high in the wind-sheltered shoulder of Ward Mountain, Camas Lake lacks the austere majesty of many of its Bitterroot neighbors. But the hike through cool, north-facing fir forest is ideal for a hot summer day, and though ambitious hikers can use the lake as a jumping-off point for several higher bodies of water, Camas Lake holds enough quiet charm to sustain simply staying put on its quiet shores.

GETTING THERE

From Hamilton, drive south on US Highway 93 for 9 miles to Lost Horse Road (Forest Road 429), near milepost 38. Turn right (west) and continue 2.4 paved miles; bear right at the Y-junction onto Camas Creek Road (FR 496), and continue 6 miles on good gravel to the trailhead pullout (elev. 5680 feet). The large parking area can accommodate a dozen vehicles.

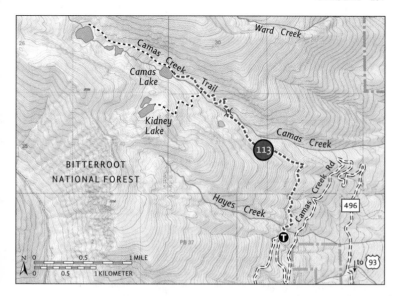

ON THE TRAIL

From beyond the road barricade, Camas Creek Trail 125 follows an old logging road—recently improved for a firebreak during the

A hiker and her dog cruise on an inflatable stand-up paddleboard in Camas Lake.

2016 Observation Point and Roaring Lion Fires—as it traverses a regenerating clear-cut. At 0.9 mile (elev. 5850 feet), at road's end, veer left (northwest) onto smooth, well-shaded trail. Thick firs limit any views of the steep drainage of Camas Creek in this cool north-facing forest of fir.

After three-quarters of a mile, the trail eventually enters a broad apron of massive granite and equally massive Douglas-firs, the talus field revealing a view down valley of the Sapphire Range's sere foothills. Enter a verdant forest of fir and fool's huckleberry as the boulder-studded trail closes in on Camas Creek and eventually crosses it and a small tributary on two sagging split-log bridges in quick succession at 1.9 miles (elev. 6480 feet). On the north side of the drainage, a half mile of switchbacks ascend a granite incline, the thinning forest cover once again allowing views of the distant

Bitterroot Valley. Reaching level terrain, the path continues another quarter mile or so through the dense undergrowth of Camas Lake's outlet to reach the lake at 2.8 miles.

Reeds ring much of the lake's immediate shoreline, its deep green waters dutifully reflecting the larch and talus of Ward Mountain's austere slopes above to the north. Small hanging valleys hint at the other lakes and invite off-trail exploration, but the quiet environs—and the presence of hungry pan-sized cutthroats among the long-submerged logs of the lake's shore—invite staying put awhile too.

EXTENDING YOUR TRIP

Several lakes occupy the hanging valleys above Camas, the most attractive being Kidney Lake. To reach it, look for a cairn-marked but easy-to-miss side trail on the creek side of the main path (no longer maintained by the Forest Service, but easy to follow once you locate its beginning) about 2.5 miles from the trailhead. An early-season crossing of Camas Creek immediately after leaving the main trail may turn back some hikers, but from here, it's an easy half mile of climbing to appropriately named Kidney Lake. Several large tent sites look out toward the island in the center of this attractive tarn.

114 Bailey Lake

RATING/ DIFFICULTY	ROUNDTRIP	ELEV GAIN/ HIGH POINT	SEASON
****/2	2.4 miles	690 feet/ 6660 feet	Late June–Oct

Maps: USGS Saddle Mountain, ID-MT, USGS Tenmile Lake, ID-MT; **Contact:** Bitterroot National Forest, Darby Ranger District; **Notes:** Dogs, horses, and bicycles permitted. Wilderness rules apply. See road closure dates below; **GPS:** 46.1287°, -114.4941°

Subalpine forest and small pocket meadows characterize most hikes in the Lost Horse

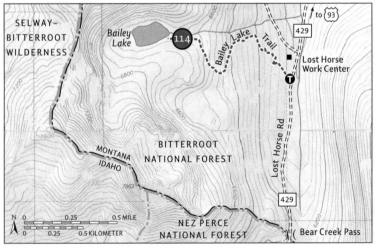

Sunning among the boulders of Bailey Lake

drainage. Not so Bailey Lake, which sits in a sunny, snag-flanked cirque high on the Bitterroot Crest. *Rough tread and relatively untouched shores belie Bailey's ease of access; this is about as kid-friendly as Bitterroot lakes get.*

GETTING THERE

From Hamilton, drive south on US Highway 93 for 9 miles to Lost Horse Road (Forest Road 429), near milepost 38. Turn right (west) and continue 2.4 paved miles; bear left at the Y-junction to continue on FR 429 for 15.4 miles of good gravel, keeping left at the Lost Horse Work Station and continuing another quarter mile to the easily missed trailhead on the right (elev. 6030 feet). A small parking area fifty yards beyond the trailhead accommodates a half dozen

vehicles. Privy and primitive camping available at Bear Creek Pass another 0.75 mile beyond the trailhead. (Note: The upper 6 miles of FR 429 are closed to all motorized use from December 1 to June 15.)

ON THE TRAIL

From the unremarkable trailhead for Bailey Lake Trail 293, bear northwest on rough, root-crossed tread. Fool's huckleberry and moist open-forest flowers—aster, gentian—frequently threaten to overwhelm the narrow trail corridor. After a quarter mile or so of thick tree cover, the trail enters an open landscape slowly recovering from a 1988 wildfire, the skeletal snags revealing the rough, rocky crest of the Lost Horse drainage. Ample huckleberry patches flank the trail as it angles aimlessly up the creek drainage, eventually gaining a boulder-studded beargrass meadow. The trail sometimes grows faint as it navigates the granite, but the occasional cairn marks the generally northwesterly course.

A mile in (elev. 6610 feet), the tread levels as it parallels Bailey Lake's outlet stream, passing a handful of small ponds before reaching lake at 1.2 miles (elev. 6660 feet).

Reflecting the grassy cirque near the crest of the Bitterroots in its often-calm waters, Bailey Lake lacks the slightly eerie feel common to other snag-encircled lakes in the Bitterroots, perhaps owing to its airy perch. Granite boulders, scattered like sun-bleached bones, lie among a low carpet of beargrass and diminutive huckleberries; scattered snags provide the only shade. The irregular-shaped granite on the lake's edge makes for fine reclining. Few flowers grow here, but the tawny late-summer color of huckleberry and high-elevation heath plants makes this a fine September outing. Surprisingly, given the setting and the short hike, Bailey's shores are not nearly as denuded as those of some of its neighbors; observing leave-no-trace practices in this fragile environment will keep it that way.

115 Fish Lake

RATING/ DIFFICULTY	ROUNDTRIP	ELEV GAIN/ HIGH POINT	SEASON
*****/4	8.6 miles	1930 feet/ 7200 feet	July–Oct

Map: USGS El Capitan, MT-ID; **Contacts:** Nez Perce National Forest, Moose Creek Ranger District; Bitterroot National Forest, Darby Ranger District; **Notes:** Dogs and horses permitted. Wilderness rules apply. See road closure note below; **GPS:** 46.1145°, -114.4924°

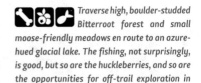 *Traverse high, boulder-studded Bitterroot forest and small moose-friendly meadows en route to an azure-hued glacial lake. The fishing, not surprisingly, is good, but so are the huckleberries, and so are the opportunities for off-trail exploration in the lightly traveled Lost Horse portal.*

GETTING THERE
From Hamilton, drive south on US Highway 93 for 9 miles to Lost Horse Road (Forest Road 429), near milepost 38. Turn right (west) and continue 2.4 paved miles; bear left at the Y-junction to continue on FR 429 for 16.4 miles of good gravel, keeping left at the Lost Horse Work Station and continuing another mile to Bear Creek Pass trailhead. There is both a Bear Creek and Bear Creek Pass trailhead; the correct trailhead is at the southwest end of the large parking area (elev. 6230 feet). Privy and primitive camping available at Bear Creek Pass. (Note: The upper 6 miles of FR 429 are closed to all motorized use from December 1 to June 15.)

ON THE TRAIL
Heading southwest from the pass on Bear Creek Pass Trail 613 into Idaho, amble among a boulder-strewn forest of skinny subalpine timber, all the while navigating a couple horse-chewed wallows in addition to granite underfoot. Soon, the trees unveil a view of rounded and ragged granite peaks before the trail enters the wilderness at 1.1 miles (elev. 6620 feet). The tread dips downward slightly and then traverses above the moose-friendly environs of Lower Bear Lake. A glance downstream reveals the serrated skyline of the Bitterroot Range; to the south struts the granite band of Elk Ridge.

Reach a junction at 1.9 miles (elev. 6720 feet); bear left for Fish Lake. Ascend a series of switchbacks among the tiny wet meadows characteristic of Lost Horse drainage. Soon a backward glance will grant a view of the upper Bear Creek drainage, including Upper Bear Lake and its grassy shores. At 2.6 miles (elev. 7180 feet), crest the Bitterroot Divide in a flat wooded pass; a moment's walk south off the trail reveals a nice visual preview of Fish Lake's azure waters. Reentering Montana, the trail jogs north as the destination, Fish Lake, comes into view to the south, its blue island-topped waters set at the head of the South Lost Horse Creek canyon. The trail descends through pleasant subalpine heath undergrowth of heather, grouseberry, and huckleberry into the South Lost Horse

Granite and penstemon frame Fish Lake below.

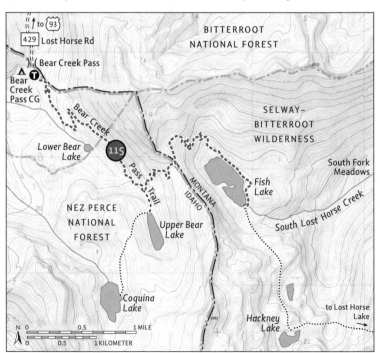

drainage, making use of long, aimless switch-backs to eventually reach the head of Fish Lake at 3.7 miles (elev. 6690 feet).

Glacially made, its timbered peninsula and islets likely the leftovers of a recessional moraine, Fish Lake exhibits a striking blue hue in its deep waters. Purple gentian and plump huckleberry line the shore, while several rock outcroppings give anglers plenty of room for a backcast. The horn of White Mountain rises to the southeast, its double-scooped cirque holding patchy snow all summer.

The trail continues another 0.6 mile on increasingly braided and brushy tread to its terminus at the Fish Lake Dam, which, screened by trees, does not mar the aesthetic of this attractive lake. Several nice campsites invite fishing or you may consider bushwhacking to Hackney and Lost Horse Lakes (farther east).

EXTENDING YOUR TRIP
An old trail, never officially maintained, continues from the outlet dam of Fish Lake first to Hackney Lake and then to Lost Horse Lake, both bodies of water granite-shelved and secluded. From Fish Lake it's 3 miles to Lost Horse Lake.

Camas carpets the meadows above Lake Como.

For a shorter side trip, bear right at the unmarked junction at 1.9 miles, following the creek channel to grass-fringed Upper Bear Lake. From here, an unmarked but obvious path—when the trail disappears, follow the cairns—crests a low wooded bench before reaching Coquina Lake. It's less than a mile from the junction to this popular tarn.

Lake Como Loop

RATING/ DIFFICULTY	LOOP	ELEV GAIN/ HIGH POINT	SEASON
****/3	7.7 miles	950 feet/ 4360 feet	Apr–Nov

Maps: USGS Como Peaks, MT; USGS Darby, MT; **Contact:** Bitterroot National Forest, Darby Ranger District; **Notes:** Dogs must be on leash in all Lake Como campgrounds. Lake Como Recreation Area daily fee applies Memorial Day weekend through Labor Day weekend. Open to horses and bicycles; **GPS:** 46.0657°, -114.2475°

Named by Jesuit missionary Father Ravalli after the Lake Como in his home country of Italy, Lake Como occupies a vast glacial basin at the feet of the Como Peaks, some of the most imposing of the Bitterroots. Boats crowd Lake Como in midsummer, so save this hike for shoulder season, when it's at its best: in the spring, for early-season conditioning when other Bitterroots areas are snowbound, or in the autumn when aspen provide close-up color.

GETTING THERE
From Hamilton, head south on US Highway 93 for 12 miles to Lake Como Road (between mileposts 34 and 35). Turn right (west) and drive 2.9 miles to Lick Creek Road (Forest

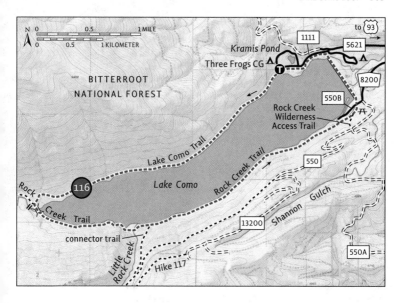

Road 5621). Turn right, following signs for the day-use area, and continue 0.7 mile to the campground entrance. Turn left and then immediately right onto FR 1111, and follow it to its end at the trailhead parking area just before Three Frogs campground (elev. 4300 feet). Privy available.

ON THE TRAIL

On Lake Como Trail 502, begin on a paved, ADA-accessible path. Numerous side trails on the shore side access picnic spots at water's edge. After 0.25 mile, the pavement ends; continue on wide, nearly level tread as it traces a contour through the trees well above the shoreline. Through gaps in the timber admire the Alps-like granite battlements of the Como Peaks, their east-facing couloirs often holding snow well into summer.

As the trail nears the lake's narrow inlet, it passes through an open landscape of aspen and gray granite. Late in the summer, the lake here may be little more than a mudflat bisected by Rock Creek.

At 2.9 miles (elev. 4290 feet), bear left as the trail descends to a sturdy footbridge over Rock Creek (the way straight is a popular portal for extended trips into the Selway-Bitterroot Wilderness, the boundary of which is just upstream of the lake). Upstream of the bridge, Rock Creek cuts a slick course of cascades through the water-pocked bedrock, its wavy contours and water-carved cups holding water long after the lake has receded. Cross the bridge, and climb a slight rise for views down into Rock Creek and downlake across Lake Como.

Ankle-taxing talus underfoot, contour around the south side of the lake, crossing Little Rock Creek at 4 miles (elev. 4270 feet) and then climbing higher above lake level. Now in open ponderosa forest, pass the junction with the Rock Creek Wilderness Access Trail. Be prepared to yield to equestrians; this is a popular ingress for pack trains into the southern Selway-Bitterroot Wilderness.

At 6.6 miles (elev. 4260 feet), drop down to the boat launch area, then cross the lake's nearly half-mile-wide outlet dam, bearing left at its far end to follow the access road back to the trailhead.

117 Little Rock Creek Lake

RATING/ DIFFICULTY	ROUNDTRIP	ELEV GAIN/ HIGH POINT	SEASON
*****/4	8.4 miles	2550 feet/ 6550 feet	July–Oct

Map: USGS Como Peaks, MT; **Contact:** Bitterroot National Forest, Darby Ranger District; **Notes:** Wilderness rules apply. Open to horses; **GPS:** 46.0409°, -114.2667°

 One of the few Bitterroot lakes cradled at the head of a canyon that is also within easy reach of the day hiker, Little Rock Creek Lake provides a rugged alternative to Lake Como's crowded shores. And there's nothing little about the dramatic canyon relief from the wind-frothed water of Little Rock Creek Lake to the wind-swept summit of El Capitan.

GETTING THERE

From Hamilton, head south on US Highway 93 for 12 miles to Lake Como Road (between mileposts 34 and 35). Turn right (west) and drive 3.7 miles, past the boat launch, to Rock Creek Road (Forest Road 550). Drive this good gravel road 2.2 miles to its continuation as FR 13200, and proceed on this increasingly rough unimproved road 0.5 mile to the

The small cascades at the outlet of Little Rock Creek Lake

large trailhead parking area overlooking Lake Como (elev. 5190 feet).

ON THE TRAIL

Beginning in a tightly knit post-fire stand of lodgepole straplings that are showing the signs of pine beetle infestation, Little Rock Creek Trail 57 quickly reaches a nice vista of Lake Como and the Little Rock Creek drainage capped by the granite arête of El Capitan. From this rock overlook, steadily lose elevation as the trail bends southwest into the Little Rock Creek drainage. Fire-singed old-growth ponderosa screen any views of the creek, which crashes through the narrow canyon below.

Having descended into stream-braided bottomland forest, enter the wilderness at 1 mile (elev. 4940 feet). Aspen-shaded talus aprons occasionally flank the trail,

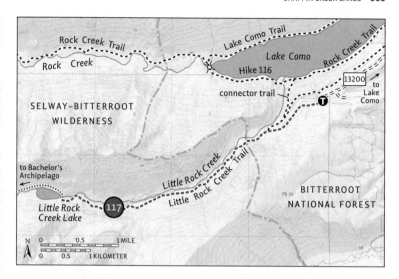

affording views of the water-stained needles and gendarmes of the canyon walls. Continuing through a pleasant forest of yew, currant, and moss-frocked rock, the trail gains ground in a stairstep fashion, the tread frequently coarse underfoot. Entering more montane forest, pull within view of smooth bedrock cascades of the creek at 2.5 miles (elev. 5600 feet). Navigate carefully through the cairn-aided remains of badly eroded trail and reach larger falls at 2.9 miles (elev. 5870 feet). Ascend a series of bedrock benches, then, in a thick forest of spruce and fool's huckleberry, cross the first in a series of shallow rivulets. Ascending across open bedrock with nice views of the larch-crowned peaks above, make one final log crossing of the creek at 3.7 miles (elev. 6270 feet), then climb the bedrock bowl in which the lake sits to reach its outlet at 4.2 miles (elev. 6550 feet).

El Capitan hides mostly from view several miles beyond the lake's head. A waterfall issues from the old outlet dam; a thicket of bleached branches and logs encircles the outlet, a testament to the seemingly ever-present gales that pour down the canyon. Fortunately there's no shortage of firewood for the spacious, wind-sheltered sites on the south shore. To the north, vertical ramparts reflect in the water in its fleeting calm moments.

EXTENDING YOUR TRIP
The Bachelor's Archipelago, a trio of sparkling subalpine pools, lies 2 trail-less miles beyond the head of Little Rock Creek Lake. It's slow going through talus aprons and shaded defiles, but intrepid hikers will find little competition for campsites.

118 Chaffin Creek Lakes

RATING/ DIFFICULTY	ROUNDTRIP	ELEV GAIN/ HIGH POINT	SEASON
*****/4	12.2 miles	3000 feet/ 7440 feet	July–early Oct

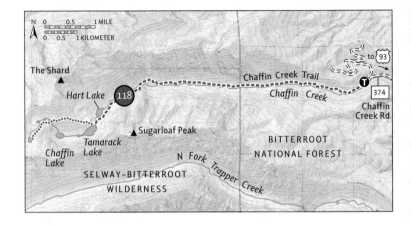

Maps: USGS Burnt Ridge, MT; USGS Trapper Peak, MT; **Contact:** Bitterroot National Forest, Darby Ranger District; **Notes:** Wilderness rules apply. Open to horses; **GPS:** 45.9542°, -114.2146°

![icons] *Follow a gently ascending stream-gradient trail along Chaffin Creek to a chain of subalpine lakes nestled between Sugarloaf Peak and the Shard. As worthwhile as these lakes are, though, the main attraction is the opportunity to reach a seldom-visited Shangri-La high on the Bitterroot Crest: the highest lakes in the range.*

GETTING THERE

From Darby, drive 4 miles south on US Highway 93 to West Fork Road (Montana Highway 473). Turn right, and in one hundred yards turn right again on Trapper-Chaffin Road (Forest Road 374). Drive 3 miles and bear right onto Chaffin Creek Road, continuing another mile to the trailhead (elev. 4810 feet). The parking area, just off a switchback in the road, accommodates a half dozen vehicles.

ON THE TRAIL

Under dry, towering pines, hike upstream; Chaffin Creek Trail 528 gains elevation at a slow drip. Aspen groves and broad talus aprons break up the proceedings, as do some impressive old-growth Douglas-fir and spruce. At one point the trail completes a long traverse across crumbled granite, the canyon opening allowing views of the arid Sapphire foothills to the east.

Soon the gargoyle-like granite knobs of Sugarloaf Peak come into view. The trail undertakes one more steep, switchbacking climb before crossing Chaffin Creek at 4.8 miles. The crossing—on a slick-rock cascade that plunges into shallow pools—would be particularly treacherous during spring runoff; if the water is running high, scout upstream twenty-five yards or so for several potential log crossings. Having passed through airy lodgepole and larch forest, the trail enters thick boggy brush just below the granite wall of Hart Lake's outlet. Cross Chaffin Creek again, and ascend one of several scattered routes over these broad rocky benches to reach Hart Lake's reedy

Leaping over the outlet creek of one of the so-called Chaffin High Lakes

waters at 5.8 miles (elev. 7360 feet). The Shard's long ridgeline towers above water-smoothed rock outcroppings. Continue along either shoreline, and at the inlet of the lake clamber over granite shelves to reach the concrete dam of Tamarack Lake at 6.1 miles (elev. 7430 feet).

Provided you don't hold too strictly to the fact that "tamarack" refers only to eastern larch, Tamarack Lake's appellation is apt: golden-hued alpine larch tenaciously color the exfoliated granite of the sheer cirque headwall above the lake's sinuous shoreline, the concrete dam at its foot doing little to mar the beauty of this high subalpine lake. The hungry pan-sized cutthroats, rainbows, and their hybrid cousins make first-cast strikes here. A few small campsites nestle among granite and small subalpine fir on the north side of the lake. Sunlight seldom

reaches the floor of this cold granite-walled lake, but it's a good place to watch the ever-changing interplay of sun and shadow on the canyon walls farther downstream and up higher on the Bitterroot Crest.

EXTENDING YOUR TRIP

An unofficial but easy-to-follow half-mile route traces Tamarack's shoreline through the huckleberry-flanked wetlands that separate it from Chaffin Lake. A small tarn tucked at the base of Chaffin Creek's head-wall, Chaffin Lake receives even less direct sunlight than Tamarack, but a variety of nice tent sites offer decent fishing.

Even more appealing is the seldom-visited hanging-valley Shangri-La (as the locals affectionately call it). It shelters a stunning grove of old-growth alpine larch around its string of parklike tarns, the uppermost

Making the final talus scramble to the summit of Trapper Peak

of which sits at more than 8600 feet—the highest lakes in the Bitterroots, and perhaps the most spectacular. The best way to reach them is to ascend the finger ridge that reaches down to Tamarack's north shore, staying as high as possible to gain nearly a thousand feet of elevation with no exposure. As the canyon walls steepen, bear left (west) and complete a boulder-hop traverse toward the head of Chaffin's cirque, gradually moving in toward the canyon walls as it cliffs out. The outlet cascades of the first tarn are less than a mile from Tamarack; another half mile of climbing separates it from the highest of the four lakes, any of which makes an unparalleled weekend camp or a base for an ascent of the Shard to the north.

⑪⑨ Trapper Peak

RATING/ DIFFICULTY	ROUNDTRIP	ELEV GAIN/ HIGH POINT	SEASON
*****/5	8 miles	3740 feet/ 10,157 feet	July–Sept

Maps: USGS Trapper Peak, MT; USGS Boulder Peak, MT; **Contact:** Bitterroot National Forest, West Fork Ranger District; **Notes:** Wilderness rules apply. Open to horses; **GPS:** 45.8471°, -114.2647°

A nontechnical, if tiring, talus hop, this 10,157-foot summit—the highest in the Bitterroots and second only to Mount Cleveland in western Montana—yields some of the best views in the region. This is the granite-topped roof of the Bitterroots.

GETTING THERE

From US Highway 93, 4 miles south of Darby (between mileposts 26 and 27), head east on West Fork Road (Montana Highway 473) for 11.5 miles to Lavene Creek Road (Forest Road 5630). Turn right and continue for 0.6 mile to Troy Creek Road (FR 5630-A), then turn left and continue 6.5 miles to the road's end and trailhead (elev. 6380 feet). Shoulder pullouts accommodate a handful of vehicles.

ON THE TRAIL

From the unassuming trailhead, Trapper Peak Trail 133 ascends at a steep clip through open Douglas-fir and lodgepole pine forest. After the trail assumes a more casual pitch on the east side of one of Trapper's long forested ridges, enter the wilderness at 1.6 miles (elev. 7670 feet). A spring provides a chance for refreshment before the trail resumes a fall-line bearing uphill. At 2.5 miles (elev. 8500 feet), windswept alpine larch yield to an austere alpine environment streaked with late-lingering lobes of snow. Below sits an unnamed tarn above the popular picnicking destination of Baker Lake (see Extending Your Trip). Trapper's summit massif dominates the western skyline. If the sky appears threatening whatsoever, turn around here; there is no cover beyond this point.

Follow cairns as the trail, now a faint mountaineers' path, steadily climbs north and west toward Trapper's summit. Reach a high saddle just east of the true summit; from here it's a brief talus scramble to Trapper's crown.

Sign the summit register and scan the horizon. This is one of the loftiest views in Glacier Country, the endless blue-hazed ridges of the Bitterroots and the Salmon River country extending as far as the eye can see to the west and south. To the southeast stands 11,147-foot Torrey Mountain, seemingly a mirage floating above its East Pioneer Mountains neighbors.

EXTENDING YOUR TRIP

An open loop can be made by descending off the northeast face of Trapper toward Gem Lake and then exiting via the Baker Lake Trail to Pierce Creek Road (FR 5634). Some consider this a finer summit approach to Trapper Peak; try it both ways and decide for yourself.

120 Boulder Creek Falls

RATING/DIFFICULTY	ROUNDTRIP	ELEV GAIN/HIGH POINT	SEASON
****/3	8 miles	2020 feet/5610 feet	May–Oct

Map: USGS Boulder Peak, MT; **Contact:** Bitterroot National Forest, West Fork Ranger District; **Notes:** Wilderness rules apply. Open to horses; **GPS:** 45.8291°, -114.2521°

Amble among aspen groves and under broad ponderosa pines in earshot of stone-studded Boulder Creek to the churn of Boulder Creek Falls.

GETTING THERE

From US Highway 93, 4 miles south of Darby (between mileposts 26 and 27), head east on West Fork Road (Montana Highway 473) for 13.2 miles to Boulder Creek Road (Forest Road 5631). Turn right and continue 1.3 miles, passing the Sam Billings Memorial Campground, to the road's end and large trailhead parking area (elev. 4520 feet).

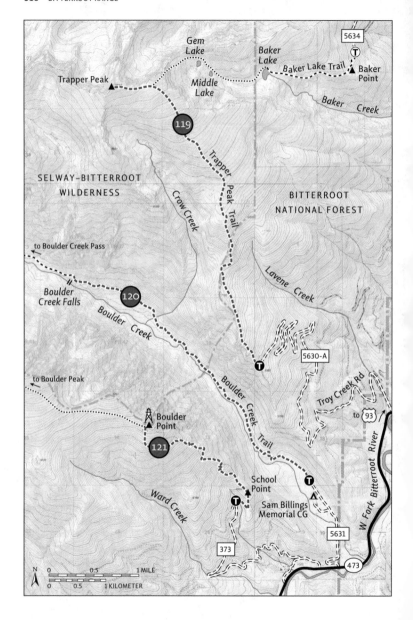

Gem Lake

Baker Lake

5634

Baker Lake Trail

Baker Point

Trapper Peak

Middle Lake

Baker Creek

119

Trapper Peak Trail

SELWAY–BITTERROOT WILDERNESS

Crow Creek

BITTERROOT NATIONAL FOREST

to Boulder Creek Pass

Lavene Creek

Boulder Creek Falls

120

Boulder Creek

5630-A

to Boulder Peak

Boulder Creek Trail

Troy Creek Rd

to 93

Boulder Point

121

Ward Creek

School Point

Sam Billings Memorial CG

5631

W Fork Bitterroot River

373

473

N

0   0.5   1 MILE

0   0.5   1 KILOMETER

Boulder Creek Falls with early autumn rain

A set of these switchbacks takes you sharply uphill to Boulder Creek Falls at 4 miles (elev. 5600 feet). Here, Boulder Creek sluices straight down a broad granite slab, gaining speed before tumbling down a 20-foot cascade and disappearing into the forest. Several large campsites above the falls make for an attractive picnic spot; just be careful on the granite slabs, where wet moss can be treacherous.

EXTENDING YOUR TRIP

The Boulder Creek Trail continues another half dozen miles to Boulder Creek Pass, where it descends on the Idaho side of the Selway-Bitterroot Wilderness to Paradise Guard Station nearly thirty miles from the trailhead. Weekend backpackers may wish to come within a mile of the pass and take the 1-mile side trail to forested Boulder Lake; it's a 19-mile roundtrip.

121 Boulder Point Lookout

RATING/ DIFFICULTY	ROUNDTRIP	ELEV GAIN/ HIGH POINT	SEASON
*****/5	4.6 miles	2500 feet/ 7753 feet	Late June–Sept

Map: USGS Boulder Peak, MT; **Contact:** Bitterroot National Forest, West Fork Ranger District; **Notes:** Wilderness rules apply. Open to horses; **GPS:** 45.8259°, -114.2700°

Climb to a lightly used yet lovingly restored lookout high on the crest of Boulder Creek canyon opposite Trapper Peak's summit massif. Use the lookout as a base for a summit attempt of Boulder Peak, or content yourself with a climb that rivals any on-trail ascent in the Bitterroots for difficulty.

ON THE TRAIL

Beginning on an old roadbed, Boulder Creek Trail 617 quickly joins the boulder-rimmed riffles of its namesake creek. Composed of tall, armor-barked ponderosa, the surrounding forest is more open than many Bitterroots canyons. Aspen sprout from broad fans of talus, which spill down from the steep canyon walls above. Here, Boulder Creek's churn competes with the flapping of thousands of aspen leaves.

The trail undulates as it gradually gains elevation, entering the wilderness and then crossing shallow Crow Creek at 2.8 miles. In typical Bitterroots fashion, the occasional steep pair of switchbacks jogs up the canyon walls, gaining elevation in gulps.

Sunrise from Boulder Point

GETTING THERE

From Darby, drive 4 miles south on US Highway 93 to West Fork Road (Montana Highway 473). Turn right (west), and continue 13.4 miles, just past the Sam Billings Memorial Campground turnoff, to Barn Draw Road (Forest Road 373). Turn right, and drive 2 miles; bear right at the signed junction, and continue another 1.1 miles to the tank-trap trailhead (elev. 5280 feet) at the road's final switchback. The road ends in another fifty yards; don't take the old roadbed that continues beyond this last tank trap.

ON THE TRAIL

From the tank-trap road closure at the trailhead, follow the old roadbed as it angles northeast across open timber, seemingly away from your destination, before doubling back and doubling down on climbing. Now on two-track, make a straight-line ascent of School Point and its grassy balsamroot slope, reaching its crest and real—albeit faded—singletrack at 0.4 mile (elev. 5559 feet).

From here the trail launches into an incredibly steep climb of Boulder Point's east flank, the trail occasionally batting around the idea of switchbacks before abandoning them for all-out ascent. The route initially veers near the wall of Boulder Creek before plunging back into the trees where thick timber limits any views, but impressive old-growth ponderosa pine and Douglas-fir close at hand give some visual distraction.

Having climbed about 1700 feet in the preceding mile and a quarter, the trail finally relents at 1.8 miles (elev. 7220 feet), leveling out and swinging wide west to avoid steep talus. Of course, at this point the reprieve seems sadistic when, 500 vertical feet from the summit, the route suddenly swings away from its destination. Nonetheless, having rounded the south side of the mountain, make one final fall-line push: reach first the privy—one of Montana's highest—and then the lookout at 2.3 miles (elev. 7753 feet).

Built in 1937 and in the process of a loving restoration by a local cross-country ski club, Boulder Point's white clapboard exterior houses cozy confines complete with the original alidade—the fire-plotting map board—and cast-iron stove. A bed, cast-iron skillets, a full load of wood, and a propane cook stove round out the free first-come, first-served accommodations. A base for year-round attempts at Boulder Peak, fourth highest in the Montana Bitterroots, the lookout, perched on a jutting aerie of bedrock, is a worthy destination in its own right, with front-door views of Trapper and Boulder Peaks above and Boulder Creek's noisy tirade below. To the east stand the sere foothills of the Sapphires, to the south the endless blue-green waves of central Idaho's Frank Church–River of No Return Wilderness. It's perhaps the most underrated vista in the Bitterroots.

Be warned: the descent back to the trailhead will test the toe boxes of your shoes.

EXTENDING YOUR TRIP

Climbers with 9804-foot Boulder Peak as their objective use Boulder Point Lookout as a base camp for summit attempts. It's another 3 miles and 2100 feet of off-trail scrambling on the south face of the ridge; all things considered, it's an easier ascent than from the trailhead to the lookout.

122 Nelson Lake

RATING/ DIFFICULTY	ROUNDTRIP	ELEV GAIN/ HIGH POINT	SEASON
****/4	5.6 miles	2580 feet/ 7470 feet	June–Oct

Map: USGS Boulder Peak, MT; **Contact:** Bitterroot National Forest, West Fork Ranger District; **Notes:** Wilderness rules apply. Open to horses; **GPS:** 45.8106°, -114.3170°

Lightly traveled and slow going owing to its up-and-down nature and rough, often obscure tread, the hike to Nelson Lake provides a wilderness experience that belies its relatively short distance. The vast granite impoundment at its foot, the result of a slide thousands of years ago, dwarfs any of the manmade dams in the Selway-Bitterroot Wilderness.

GETTING THERE

From Darby, drive 4 miles south on US Highway 93 to West Fork Road (Montana Highway 473). Turn right (west), and continue 14.8 miles to Nez Perce Road. Turn right, and drive 2.9 miles to Gemmell Creek Road (Forest Road 5633). Turn right (north) and continue 5.1 miles on good gravel and dirt to the unmarked trailhead at a switchback (elev. 6070 feet); if you get to road's end you've gone 0.3 mile too far. The small

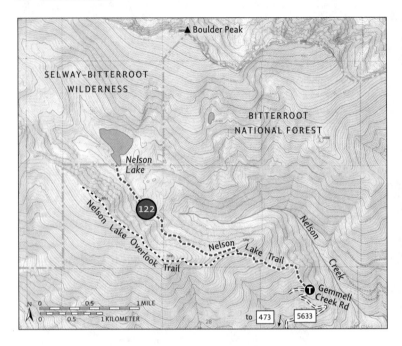

pullout on the road's shoulder accommodates three vehicles.

ON THE TRAIL

Beginning on a steep old skid road, climb on Nelson Lake Trail 135 among huckleberries, beargrass, and balsamroot, the cinnamon-brown puzzle pieces of ponderosa bark towering over all. Eventually, gaps in the trees afford a view up canyon of the talus-strewn Nelson Creek drainage and the barren, arid arête of Boulder Peak above. Just shy of half a mile, the trail bears west along the ridge, now on true singletrack, then gains the ridge at 1 mile (elev. 7220 feet). Ascend again, and at 1.3 miles (elev. 7400 feet), turn right at an unmarked junction (continuing straight is

the long-abandoned but easy-to-follow route to Nelson Lake Overlook).

On rougher, rockier tread, follow the contours of the ridge as it generally descends through head-high fool's huckleberry and across talus slopes, Boulder Peak and its surroundings now largely obscured by lodgepole forest. At 1.8 miles (elev. 7210 feet) enter a large talus slope of refrigerator-sized rocks at the base of the cliff band. The tread occasionally trails off here among riotous hyssop, lomatium, paintbrush, columbine, and wild raspberry; but it is generally easy to follow as it contours around the flower-filled bowl to the copse of trees on the far side. Once in the small stand of trees, head straight, following small cairns. The tread reappears intermittently, generally following

The natural granite dam of Nelson Lake

a contour line through talus fields and young aspen. It's still rocky and rough underfoot, but the trail corridor appears to get brushed with some regularity. When in doubt, don't drop in elevation. This is a good spot to watch for moose, the young aspen thickets providing excellent browse and cover for the animals. The open sweep of the canyon here directs the eye southeast toward the West Fork drainage.

Eventually a massive natural rock wall appears, some thirty feet higher than the basin below. This massive rock slide thousands of years ago permanently impounded the lake; it dwarfs by orders of magnitude any of the manmade dams in the Bitterroots. Dotted by a few skeletal snags, the wall is a slightly unsettling sight. Follow cairns through the rocks to the lake's foot, and the wilderness boundary, at 2.8 miles (elev. 7370 feet). Forming a deep, diamond-shaped bowl, austere gray peaks surround the lake on three sides, the prominent peak to the north, 9804-foot Boulder Peak, the source of the massive slide. An inlet stream echoes loudly across the lake; the body of water appears to lack an outlet, but water percolates through the porous rock impoundment only to reappear as Nelson Creek downstream. The rocky shore provides few camping spots or spots to relax, with tent sites limited to the timbered inlet.

EXTENDING YOUR TRIP

Although long abandoned, the Nelson Lake Overlook Trail remains in good shape and accesses a pleasant ridgeline objective that's accessible when other high points are snowbound. From the junction at 1.3 miles, continue straight, stepping over Lincoln-Log-like piles of lodgepole as the trail gains a wide ridge. Another mile or so of easy routefinding deposits hikers at Nelson Lake Overlook, which, as the name suggests, provides an aerial view of the namesake lake.

123 Castle Rock

RATING/ DIFFICULTY	ROUNDTRIP	ELEV GAIN/ HIGH POINT	SEASON
***/3	5 miles	1770 feet/ 7722 feet	June–Oct

Maps: USGS Bare Cone, MT-ID; USGS Nez Perce Peak, ID-MT; **Contact:** Bitterroot National Forest, West Fork Ranger District; **Note:** Wilderness rules apply; **GPS:** 45.7160°, -114.5023°

Follow a section of the old South Nez Perce Trail to the bare volcanic bastion of Castle Rock. The 7722-foot peak, an old volcanic plug, has resisted the eons-long siege against erosion that claimed the surrounding sedimentary rock. It is also a centerpiece of the 61,000-acre Blue Joint Wilderness Study Area, an annex of thick pine forest and small, grassy pocket meadows that abuts the largest contiguous wilderness in the Lower 48.

GETTING THERE
From Darby, drive 4 miles south on US Highway 93 to West Fork Road (Montana Highway 473). Turn right (west), and continue 14.8 miles to Nez Perce Road (MT 468). Turn right, and drive 16.8 miles—paved for the first 4 miles, gravel the following 6, and paved the remainder—to the large trailhead at Nez Perce Pass (elev. 6590 feet). Privy available. Please do not park on the helicopter landing pad.

ON THE TRAIL
From the pass, Nez Perce Pass Trail 16 climbs steeply south, the thick Douglas-fir

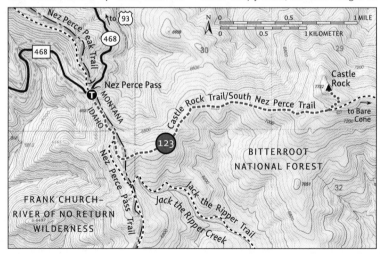

The view of Mount Jerusalem and the southern Selway-Bitterroot Wilderness from Castle Rock

forest screening any meaningful views of Castle Rock to the east. After a short time, the trail reaches a junction where you head left; a sign nailed to a tree indicates Castle Rock, the unassuming sign belying the historical significance of the South Nez Perce Trail, one of two trans-Bitterroots routes the Nez Perce used. A bit of steep climbing ensues before the trail levels in small grassy parklands typical of the Blue Joint Wilderness Study Area: widely spaced old-growth Douglas-fir and ponderosa underlain by pine grass and the cream-and-purple parade of wildflower blooms—yarrow, lupine, buckwheat. The Blue Joint is revered for its elk herds, and although you're unlikely to see one, deer abound, and a genetically pure herd of bighorn sheep use the area around Castle Rock for lambing.

Thick understory encroaches for a time as the trail undulates along the ridge, bearing generally downward. Crest a small rock helm at 1.8 miles (elev. 7140 feet), the opening understory allowing a brief view of Castle Rock's western buttress. Ascend, and at 2 miles (elev. 7310 feet), cross a rocky delamination deposit field from Castle Rock. This is the closest the approach trail gets to the summit, and from here it's off-trail to the destination. However, the best approach is to continue another one hundred yards or so on the trail, then skirt the right side of the talus apron, following cairns. Concentric rock benches guard the summit, but on the east side of peak is an easy route through fist-sized rock to the top; look for the obvious embrasure to the summit (elev. 7722 feet).

Low juniper and a handful of trees surround a single large summit cairn of red rock. Although the immediate setting is rather austere, the views are grand. To the north stand the scalloped peaks of the southern Selway-Bitterroot Wilderness, Mount Jerusalem most prominent. Below is the Magruder Corridor, a thin ribbon of rough road that bisects the largest unroaded block of land in the Lower 48 and separates the Selway-Bitterroot Wilderness and the Frank Church–River of No Return Wilderness. The Blue Joint, over which Castle Rock lords, would make a small but fine addition to these wilderness areas.

EXTENDING YOUR TRIP

Bare Cone and its car-accessible lookout make for a possible shuttle-assisted hike another few miles farther east on the South Nez Perce Trail.

Opposite: *Sunrise above Stony Lake from the Sapphire Divide*

sapphire mountains

The Sapphire Mountains once formed the cap of the Bitterroot Mountains before sliding east, leaving the Bitterroot Valley in their wake. In contrast to the latter's shattered granite silhouette, the Sapphires offer tight creek canyons and mellow ridgetop wandering on faint, flower-flanked tread. From the Sapphire Divide, peer down limestone cliffs into the stark east side of the Sapphires, so named for being one of the world's foremost producers of this light blue gem.

Map: USGS Grizzly Point, MT; **Contact:** Lolo National Forest, Missoula Ranger District; **Notes:** Wilderness rules apply. Open to horses; **GPS:** 46.5600°, -113.7041°

Wander in one of Montana's smallest wilderness areas and see why its tight timbered canyons have hidden scofflaws and strike-it-rich schemers in addition to eagles and elk.

GETTING THERE

From Interstate 90 about 23 miles east of Missoula, take exit 125 (Rock Creek). Drive south on Rock Creek Road 14.2 miles—the first 12 miles paved, the remainder narrow and pot-holed—to the Welcome Creek trailhead on the right (elev. 4010 feet). Privy available. There is enough parking space for about ten vehicles.

124 Welcome Creek

RATING/ DIFFICULTY	ROUNDTRIP	ELEV GAIN/ HIGH POINT	SEASON
***/4	5.2 miles	900 feet/ 4500 feet	May–Nov

Wandering among the towering ponderosa pines of Welcome Creek

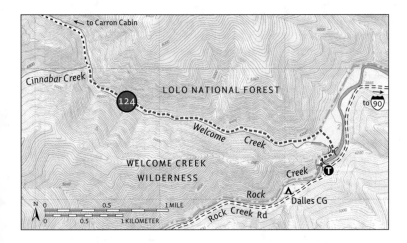

ON THE TRAIL

Welcome Creek, like Burdette Creek (Hike 100) and Fish Lakes Canyon (Hike 3), challenges the notion that only high rock-and-ice wildlands deserve our attention. The 28,135-acre Welcome Creek Wilderness forms the west slope of Rock Creek and its world-famous trout waters. Boasting no lakes and few flat places to pound a tent stake, the timbered ridges and tightly knit canyons nonetheless are a small chunk of increasingly rare relatively low-elevation forest in the wilderness system.

From the trailhead, immediately do a drunken-sailor walk across the impressive wooden suspension bridge spanning Rock Creek. Most visitors go no farther, opting to fish the pools from Rock Creek's sandy beach. Passing the beach, continue through boulder-studded Douglas-fir forest, crossing Welcome Creek on a series of stepping stones to enter the wilderness. Level tread heads away from the sound of the creek through widely spaced ponderosa and fir to the edge of the canyon's talus walls. The

trail gets noticeably rougher as it enters the remains of a canyon-spanning burn; blowdowns frequently block passage, and a variety of thorny shrubs—wild raspberry, currant—will lash at unprotected legs.

At 1.9 miles (elev. 4350 feet), cross a small side channel of the creek, here only four feet wide, and continue upstream. Occasionally masses of head-high fireweed threaten to overtake the trail, and dogwood turns it into a tunnel, but overall it's easy going. Cross a split-log bridge at 2.4 miles (elev. 4460 feet). Now on the south side of the creek, reach its confluence with Cinnabar Creek at 2.5 miles (elev. 4500 feet). The Cinnabar Cabin burned in 2007, leaving the Carron Cabin 2.5 miles upstream as the only semi-intact structure in the wilderness. All that remain are a handful of rusted mining relics from the creek's rough-and-tumble past. Gold was discovered here in 1888, and one of the state's largest nuggets was pulled from the creek during this time. After the mines went bust, outlaw Frank Brady holed up here until he was killed in a 1904 shoot-out at a cabin on Welcome Creek. Opponents of wilderness designation for Welcome Creek pointed to the presence of old cabins as grounds for its dismissal from consideration, but the moldering homesites illustrate that, in wilderness, "man himself is a visitor who does not remain."

EXTENDING YOUR TRIP

The trail continues for another 5 miles up to Cleveland Mountain on the Sapphire Divide, but its condition is even spottier than the previous miles. Carron Cabin, 2.5 miles upstream of Welcome Creek, makes an attractive destination, though. Cross Cinnabar Creek just upstream of its confluence with Welcome Creek, then look for the trail up the slope (it's not down at the creek bottom).

Autumn larch shade the talus slopes south of Dome-Shaped Mountain.

125 Stony Lake and Dome-Shaped Mountain

Stony Lake

RATING/ DIFFICULTY	ROUNDTRIP	ELEV GAIN/ HIGH POINT	SEASON
***/4	7 miles	1880 feet/ 7920 feet	July–early Oct

Dome-Shaped Mountain

RATING/ DIFFICULTY	ROUNDTRIP	ELEV GAIN/ HIGH POINT	SEASON
****/5	13.2 miles	2710 feet/ 8656 feet	July–early Oct

Maps: USGS Burnt Fork Lake, MT; USGS Stony Creek, MT; USGS Skalkaho Pass, MT; USGS Mount Emerine, MT; **Contact:** Beaverhead-Deerlodge National Forest, Pintler Ranger District; **Note:** Open to horses and bicycles; **GPS:** 46.2327°, -113.7466°

 *Wander the seldom-visited Sapphire Divide, the former top of the Bitterroot Mountains. What Dome-Shaped Mountain lacks in drama it makes up for in views, of broad meadows and regal alpine larch.*

GETTING THERE

From Hamilton, drive 2 miles south on US Highway 93 to the junction with Skalkaho Road (Montana Highway 38). Turn left (east) and drive 27 miles to Skalkaho Pass—paved the first 19 miles, narrow, windy dirt (or slick mud when wet) the next 8 miles, passing stairstepping Skalkaho Falls at 22 miles. At the pass, continue on MT 38 for 2 miles to Crystal Creek Campground and the trailhead parking area (elev. 6970 feet). Privy available.

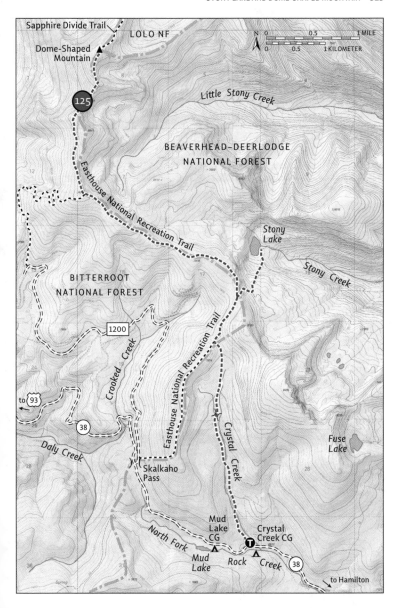

Sapphire Divide Trail

LOLO NF

Dome-Shaped
Mountain

125

Little Stony Creek

BEAVERHEAD–DEERLODGE
NATIONAL FOREST

Easthouse National Recreation Trail

Stony
Lake

Stony Creek

BITTERROOT
NATIONAL FOREST

1200

Crooked Creek

Easthouse National Recreation Trail

Crystal Creek

to 93

38

Daly Creek

Fuse
Lake

Skalkaho
Pass

North Fork

Mud
Lake
CG

Crystal
Creek CG

T

Mud
Lake

Rock

Creek

38

to Hamilton

N

0   0.5   1 MILE
0   0.5   1 KILOMETER

ON THE TRAIL

Making use of an old, rocky roadbed, gently ascend through dense lodgepole and spruce forest, Crystal Creek burbling to the right. Staying on the most well-used road as it passes numerous two-track incursions, reach an outfitters' camp at 0.4 mile, and bear right across a wooden puncheon and onto true singletrack.

Proceeding at stream gradient, cross the creek in another one hundred yards and ascend through quiet forest. Pass several colorful pocket meadows, frequently rumpled by bedding elk, as the trail crosses the creek on a log bridge and proceeds upstream. Heading up the drainage, note the talus piles, probable evidence of an old glacial moraine. Crest the ridge, and immediately bear right onto Easthouse National Recreation Trail at 2.2 miles (elev. 6970 feet).

Now in silent, graying snags, follow the ridgeline north, Dome-Shaped Mountain's gray summit straight ahead. In a timbered draw that escaped fire, reach the junction with the trail to Stony Lake at 2.9 miles.

To reach Stony Lake, go right and descend steep, rough tread through eerie standing snags to the forested east shore. Folks claim it's a mile. It only feels like one; it's closer to 0.6 mile. Aptly named, Stony offers temperamental fishing from its overused campsites. Stumps, like rotting piers, stand silent on the shore. Don't be surprised to startle a moose here.

To reach Dome-Shaped Mountain, continue straight from the junction, following a broad ridge of beargrass and burnt spires, the right edge of the ridge ending in limestone rock formations and a drop to the lake. To the west, take in views of the "flatirons," the prominent features of mylonite along the eastern front of the Bitterroots that show where the Sapphires sheared off.

The trail begins to climb in earnest through alternating patches of unburnt timber and expansive open meadows, with steep rock gullies and tiny unnamed ponds to the right. At 5 miles (elev. 8450 feet), continue straight at a T-junction. Now in alpine larch and scattered whitebark pine, descend on the west side of the crest, eventually dropping sharply into a granite saddle shaded by alpine larch. The trail, which is occasionally faint, then ascends through sparse charred snags to reach the parklike summit of Dome-Shaped Mountain at 6.6 miles (elev. 8656 feet).

Wizened whitebark pines permit views of the broad glacier-shaped valleys of the Sapphires. The 11,000-foot peaks of the East Pioneers hover over the gem-rich mining country to the east.

EXTENDING YOUR TRIP

Continue on the Sapphire Divide Trail for more seldom-visited scenes of subalpine meadows and graying snags. Beyond Dome-Shaped Mountain, the trail gets noticeably rougher and harder to follow.

Resources

Beaverhead-Deerlodge National Forest
www.fs.usda.gov/bdnf
Pintler Ranger District, Philipsburg
(406) 859-3211

Bitterroot National Forest
www.fs.usda.gov/bitterroot
Darby Ranger District, Darby
(406) 821-3913
Stevensville Ranger District, Stevensville
(406) 777-5461
West Fork Ranger District, Darby
(406) 821-3269

City of Missoula Parks & Recreation
(406) 552-6000
www.ci.missoula.mt.us/157/Parks-
Recreation

Confederated Salish and Kootenai Tribes
http://nrd.csktribes.org/fwrc/recreation

Glacier National Park
www.nps.gov/glac
(406) 888-7800

Flathead National Forest
www.fs.usda.gov/flathead
Glacier View Ranger District, Hungry
Horse
(406) 387-3800
Hungry Horse Ranger District, Hungry
Horse
(406) 387-3800
Swan Lake Ranger District, Bigfork
(406) 837-7500

Tally Lake Ranger District, Kalispell
(406) 758-5204

Kootenai National Forest
www.fs.usda.gov/kootenai
Cabinet Ranger District, Trout Creek
(406) 827-3533
Fortine Ranger District, Eureka
(406) 296-2536
Libby Ranger District, Libby
(406) 293-7773
Rexford Ranger District, Eureka
(406) 296-2536
Three Rivers Ranger District, Troy
(406) 295-4693

Lolo National Forest
www.fs.usda.gov/lolo
Missoula Ranger District, Missoula
(406) 329-3814
Ninemile Ranger District, Huson
(406) 626-5201
Plains/Thompson Falls Ranger District,
Plains
(406) 826-3821
Seeley Lake Ranger District, Seeley Lake
(406) 677-2233
Superior Ranger District, Superior
(406) 822-4233

Lone Pine State Park
http://stateparks.mt.gov/lone-pine/
(406) 755-2706

Nez Perce National Forest
www.fs.usda.gov/nezperceclearwater/
Moose Creek Ranger District, Kooskia, ID
(208) 926-4258

Pacificorp
recreation@pacificorp.com
(503) 813-6666
825 NE Multnomah Street
Portland, OR 97232

Stillwater State Forest
(406) 881-2371

CONSERVATION AND TRAIL ORGANIZATIONS

Bob Marshall Wilderness Foundation
www.bmwf.org
(406) 387-3822
PO Box 190688
Hungry Horse, MT 59919

Continental Divide Trail Coalition
www.continentaldividetrail.org
(303) 996-2759
PO Box 552
Pine, CO 80470

Crown of the Continent Geotourism Program
https://crownofthecontinent.natgeotourism
   .com
(406) 407-0421

Five Valleys Land Trust
www.fvlt.org
(406) 549-0755
120 Hickory Street, Suite B
Missoula, MT 59801

Flathead Land Trust
www.flatheadlandtrust.org
(406) 752-8293
PO Box 1913
Kalispell, MT 59903

Friends of Scotchman Peaks Wilderness
www.scotchmanpeaks.org
(208) 946-9127
PO Box 2061
Sandpoint, ID 83864

Great Burn Study Group
www.greatburnstudygroup.org
(406) 240-9901
1434 Jackson Street
Missoula, MT 59802

Glacier National Park Conservancy
https://glacier.org
(406) 892-3250
PO Box 2749
402 9th Street West
Columbia Falls, MT 59912

Montana Wilderness Association
www.wildmontana.org
(406) 443-7350
80 South Warren
Helena, MT 59601

Pacific Northwest Trail Association
www.pnt.org
(360) 854-9415
1851 Charles Jones Memorial Circle #4
Sedro-Woolley, WA 98284

Selway-Bitterroot Frank Church Foundation
www.selwaybitterroot.org
(208) 871-1906
120 Hickory Street, Suite A
Missoula, MT 59801

Swan View Coalition
www.swanrange.org
(406) 755-1379
3165 Foothill Road
Kalispell, MT 59901

Whitefish Legacy Partners
www.whitefishlegacy.org
(406) 862-3880
PO Box 1895
Whitefish, MT 59937

RECOMMENDED READING

Alt, David D., Donald W. Hyndman. *Roadside Geology of Montana*. Missoula: Mountain Press Publishing Company, 2013.

Egan, Timothy. *The Big Burn: Teddy Roosevelt and the Fire That Saved America*. Boston: Houghton Mifflin Harcourt, 2009.

Glover, James. *A Wilderness Original: The Life of Bob Marshall*. Seattle: Mountaineers Books, 1996.

Gnam, Steven. *Crown of the Continent: The Wildest Rockies*. Seattle: Braided River, 2014.

Hansen, Heather. *Wildfire: On the Front Lines with Station 8*. Seattle: Mountaineers Books, 2018.

Acknowledgments

Thanks to the team at Mountaineers Books, in particular publisher Helen Cherullo, editor Laura Shauger, and editor in chief Kate Rogers. In addition, I thank Rebecca Friedman for her keen eye and insightful comments, and Ben Pease for his excellent map making.

Thanks to Western Montana's Glacier Country Tourism for project support when I was first developing the idea that became this book.

I could have not hiked thousands of miles within western Montana without the help of friends and family, too numerous to name here. To all of you, whether you shared the trail, a campsite, a place to crash or your love and support: thank you.

Index

1% for Trails: Partnerships with Outdoor Nonprofits

Mountaineers Books designates 1 percent of the sales of select guidebooks in our Day Hiking series toward trail stewardship. Since launching this program, we've contributed more than $14,000 toward improving access to our public lands.

For this book, our 1 percent of sales is going to the Montana Wilderness Association. For 60 years, Montana Wilderness Association has worked with local communities throughout the state to preserve wilderness and traditional recreation heritage. The organization puts boots on the ground, from hiking trails to the halls of Congress, to steward common-sense solutions to conservation issues. And with increasing strains on our public lands—and outright assaults on their protections—the work of Montana Wilderness Association matters now more than ever.

Mountaineers Books donates many books to nonprofit recreation and conservation organizations. Our 1% for Trails campaign is one more way we can help fellow nonprofit organizations as we work together to get more people outside, to both enjoy and protect our wild public lands.

If you'd like to support Mountaineers Books and our nonprofit partnership programs, please visit our website to learn more or email mbooks@mountaineersbooks.org.

About the Author

An accomplished editorial and commercial writer and photographer, **Aaron Theisen** has contributed to numerous regional and national sports and lifestyle publications, including *Powder*, *Backpacker*, *British Columbia*, and *Northwest Travel & Life*. Aaron is coauthor, with Craig Romano, of *Day Hiking Mount St. Helens*.

MOUNTAINEERS BOOKS, including its two imprints, Skipstone and Braided River, is a leading publisher of quality outdoor recreation, sustainability, and conservation titles. As a 501(c)(3) nonprofit, we are committed to supporting the environmental and educational goals of our organization by providing expert information on human-powered adventure, sustainable practices at home and on the trail, and preservation of wilderness.

Our publications are made possible through the generosity of donors, and through sales of more than 800 titles on outdoor recreation, sustainable lifestyle, and conservation. To donate, purchase books, or learn more, visit us online:

MOUNTAINEERS BOOKS
1001 SW Klickitat Way, Suite 201 • Seattle, WA 98134
800-553-4453 • mbooks@mountaineersbooks.org • www.mountaineersbooks.org

Leave No Trace strives to educate visitors about the nature of their recreational impacts and offers techniques to prevent and minimize such impacts. Leave No Trace is best understood as an educational and ethical program, not as a set of rules and regulations. For more information, visit www.lnt.org or call 800-332-4100.

OTHER MOUNTAINEERS BOOKS TITLES YOU MAY ENJOY!